Y0-CBW-568

PUBLIC BROADCASTING
AND THE PUBLIC TRUST

i

PUBLIC BROADCASTING AND THE PUBLIC TRUST

Edited by David Horowitz and Laurence Jarvik

SECOND THOUGHTS BOOKS is an imprint of the Center for
the Study of Popular Culture, P.O. Box 67398, Los Angeles,
CA 90067, 800-752-6562.

Copyright ©1995 by the Center for the Study of Popular
Culture. All rights reserved. No part of this publication may
be reproduced, stored in a retrieval system, or transmitted in
any form or by any means, electronic, mechanical, photo-
copy, recording, or otherwise, without the prior written
consent of the publisher.

ISBN 1-886442-03-7

Printed in the United States of America
1 2 3 4 5 6 7 8 9 10

President: David Horowitz
Vice President: Peter Collier
Publications Director: Elizabeth Larson
Art Director: Jean-Paul Duberg

ACKNOWLEDGMENTS

Wendy Lee Nentwig and Bruce Donaldson assisted in the preparation of this book. The authors would also like to thank the Sarah Scaife Foundation, the Bradley Foundation, the Olin Foundation, the Elizabeth S. Hooper Foundation, Wally Nunn, Bruce Hooper, and the 40,000 member-supporters of the Center for the Study of Popular Culture for sponsoring COMINT and making this work possible.

TABLE OF CONTENTS

PREFACE

For its first 23 years of existence, the public-broadcasting system had no formal community of critics to whom it had to answer. Its creator and funder, the U.S. Congress, was comfortably controlled by Democrats, who were in profound sympathy with the liberal culture of the system itself. The same held true of the pundits of the commercial media, for whom public broadcasting was something like a favorite godchild. The centers of the academic world, even more firmly dominated by a left-wing culture, viewed public broadcasting as the fragile beacon of a future freed from the taint of commerce and the democratic constraints of the economic market. The relationships between these liberal subcultures, which provided the critical environment of public broadcasting, has been developed over the last two decades to an incestuous degree. To cite one paradigm case, the dean of the Columbia School of Journalism, which administers prestigious awards in journalism and publishes a leading critical magazine about the profession, is Joan Konner, who came to the post after an apprenticeship as a producer for public television and a protégé of Bill Moyers, former press secretary for Lyndon Johnson, an architect of the public-broadcasting system, a ubiquitous presence on its airwaves and its leading liberal voice. Ms. Konner is also the publisher of the *Columbia Journalism Review*.

For years, the only anomalous element in this cosy environment was the lonely (and therefore marginalized) voice of Reed Irvine and his organization Accuracy in Media. Over the years, his publication, *Accuracy in Media Reports*, intermittently published analyses of PBS documentaries that examined their tendentious claims and political biases. Irvine even attempted to sue the Corporation for Public Broadcasting for its systematic violation of the fairness doctrine of the Public Broadcasting Act of 1967. The courts ruled that the law had no teeth. It was Congress' responsibility to enforce its own act, which its Democratic majority chose not to do. In the 1980s, Reed Irvine was joined by the Center for Media

ix

and Public Affairs and the Media Research Center, which focused principally on commercial media but published occasional studies of the public-broadcast output.

In the spring of 1989, this situation began to change when the Center for the Study of Popular Culture decided to focus its attention on public broadcasting. Its first project was to prod PBS to provide airtime for the late Nestor Almendros' documentary on Castro's prisons, *Nobody Listened*. Eventually PBS agreed to air the documentary but under circumstances that were demeaning to Almendros and his film. *Nobody Listened* was aired alongside a propaganda film by long-time Castro crony Saul Landau. This was PBS's idea of "balance." Then in the winter of 1990, the Center for the Study of Popular Culture began publication of a new journal, COMINT, which undertook to examine public broadcasting from a conservative point of view. COMINT's first issue reminded public broadcasters of their forgotten mandate to be guardians of the public trust. Under the Public Broadcasting Act of 1967, they were required to "balance" their programming schedules to prevent their taxpayer-funded entities from falling under the sway of one political party, thereby becoming an element subversive of the democratic process itself. The Voice of America, another government entity, is forbidden by law to broadcast domestically for precisely this reason. Yet, as the ensuing pages show, public broadcasters have ignored this mandate for the entire history of the system.

The present volume is composed of articles from COMINT's first four years. It is the only critical account of public broadcasting from a conservative perspective that has been published in the entire 28-year history of the modern public-broadcasting system. This, in itself, speaks volumes about the political bias in America's academic and cultural institutions and, specifically, in the world of broadcasting criticism. The pages that follow document the overweening political bias in the universe of public broadcasting. They also document the failure of public broadcasters to live up to their own standards or to be accountable to the public they claim to serve.

Because COMINT was intended to promote the reform of the system, this volume is also a record of the system's resistance to change, including an attempt made by Congress in the Telecommunications Act of 1992 to induce it to reform itself. In that year Congress, at the behest of Republican Leader Robert Dole, passed a series of amendments designed to bring public broadcasting into conformity with the law. This effort was met with resistance throughout the system, including from the Republican-dominated board of the Corporation for Public Broadcasting, so effectively have public broadcasters been able, until now, to take their opponents into camp and to insulate themselves from accountability. The failure to reform in 1992-94 set the stage for the confrontation with the new Republican majority in Congress in 1995.

David Horowitz
Laurence Jarvik
January 19, 1995

PART I

MISSING BALANCE

THE PROBLEM WITH PUBLIC TV

"Public television's greatest weakness today is not its lack of money but its lack of mission. It doesn't know what it's there for."
—James Day, former president of
National Education Television

Iagree with Henry Kissinger that war is the normal state of mankind and peace is an aberration." The improbable speaker of this statement was Donald Ledwig, president and chief executive officer of the Corporation for Public Broadcasting, which annually distributes $250 million in taxpayer funds to more than 300 public TV stations, whose signals are seldom seen to transmit sentiments so illiberal. "When governments are delegitimized and the balance of power is destabilized," Ledwig continued, "the normal state of affairs reasserts itself. When the Berlin Wall came down, there was a delegitimization of governments in the Soviet bloc; people began talking about peace dividends and disarmament. The inevitable question was: Where would the next conflict erupt?"

Ledwig was holding forth in his office at the corporation's new marble and brass headquarters in Washington, D.C. I was meeting with him as an advocate for the Committee on Media Integrity, a group concerned about the absence of just those perspectives on a public network whose programs regularly promote the delegitimization of governments (especially those of America and its allies) and disarmament fantasies (like those recently featured in Gwynne Dyer's eight-part series, *War*).

During his ruminations, Ledwig revealed that he was a graduate of the Naval War College, an admission accompanied by an almost poignant aside. Reed Irvine of Accuracy in Media had organized a campaign to protest a recent PBS program. One of the pre-typed AIM postcards sent to Ledwig had contained a handwritten scrawl from an old naval buddy: "What the hell is going on at your station?"

It was a good question, and one that I put to Ledwig myself. Instead of responding directly, the head of the free world's largest government-funded television network rummaged through the clutter on his desk to retrieve a remote-control device. Holding it up, he said "There are 80 channels at your finger tips. You don't have to watch this one."

If the moment was surreal, it accurately summed up the complexities of the public-television system. These began with the very name of the entity that manages the national distribution of its programs and is most familiar to its audiences. PBS officials stress that the initials "PBS" stand for Public Broadcast Service, not "System"—as though the latter might betray an unseemly ambition, even a dangerous one. In 1973, the Nixon White House had, in fact, vetoed funding for the corporation, citing its alleged ambition to become a "fourth network." Indeed, many of the organizational anomalies of public television (for example, the fact that Ledwig's corporation funds programs but is barred from producing or distributing them) are part of an elaborate bulwark to prevent the recurrence of such attacks.

By any measure, these devices have been effective. After 12 years of Reagan and Bush appointees to the corporation board, there is little more than a Donald Ledwig to show for their efforts. But even if the system had not produced a leader so disarmingly reconciled to his own impotence, things would not be much different. Under present arrangements, Ledwig has little control over the money he spends. Of the funds Congress makes available through the corporation, 93 percent are distributed to the stations under a formula that he cannot alter. The situation inspired former director Richard Brookhiser to describe CPB as nothing more than a "bag man" for the self-appointed and self-appointing bureaucracy that has ruled public broadcasting since its creation and under whose guidance it has grown to a $1.2-billion leviathan virtually free of public accountability and control.

◆ ◆ ◆

Created by the Public Broadcasting Act of 1967, the present system is one of the last El Dorados of the Great Society. Non-commercial television became a possibility in 1952, when the FCC reserved 242 channels for educational purposes. But in the Eisenhower era, the idea of government-sponsored media of any kind would have been rejected as "creeping socialism." In 1961, however, Kennedy's new FCC chairman Newton Minow condemned commercial television as a "vast wasteland" and pledged his support to its educational rival. The following year, Kennedy signed the Educational Television Facilities Act, providing government funds to build new stations, and in the same year Congress passed the All-Channel Receiver Bill, requiring new television sets to include the UHF channels on which most educational programs were carried.

The New Frontiersman who would prove most crucial to the new system was the president's National Security Advisor, McGeorge Bundy, one of "the best and the brightest." The precocious Bundy had orchestrated the Vietnam crusade for both Kennedy and Johnson, until running it into the quagmire from which it never recovered. In 1966, he became one of the first in a long line to leave the sinking ship of the policy he had charted, finding refuge in the presidency of the Ford Foundation.

On taking the presidency at Ford, Bundy told intimates that he intended to make educational television one of two objects of his attention (the other was race relations). Ford had funded all 30 of the first (and most important) educational stations and many of those that followed as well. In making its grants, Ford did not hesitate to use the leverage its vast resources created. In Los Angeles, a group of local businessmen and community leaders had spent a decade developing KCET as a community station; then Ford stepped in and demanded the removal of the founders and the appointment of its hand-picked executive as a condition of the grant that made the station viable. By the mid-'60s, Ford had spent a prodigious sum—$150 million—to transform the more than 100 existing stations into the beginnings of a national network.

Before Ford entered the picture, educational stations were distinctly homegrown, do-it-yourself, garden variety in character. Operating an average of only eight hours a day and mainly associated with universities and schools, their programming was devoted to no-frills instructional fare tailored to their respective locales. *Shakespeare in the Classroom, Today's Farm, Parents and Dr. Spock,* and *Industry on Parade* were typical titles of the programs that were often "bicycled" from one station to the next because the stations had no cable interconnection link at the time. The unifying factor among these educational productions, and the one that distinguished them most clearly from commercial TV, was their low budgets—the factor that Ford had set out to change.

Transformed by the infusion of this capital, the medium rapidly became the public television with which we are familiar today. There is no organic relation between the high-tech professionalism of this medium and the modest, if sincere, efforts of the educational pioneers. An hour of *MacNeil/ Lehrer* costs $96,000 today, while a similar segment of a series like *Cosmos* or *Masterpiece Theater* might run up budgets three or four times that size. These budgets may be less than those of comparable commercial shows (thanks to special discount arrangements with unions and talent), but they are still out of reach of any university or community group.

Despite this reality, the pre-lapsarian era lives on as an image central to public television's self-understanding. It is also a featured item in the PBS promotional package. Today, PBS executives still portray their network as if it were a decentralized service to diverse publics, the very incarnation of America's democratic spirit:

> PBS is owned and directed by its member public television stations, which in turn are accountable to their local communities. This grassroots network is comprised of stations operated by colleges, universities, state and municipal authorities, school boards, and community organizations across the nation.

To be a *vox populi* and to provide a quality and range of programming that commercial stations presumably cannot is the rationale by which public television justifies its existence to its five million viewer-contributors and congressional funders.

Yet, as the familiar profile of PBS programs would suggest, there is less populism in these structures than meets the eye. Despite organizational complexities of Rube Goldberg dimensions and the lack of a single programming authority, centralized power dominates the system and creates its characteristic voice. Of the $44 million in program grants that Donald Ledwig's corporation makes available to the 341 separately owned PBS stations across the nation, fully half that total—$22 million—goes to just two: WGBH in Boston and WNET in New York. (Another $10 million goes to a group of producers affiliated with WNET, to three other stations, and to PBS itself, accounting for 77 percent of the total funds.) This money is then leveraged against grants from private foundations and other sources by a factor as great as two, three, or even five times the original amount. The result is that most major public television series— *MacNeil/Lehrer, American Playhouse, Frontline, NOVA, Sesame Street, Great Performances, Masterpiece Theater,* or any of Bill Moyers' various offerings—are produced or "presented" by WNET and WGBH. Others are produced by a group of stations known as the "G-7" (after the tag given to the major industrial powers at the last economic summit).

Not coincidentally, WNET and WGBH are the stations with which Bundy and Ford were most intimately connected. Hartford Gunn, the president of WGBH, was a Harvard colleague of Bundy's, and the station itself was run by Harvard, the Massachusetts Institute of Technology, the Lowell Institute, and four other Boston-area institutions. As an early recipient of Ford money, WGBH collaborated with the foundation on the first link connecting the stations (the Eastern Educational Network). Under Bundy's direction, WGBH executive David Davis (now the head of *POV* and *American Playhouse*) was recruited to Ford, where he engineered the creation of PBS.

Ford also created the other half of public television's present duumvirate, conceiving its precursor, The National Educational Television and Radio Center, as the first and only national producer of programs. (The stations' own production capabilities were severely restricted by budgetary constraints.) As the number of stations grew, Ford moved the center from

Ann Arbor, Michigan, to New York, renaming it NET, and then merged it with New York's channel 13 to create WNET as the most powerful station in the emerging network.

Almost as important in shaping the new system were the radical currents of a decade in which America's political culture seemed to be coming apart. Before leaving the White House, Bundy recruited Fred W. Friendly, a former Johnson advisor and CBS executive who had become the focus of a celebrated incident of the Vietnam era. The Fulbright Hearings on Vietnam were the first congressional challenge to the war. Outraged by CBS's refusal to air a segment of the hearings that featured war critic George Kennan (CBS ran an *I Love Lucy* episode instead), Friendly resigned in a widely publicized protest. Hours later he received Bundy's call. It was characteristic of the way the new system attracted personnel.

The new program director of WNET, Robert Kotlowitz, received a similar call when he and the entire editorial board at *Harper*'s magazine were purged in a conflict with management. Among other issues, according to Kotlowitz, they had antagonized the publisher by featuring the anti-war journalism of Norman Mailer and other radical outpourings. "Movement" activists, who would never consider careers in commercial media, flocked to campus and community stations with "progressive" profiles, such as San Francisco's KQED, to promote their political agendas. In 1969, Ford summoned KQED's head, James Day, to New York to become president of NET.

Few institutions reflected the changes of the times as vividly as NET. A decade earlier, the fledgling institution had regarded itself as part of the national establishment. When Kennedy called for a national mobilization during the Berlin crisis of 1961, NET's president at the time, John White, volunteered the services of educational TV. "As the nation makes plans for its defense...," he wrote Kennedy, "the facilities of the educational television stations are an important national asset, ready to play an appropriate role in conveying information to youngsters in school and to adults at home, as well as for the training of specific civilian groups."

Yet by decade's end, NET productions were regularly expressing not only the anxious doubts of liberals and moderates but the seditious humors of the '60s New Left. A controversial NET production, *Who Invited Us?*, was a sneering history of U.S. interventions abroad (pointedly omitting World War II) in which America was portrayed as an imperial meddler. *Inside North Vietnam* was a "documentary" by Mao apologist Felix Greene that had previously been rejected by CBS as "too pro-Hanoi." It was aired on the eve of the Tet Offensive and featured a smiling "Uncle Ho" amidst his adoring subjects. Thirty-three Congressmen signed a letter criticizing NET for acting as "a conduit for enemy propaganda." Other NET shows included a pro-Castro report on Communist Cuba, an investigation of the FBI by New Left radical Paul Jacobs, and a populist *j'accuse* called *The Banks and the Poor*, which ended with a list of 133 congressmen and their alleged connections to the banking industry played over the strains of *The Battle Hymn of the Republic*.

◆   ◆   ◆

By the mid-'60s, an integrated public-television network had taken shape under the spell of Ford's largesse. But Ford had no intention of footing the bill for its creation, a task it reserved for the taxpaying public. In 1965, WGBH patron Ralph Lowell had already persuaded Carnegie to promote such an agenda. The Carnegie Commission was graced by the presidents of Harvard and MIT, and its recommendations quickly resulted in the Public Broadcasting Act of 1967, facilitated by Bundy's former colleagues in the Johnson administration, Douglass Cater and Bill Moyers.

In creating the new system, its architects attempted to square the circle of a government-funded institution that would be independent of political influence. The result was a solution in the form of a problem: a private corporation that would distribute the government funds. Compromise was the order of the day. The Carnegie plutarchs wanted the governing board of the corporation to be composed of eminent cultural persons. Johnson wanted (and got) political appointees. Carnegie wanted a permanent funding base in the form of an excise tax on television sets to strengthen its independence. The television lobby and Congress said no. But as a sop to the broadcasters, emphasis was placed on the private nature of the corporation as a "heat shield" to insulate the system from governmental influence. "Our public broadcasting system," a PBS president would later explain, "was designed to keep the Federal Government and political influence out of program-making."

Congress also limited the corporation's mandate, insisting that it be established on the "bedrock of localism." (The idea of an elite network created by Harvard, Ford, and Lowell but financed by the taxpayer would have been political anathema.) To prevent the corporation from creating a centralized "fourth network," Congress barred it from producing programs, operating stations, or managing the "interconnection" between them.

The Republican minority understood that excluding "political influence" meant that they were going along with a Democratic majority in creating a partisan media that could do considerable damage to their own political future. To counteract this possibility, they insisted on the safeguards of a decentralized system that would not aspire to be a national network. In addition, they inserted a clause requiring "fairness, objectivity and balance" in all programming of a controversial nature.

Such was the plan; the product proved otherwise. While Congress had agreed to provide a fund to finance the stations, it was left to others to connect them into a national voice. In practice this meant Ford and Bundy, who had recruited WGBH executive David Davis for the task. Working with Ward Chamberlin, Davis engineered the new interconnection, which began operations in 1970 as the Public Broadcasting Service.

In creating PBS, Ford was forced to frustrate the ambitions of its own favorite son, NET, which as the national program producer had seemed the logical choice to connect the new system and manage its programs. But NET was already too controversial for such a focal position. Its radical provocations had antagonized not only Congress but also the more conservative stations in regions outside New York, where the counter culture had yet to penetrate. To preserve NET's political influence, Ford merged it into the powerhouse New York station that became the producing head of the new system.

To meet congressional concerns about preserving localism, the new Public Broadcasting Service was to be controlled by a board of directors elected by the "grassroots" subscribing stations. But Ford ensured that they, in turn, would be dominated by the powerful inner circle of metropolitan stations it financed and favored. The new PBS president was Hartford Gunn, the manager of WGBH.

While this process of creation was working itself out, political events were moving in ways that would fatefully shape the future. Until 1968, the disaffected Democrats who had created public television were engaged in a family quarrel with the Johnson administration. The war had cast them unexpectedly in an adversarial posture towards the anti-Communist liberals, who remained committed to the Vietnam policy they had once supported. But in 1968, the White House fell into unfriendly Republican hands, and, worse still, into the hands of the man who, since the trial of Alger Hiss, had been their most hated political antagonist.

With Richard Nixon in the White House, the Vietnam nightmare no longer belonged to the liberals. Liberals, in fact, had not only joined the opposition but, behind the candidacies of Gene McCarthy, Bobby Kennedy, and, later, George McGovern, they had become its leaders. After the defeat in 1968, many took up positions in the media to assault the new administration and its now unpopular war. With this development, the partnership that had always existed between wartime Washington and the fourth estate began to fracture along the fault lines of the radical decade.

Even the commercial networks went on the attack. In 1971, CBS aired *The Selling of the Pentagon*, an unprecedented indictment of the nation's defense establishment, which was accused of illegal politicking in behalf of its war and economic profiteering. When the Nixon administration attempted to strike back, a second battlefront was opened between the media and the White House—a battlefront that would escalate right up to the Watergate crisis and the resignation of the president.

Among the disaffected Democrats who entered the media, the more liberal gravitated to public television. It was in this period that Johnson aide Bill Moyers joined WNET to begin his intellectual odyssey to the left. When he arrived, the atmosphere at the station, in the words of Robert Kotlowitz, was already one of "guerrilla warfare."

It was in this atmosphere that Ford announced it was creating and funding a PBS news center in Washington, D.C., which would be staffed by prominent media luminaries, all of whom the Nixon White House had identified as political enemies. Among them were Elizabeth Drew, Robert MacNeil, and—most egregious of all, to the White House—Kennedy crony Sander Vanocur, who came over from NBC with an $85,000 price tag, or twice the annual salary of a sitting congressman.

The loading of these cannons was duly noted by the White House, and on October 20, 1971, at a meeting of educational broadcasters in Miami, an explosion occurred. "I honestly don't know what group I'm addressing," Nixon aide Clay Whitehead told those assembled. "What's your status? To us there is evidence that you are becoming affiliates of a centralized, national network."

The line of attack had been carefully calculated. Recognizing that the White House could not win the argument if the conflict were posed in political terms, Whitehead focused on procedural issues. Ford and the PBS affiliates were violating their mandate by creating a fourth network. Instead of funding a variety of programming from which stations could pick and choose, they had created a centralized production facility. "How different will your network news programs be from the programs Fred Friendly and Sander Vanocur wanted to do at CBS and NBC?" Whitehead asked.

The present ambitions, Whitehead claimed, were at odds with the original conception as set out by Carnegie and the Public Broadcasting Act. The idea behind the creation of the Corporation for Public Broadcasting was to support grassroots television—"to serve the stations—to help them extend the range of *their* services to their communities. The idea was to break the NET monopoly of program production...."

Evidently both Congress and the public had been taken for a ride:

> In 1961, the public broadcasting professionals let the Carnegie dreamers...run on about localism and 'bedrocks' and the rest of it—let them sell the Congress on pluralism and local diversity—[but] when they've gone back to the boardrooms and classrooms and union halls and rehearsal halls, the professionals...stay in the control room and call the shots.

Whitehead's speech was but the opening salvo. The following June, Nixon vetoed the CPB funding bill. The corporation's president and several Johnson-appointed board members immediately resigned and were replaced with Nixon nominees. PBS executives issued declarations of concern. WNET invited Whitehead and the new Nixon appointees to appear on camera in public debate. But while the battles raged, the war itself was already over.

Thirteen days before, five men had been arrested while breaking into the Watergate apartment complex in Washington. By the end of the year, the most watched programming on public television stations were the hearings to decide whether to impeach the president. True to its mission of providing the public with fare that the commercial channels would not, PBS featured the hearings on prime time when the networks had turned to other entertainments.

The outcome of the battle Whitehead had begun was a complete rout for the Nixon camp. "When Watergate came along," WNET's Robert Kotlowitz recalled, "that was the whole damn thing."

With Nixon as its enemy, PBS's guerrilla army was able to cast itself as a national David. The result was a groundswell of support from new members and contributors. Even the more "conservative" stations that had been at loggerheads with PBS joined hands with the center to fight the common foe. Having humbled the president, the Democratic Congress now rushed eagerly to aid its ally in the Watergate travails. A significant increase in system funds was authorized and, more importantly, committed three years in advance. Congress also acted to tie the corporation's unreliable hands. Fifty percent of its program grants were now earmarked for the stations as "general support"—a percentage that would rise above 90 percent in the following decade. The stations, in turn, kicked back a portion of their grants into a newly created program fund, further depriving CPB of influence over the system product. When the dust had settled, the corporation, which Nixon had tried to make a conservative redoubt, was discredited and crippled, while Ford's protege, PBS, emerged as the newly dominant power at the center of the system.

Vietnam and Watergate: public television's birth by fire in the crucible of these events created its political culture that today often seems frozen in '60s amber. The one area of its current affairs programming that managed to escape this fate, ironically, is the one where the battle with the Nixon White House was most directly joined.

"When you're talking about using federal funds to support a journalism activity," Whitehead had warned, "it's always going to be a subject of scrutiny....It just invites a lot of political attention." In 1975, even as public television was making its peace with Nixon's successor, WNET launched the *MacNeil/Lehrer Report* as a half-hour nightly magazine following the network news. Devoted to a single subject per evening, *MacNeil/Lehrer* provided in-depth analysis that network sound-bites could not duplicate.

Robert MacNeil had been one of the liberal journalists singled out by the Nixon administration as a political antagonist. By avoiding an advocacy position, MacNeil's program earned the confidence of conservatives and went on to prosper more than any other public-television show besides *Sesame Street*. In 1983, it expanded to an hour and thereafter set a quality standard for prime-time news.

But *MacNeil/Lehrer* proved to be the exception. In other areas of current-affairs programming, a different standard was set. In film documentaries—where current-affairs subjects were treated in a magazine-like setting, making it possible to tell a story whole and provide an editorial thrust—the political personality of the system Bundy and Friendly had put into place, soon showed another, more radical face.

In fact, the protest culture that everywhere else had withered at the end of the '60s when its fantasies of revolution collapsed had found a refuge in public television. A cottage film industry of activist documentarians had sprung up during the '60s as the makers of promotional films for the Black Panther Party, the Weather Underground, and other domestic radical groups, and for the revolutionary future in Communist countries like Cuba and Vietnam. Felix Greene, Emile De Antonio, and the Stalinist propagandist Joris Ivens were their "politically committed" cinematic models. This group now began its own institutional "long march" by taking its political enthusiasms, its filmmaking skills, and its network of left-wing foundations (Rubin, Rabinowitz, and MacArthur) into the PBS orbit.

The integration of these radicals into the liberal PBS community was made easier by the convergence of political agendas at the end of the Vietnam War, when supporters of the Communist conquest were able to celebrate victory with liberals who had only desired an American withdrawal. Another convergence occurred in relation to the post-'60s romance between New Left survivors and the Old Left Communists, whom cold warriors like Richard Nixon had made their targets. Liberals shared the radicals' antipathy for the anti-Communist right, along with their sense that the political targets of anti-Communists were victims of persecution.

The Unquiet Death of Julius and Ethel Rosenberg, which appeared as a two-hour PBS special in 1974 and attempted to exonerate the most famous martyrs of the anti-Communist '50s, was a prime expression of this left-wing nostalgia. In introducing its special, PBS described it as "the kind of programming that we enjoy presenting [and] hope to continue to present."

What was striking about the film was not just that it cast doubt on the verdict of the Rosenberg trial, or that it did so even as massive FBI files released under the new Freedom of Information Act were confirming their guilt, or even that it went beyond the airing of doubts about the case to imply that there had been a government "frame-up" and that the verdict was an indictment of American justice. What was disturbing (and, it turned out, prophetic in terms of future PBS productions) was that it was also a political brief for the Communist left to which the Rosenbergs had belonged.

The narration introduced the Rosenbergs thus: "With millions of others they question an economic and political system that lays waste to human lives. Capitalism has failed. A new system might be better. Socialism is its name. For many the vehicle for change is the Communist Party." The film then cut to an authority explaining that Communists were people who "believed that you couldn't have political democracy without economic democracy....Being a Communist meant simply to fight for the rights of the people." The authority was longtime Stalinist Carl Marzani, a fact the program neglected to mention.

In 1978, to mark the 25th anniversary of the Rosenberg's execution, PBS ran the four-year-old program again, adding a half-hour update. The update confirmed just how determinedly ideological some regions of PBS had become. The original two-hour program had been based on the standard defense of the Rosenbergs' innocence written by fellow-travelers Walter and Miriam Schneir. In the interim, *The Rosenberg File* by Ronald Radosh and Joyce Milton was published, based on the new FBI materials and on original interviews with principals in the case. While concluding that Julius was guilty as charged, the authors were critical of the death penalty and of the prosecution of Ethel, against whom they believed no credible case had been made.

Because *The Rosenberg File* had been so widely praised as a "definitive" account, PBS executives asked producer Alvin Goldstein to include the "update" and to interview Radosh on camera. When Goldstein edited the interview, however, he did so with the scruples of a Party censor. "I couldn't believe the final product when I saw it," Radosh said later. "He cut out everything I said that contradicted his film, and left only the parts that supported his claims—the failure of the government to make its case against Ethel, the injustice of the sentence. Whereas our book totally demolished the argument of his film, viewers watching it would think I endorsed his claims. Moscow television couldn't have done better. It was outrageous."

Far from being an isolated example, the PBS treatment of the Rosenberg case proved typical. Politically "committed" profiles of individual Communists that appeared as PBS specials included Paul Robeson, Angela Davis, Dashiell Hammet, and Bertolt Brecht, in addition to Stalin propagandist Anna Louise Strong, Marxist martyr Victor Jara, and Stalin idolater Frida Kahlo. These were amplified by the collective portraits *Seeing Red* (1986), a 90-minute profile of American Communists as progressive idealists, and *The Good Fight*, a nostalgic tribute to Stalinism's international contingent in the Spanish Civil War.

This opening to the discredited pro-Soviet left was not only not balanced by any reasonably truthful portrait of American Communism, it was pointedly not matched by any equal-opportunity offering to anti-Communists, whether of the left or right. Thus, there was an *American Playhouse* mini-series sympathetic to the claims of Alger Hiss, the man charged with betraying his country, but not to the courage of Whittaker Chambers, the man who risked his life attempting to save it. There were specials on Robert Oppenheimer but not Edward Teller, on Carlos Fuentes but not Vargas Llosa, on Brecht but not Solzhenitsyn (or Sakharov or Sharansky), on the Communist Party but not the Congress for Cultural Freedom, on the personal trials of American radicals who had devoted their lives to a political illusion and enemy power but not on the tribulations of those who changed their minds in order to defend their country and its freedom. No homages to Max Eastman, Jay Lovestone, James Burnham, Bayard Rustin, or Sidney Hook.

While PBS searched for silver linings in the dark clouds of the Communist left, it found mainly negative forces at work in those American institutions tasked with fighting the Communist threat, in particular the Central Intelligence Agency, which became a PBS symbol of American evil. In 1980, PBS aired a three-hour series called *On Company Business*, which its New Left producers described as "the story of 30 years of CIA subversion, murder, bribery and torture as told by an insider and documented with newsreel film of actual events." The makers of *On Company Business* made it clear that, unlike the Church Committee, they were not concerned about the CIA being a rogue elephant but regarded its actions as an expression of policy "determined at the highest levels of the US government."

The CIA "insider" on whom PBS relied for editorial guidance was Philip Agee—not so much a dissenter from CIA policy as a defector to the Soviet side. Working closely with Cuban intelligence, Agee had "outed" CIA and other Western intelligence agents, destroying their operations and endangering their lives. In a 1975 *Esquire* article, Agee had written: "I aspire to be a communist and a revolutionary." The same year, a Swiss magazine asked his opinion of U.S. and Soviet intelligence agencies. He replied:

> The CIA is plainly on the wrong side, that is the capitalistic side. I approve of KGB activities, communist activities in general, when they are to the advantage of the oppressed. In fact, the KGB is not doing enough in this regard because the USSR depends upon the people to free themselves. Between the overdone activities that the CIA initiates and the

more modest activities of the KGB there is absolutely no comparison.

PBS viewers of *On Company Business*, however, were kept ignorant of Agee's political commitments. Agee had been expelled from the Netherlands, France, and England because of his contacts with Soviet and Cuban intelligence agents, but the PBS special identified him only by the caption "CIA: 1959-1969." When Reed Irvine and other critics objected to the program's "disinformation," they were dismissed out of hand by PBS vice president for news and public affairs Barry Chase. Chase sent a memo to all PBS stations describing *On Company Business* as "a highly responsible overview of the CIA's history and major contribution to the ongoing debate on the CIA's past, present and future."

PBS's next summary view of American intelligence was a Bill Moyers special called *The Secret Government* (1987), which insinuated what no congressional investigation had ever established: that the CIA was indeed a rogue institution subverting American policy. The wilder shores of this kind of conspiracy thesis were subsequently explored in two *Frontline* programs, *Murder on the Rio San Juan* and *Guns, Drugs, and the CIA*, which leaned heavily on the discredited "secret team" fantasies of the Christic Institute. *The Secret Government* was followed by a four-part series called *Secret Intelligence* (1989), which, like all three of its predecessors, rehearsed the standard litany of left-wing complaints—Iran, Guatemala, Bay of Pigs, Chile—and culminated in a one-sided view of Iran-Contra as an anti-Constitutional plot. Like its predecessors, *Secret Intelligence* found the agency more of a threat to American institutions than a guardian of American security.

Although PBS officials continued to pay lip service to "balance," no sympathetic portrait of the CIA's Cold War activities was aired, no equally partisan account of its role in supporting the anti-Communist rebels in Afghanistan or Angola or of the costly destruction of the CIA's assets in the Middle East as a result of the liberal and radical attacks on its integrity. In the absence of countervailing portrayals of American cold war policies and institutions, the indictments presented in PBS documentaries amounted to an editorial position. In the PBS perspective, the United States was seen as an imperialist, counter-revolutionary power whose national security apparatus was directed not at containing an expansionist empire but (in the words of the producers of *On Company Business*) at suppressing "people who have dared struggle for a better life."

Ironically, this Marxist caricature received a full-dress treatment on PBS channels in 1989, the year the Communist utopia collapsed in ruins. *The American Century* was a five-part, five-hour British financed series, written and produced by *Harper's* editor Lewis Lapham, which purported to chart the course of American foreign policy from 1900. The final segment traced American Cold War policy from 1945 to 1975. It did not pay tribute to the heroic efforts of Cold War containment that had resulted in the liberation of a billion people from the chains of a tyranny as great as the world has ever known. It rehearsed, instead, the same left-wing litany— Guatemala, Iran, Bay of Pigs—to claim that under the cloak of anti-Communism, third-world progress had become the victim of greedy U.S. corporations and their secret allies in the U.S. government (described by Lapham in relation to Cuba as "the agent of the reactionary past"). This summary segment of the series was called "Imperial Masquerade," and it appeared in December 1989 even as East Berliners were tearing down their Wall.

This view of America as an evil empire was powerfully reinforced by PBS's treatment of post-Vietnam Communism in other documentary shows. In 1975, PBS aired Shirley MacLaine's *China Memoir*, a view of the Maoist paradise so wide-eyed that PBS's own chairman was forced to concede that it was "pure propaganda." *China Memoir* was followed by *The Children of China* (1977), praised by Communist officials who thought it would help Americans to "understand the 'new' China." The "new" North Korea and the "new" Cuba were also the focus of promotional features in *North Korea* (1978), *Cuba, Sport and Revolution* (1979), *Cuba: The New Man* (1986), and *Cuba—In the Shadow of Doubt* (1986), about which the *New York Times* commented: "At its best, the documentary has a romantic infatuation with Cuba; at its worst, it is calculated propaganda."

As the locus of the cold war shifted to Central America in the 1980s, Marxist agitprop established itself on PBS as a new wave aesthetic. Documentary after documentary appeared as briefs for the Sandinista dictatorship in Nicaragua and for the FMLN terrorists in El Salvador. These included *El Salvador, Another Vietnam?* (1981), *Nicaragua: These Same Hands* (1982), *Nicaragua...From the Ashes* (1982), and *Target Nicaragua* (1983). The producers of these programs, presented by WNET, were the radical activist filmmakers who had come in from the '70s cold (among them, World Focus Films of Berkeley, The Women's Film Project, and The Institute for Policy Studies).

As with its celebrations of American Communism, PBS showed no eagerness to balance this advocacy with other views. In 1983, The American Catholic Committee offered WNET a program critical of the Marxist regime, *Nicaragua: A Model for Latin America?* The Catholic film was based on documentary footage and dealt with government repression of the press, the Roman Catholic church, and independent labor unions. WNET rejected the film while denying the rejection was made on political grounds. "We thought we had a better way to handle this information," said WNET president Jay Iselin in explaining his decision.

In 1985, a *Frontline* series called Central America in Crisis did depart momentarily from the propagandizing trend of PBS documentaries to look critically at the various sides of the conflict, and in 1986, *Nicaragua Was Our Home,* a film focusing on the plight of the Miskito Indians, was aired in response to the protests over WNET's previous offerings. But for the most part, the "better way" to handle information about Nicaragua turned out to be pretty much the way it had been handled before.

In 1984, WGBH's *Frontline* series featured *Nicaragua: Report from the Front,* produced by Pam Yates' Skylight Productions, whose message (in the words of *New York Times* reviewer John Corry) was: "Sandinistas are good; their opponents are bad. There is no middle ground." The same wisdom was the message of two subsequent *Frontline* reports: *Who's Running This War?* (1986), which portrayed the Contras as Somozcistas bent on violating human rights, and *The War On Nicaragua* (1987) by William Greider and producer Sherry Jones, which was named one of the worst shows of the year by the liberal critic of the *San Francisco Chronicle,* John Carman. Carman called it "shoddy, unfair and manipulative journalism." (In a typical scene, Carman noted, a

U.S. General remarked that bringing troops to Honduras was an education for them; his words were illustrated by film footage of U.S. servicemen "throwing grenades and shooting up the countryside.")

Nor did the PBS approach to Communist movements alter when addressing the conflicts in other Central American countries. Skylight Productions' *Guatemala: When the Mountains Tremble* (1985), for example, was panned by the *New York Times* as a "vanity film" because of its agitprop character. *Washington Post* TV critic Tom Shales summed it up in the following terms: "The film is bluntly didactic and one-sided in portraying Guatemalan rebels as noble freedom fighters and Guatemalan peasants opposed to the present regime as the victims of repression, torture and squalor."

Five of the programs on Central America that PBS chose to air during this crucial decade before Com-munism's collapse were, in fact, the work of a single director and radical ideologue, Deborah Shaffer, whose "solidarity" with the Communist dictators of Nicaragua and their guerrilla allies in El Salvador and Guatemala, far from being hidden, was a proudly displayed item in her curriculum vita. Her most celebrated documentary, *Fire From the Mountain* (1986), an aggressive promotion of Sandinista myths, was based on the autobiography of Sandinista secret police chief Omar Cabezas, while her other films—*El Salvador: Another Vietnam?*, *Central America in Revolt*, *Witness to War: Dr. Charlie Clements*, and *Nicaragua: Report From the Front* (the latter two were Skylight productions)—all reflected her commitment to the Communist politics of the Central American guerrillas.

In 1988, the congressional oversight committees for public television, led by Democratic chairs Rep. Markey and Sen. Inouye, institutionalized this revolutionary front inside PBS by authorizing the transfer of $18 million of CPB moneys to set up the Independent Television Service (ITVS) as a separate fund for "independent" filmmakers.

Representing the independents in testimony before the committees were Deborah Shaeffer's producer Pam Yates of Skylight Productions and Larry Daressa, co-chair of the National Coalition of Independent Public Broadcasting Producers. Daressa, who later turned up on the ITVS board, was also the 20-year president of California Newsreel, flagship of the radical film collectives and producer of such '60s classics as *Black Panther* and *The Peoples War*, a triumphalist view of the Communist conquest of Vietnam.

Daressa made the strong case, attacking PBS for its "betrayal" of trust. PBS had become commercial, he claimed, and—knuckling under to "corporate interests"—conformist. "Independent producers have found themselves progressively marginalized in this brave new world of semi-commercial, public pay television," he says. "Our diverse voices reflecting the breadth of America's communities and opinions have no place in public television's plans to turn itself into an upscale version of the networks. We have found that insofar as we speak with an independent voice we have no place in public television."

One longtime member of the public-television community commented on this testimony: "These people are not 'diverse,' they're politically correct. Nor are they 'independent.' These are the commissars of the political left. These are the people who basically owned the Vietnamese and Cuban and Nicaraguan franchises, who got so close to Communist officials and guerrilla capos that if you wanted to get access for interviews or permission even to bring camera equipment into the 'liberated zone' in certain cases, you had to go through them."

By authorizing $18 million in public funds to the artistic commissars of ITVS, Congress had provided the extreme left with an institutional base in public television.

Throughout its tenure, the Reagan administration had waged a front line battle against Soviet-backed Marxists in Central America and the Sandinista dictatorship in Nicaragua. Yet there was no direct White House response to the PBS attacks on its Central American policies, or even to PBS's propaganda war on behalf of its Communist enemy. "PBS never came up as an issue," recalls Reagan's chief domestic advisor, Martin Anderson, "We just never focused on it."

Far from attempting to control public television through its funding corporation, as the Nixon administration had, the Reagan White House had even reappointed CPB chairman Sharon Rockefeller, a Carter nominee and liberal Democrat. "Our intention had been to remove her as chairman, just as we tried to do with every other agency" recalls Penn James, who handled White House appointments. "But when we announced our intention, her father, Sen.

Charles Percy, was outraged. He went storming over to the White House and told the president, 'If you want my cooperation on the foreign relations committee, you'd better reappoint my daughter.' So we did."

During her tenure, Rockefeller acted to insulate the system from political accountability even more. She changed the corporation by-laws to further curtail its discretion over programming so that the new Reagan appointees were confronted with an official policy under which they were not even to mention programs by name. New board member Sonia Landau found that directors were discouraged from even asking questions about programs: "Once you start asking, everybody starts hollering, 'Heat shield!'"

But with Reagan's re-election and her father's defeat, Rockefeller was replaced as the chairman by Landau. The following spring, Reagan appointee Rick Brookhiser offered a modest proposal to the corporation board. Brookhiser suggested that the corporation undertake a scientific "content analysis" of the current-affairs programs it had funded to see if they were indeed tipped to one side of the political scale. The board would be "derelict" he said, if it did not try to assure the "objectivity and balance" of its programming as the 1967 act had mandated.

It seemed a straightforward request, but the reaction was almost entirely negative. "Any signs that the corporation might think of itself as more than a conduit, draws the alarm of the system," Brookhiser reflected afterwards. "The system rushes to the scene like phagocytes in the bloodstream to an infection. Sharon Rockefeller hated my proposal. The station heads complained. I remember going up to a meeting of public TV stations in Boston where I tried to argue the case. When they took a vote, it was unanimous against."

Charges of "neo-McCarthyism" were hurled in Brookhiser's direction, and PBS vice president Barry Chase scolded: "It is inappropriate for a presidentially appointed group to be conducting a content analysis of programming. It indicates that some people on the CPB board don't fully understand the appropriate constraints on them."

In an interview with the *Los Angeles Times*, Bruce Christensen, president of PBS, was less restrained: "In 1973, President Nixon in fact tried to kill federal funding for public television through his political appointees to the board and the kind of chicanery that went on at the time. They didn't do a 'content analysis.' Content analysis seems to me a little more sophisticated way of achieving those ends."

Such accusations were sufficiently intimidating to stall the proposal. Brookhiser could not secure enough support even from the Reagan-appointed majority to get approval. Meeting in St. Paul in June, the corporation board decided to postpone its decision on the study until September. But before it could meet, a new controversy erupted that polarized the forces even further, demonstrating just how weak the conservatives' influence on public television was and how powerful their liberal adversaries had become.

The *casus belli* was a nine-part series on Africa presented by WETA. *The Africans* had been underwritten by more than $1 million in grants from PBS, CPB, and the National Endowment for the Humanities. When NEH Chairman Lynne Cheney received an additional request from WETA for $50,000 to promote the series, she decided to screen it. Her response was outrage. "I have just finished viewing all nine hours of *The Africans*," she wrote to WETA president Ward Chamberlin. "Worse than unbalanced, this film frequently degenerates into anti-Western diatribe. I fail to understand how a public television station of WETA's stature and reputation could be involved with a series that extols the virtues of Muammar Qaddafi." She continued:

> One entire segment, called *Tools of Exploitation*, strives to blame every technological, moral and economic failure of Africa on the West....The result of all this blame-casting in Part IV is to make the Africans seem a passive, supine people, an implication insulting to Africans that is simply untrue....The film moves from distressing moment to distressing moment, climaxing in Part IX where Qaddafi's virtues are set forth. Shortly thereafter, pictures of mushroom clouds fill the screen and it is suggested that Africans are about to come into their own, because after [the] 'final racial conflict' in South Africa, black Africans will have nuclear weapons.

Cheney told WETA that not only would she not finance the promotion of the series, but she wanted the NEH credits removed from the print: "Our logo is regarded as a mark of approbation, and the NEH most decidedly does not approve this film."

Cheney's position was in striking contrast to PBS executives' defense of the series, which was to disclaim all responsibility for the product that bore their imprint: "We don't make the programs at PBS," Christensen explained in a statement that encapsulated the official defense, "and we have no editorial control ultimately over what is put in the program....Until a series is delivered to PBS for distribution, we have no editorial input or oversight over the producer or anyone connected to the project."

It was an evasion that the bureaucratic complexities of the system made possible. PBS did not actually "produce" programs and, in that most technical sense, could not be held responsible for what was in them. But this was to beg the question. As "gatekeeper" for the national distribution of programs, PBS daily rejected projects simply on the grounds that they "did not meet PBS standards." A thick volume of "Standards and Practices" was, in fact, distributed to independent producers, warning them that public television had to "maintain the confidence of its viewers" and that, consequently, producers had to adhere strictly to the official PBS guidelines for quality. Moreover, once a series like *The Africans* was aired, it bore the PBS logo and was promoted and distributed by PBS on cassette and often in companion book form, with educational aides, to schools and libraries. Such activities constituted an active endorsement and, like the decision to air the programs in the first place, was not merely an imposition, as Christensen implied.

In seeking support from the press and Congress, however, PBS executives deployed a more persuasive argument than their own impotence. For the NEH or PBS to exert any judgment on the quality of *The Africans*, they claimed, would be to engage in a form of censorship. The National Endowment, Christensen told the *Los Angeles Times*, is "not the Ministry of Truth." He warned that if Cheney were to insist on entering the editing room, "there will be no NEH funding in public television."

This line of reasoning was more effective but no less

spurious. It simply ignored the right (let alone obligations) of a funder to impose guidelines and conditions on the recipients of its gifts. It also ignored the fact that the Corporation for Public Broadcasting's own standard contract with producers stipulated that it would be allowed to see rough cuts and make changes it regarded as necessary. Christensen's argument also ignored PBS's own responsibility—emphasized by PBS officials on other occasions—for the character of programs they distributed and promoted.

With PBS again polarized as the public's David against the government's Goliath, Brookhiser's proposal failed to gain the approval of the Reagan-appointed board. A move by 57 House members to stimulate an inquiry into the matters that Brookhiser had raised was also easily rebuffed by the appropriate committee head, John Dingell. To consolidate these victories, PBS appointed a committee to review its own procedures. Stacked with an in-house majority, the committee avoided any systematic review of programming and concluded with a pat on its own back: "PBS's procedures...have encouraged programs of high quality that reflect a wide range of information, opinion, and artistic expression and that satisfy accepted journalistic standards."

◆　◆　◆

The fact that business would proceed as usual became quickly apparent. In the fall of 1989, public-television station WNYC announced the cancellation of a program about the Palestinian intifada that it had previously agreed to "present." In making the announcement, WNYC vice president Chloe Aaron characterized the program, *Days of Rage*, as "propaganda" and compared it to Leni Riefenstahl's Hitler epic *Triumph of the Will*. At this juncture, WNET stepped into the breach with an announcement that it would present *Days of Rage* instead.

The 90-minute documentary turned out to be a catalogue of horror stories about the Israeli occupation that interviewed only Palestinian moderates and Israeli extremists and omitted any mention of Palestinian terrorism. In the best tradition of PBS's "independent" documentary filmmakers, its producer, director, and narrator, Jo Franklin-Trout, was an activist with close ties to her subjects.

In 1980, she had served as a "back-door channel" for the Saudi government, which had complained about a

PBS documentary, *Death of A Princess*, that told the story of a member of the royal family who had been executed for adultery. To appease Riyadh, PBS agreed to run a three-part documentary on Saudi Arabia "slanted," in the words of *The New Republic*, "towards the Saudi perspective." The documentary was made by Jo Franklin-Trout and was paid for by four Saudi-involved multinational corporations that previously had lobbied for the sale of AWACs to the regime.

Days of Rage proved to have a similarly tainted provenance. In an article appearing in *The New Republic*, Middle East expert Steve Emerson revealed that *Days of Rage* had been produced in close cooperation with the Arab American Cultural Foundation, headed by a friend and advisor to PLO chief Yasir Arafat. The foundation had financed the film by agreeing to purchase copies if it approved the product, which it did.

During the battle over *Days of Rage*, WNET was besieged by critical press, public protests, and membership cancellations, but it held fast to its decision. Reflecting later on his role in airing the program, WNET vice president Bob Kotlow-itz displayed an attitude that was both perverse and at the same time characteristic of that of other public television officials: "I thought the *intifada* program was a horror. It was a horror. And I wasn't happy with having it on the air. But I'm still happy that we made the decision to go with it."

It was, by any standard, an extraordinary admission for a professional journalist. One would be hard put to imagine, for example, a CBS executive first acknowledging a story's indefensibility and then claiming an achievement in running it. Kotlowitz' attitude, in fact, bore a striking resemblance to Ledwig's suggestion to me to switch off his own channel because of its one-sided lobby against principles that he himself firmly believed in. Both betrayed the lack of a proprietary vision in governing their own institutions. Both were really invoking a higher principle in making judgments that otherwise seemed inexplicable.

This "higher principle" has a name within the public television community, where it is referred to as "the mission," one of the most important but least understood factors in shaping the public television persona. Simply put, the "mission" is a mandate to provide for the public what commercial television allegedly cannot—by its very nature—provide, because it is "constrained by the commercial necessity of delivering mass audiences to advertisers." The words belong to PBS president Bruce Christensen and are contemporary. But they could as well have been taken from the Carnegie Commission report 20 years earlier. The "mission" is what makes public television "public." It is its life principle and *raison d'etre*. It is what justifies the hundreds of millions of government and privately contributed dollars necessary to make the system possible.

The "mission" provides a rationale under which viewpoints that are politically and socially marginal appear to public-television executives to have a presumptive claim on public air time. And this is the rationale that justifies the indefensible propaganda of programs like *Days of Rage*, promos for Communist guerrillas in Central America, as well as the manifestos for sexual radicals and hate groups at home (*Tongues Untied* and *Stop the Church*) that have recently provoked similar public-relations problems for the system. It is also the rationale that justifies the establishment of ITVS— the institutionalization of the marginal left as a primary component of PBS's public affairs profile.

Just how much a part of public television's personality this attitude has become can be seen in a recent controversy involving Bill Moyers, the medium's most ubiquitous presence, described as a "national treasure" by the present PBS programming chief, Jennifer Lawson. Moyers had been challenged by the Committee on Media Integrity as the author of PBS's only two full-length documentaries on the Iran Contra affair, *The Secret Government* and *High Crimes and Misdemeanors*. The committee questioned whether a monopoly of views pitched to the left end of the political spectrum met the standards of fairness and balance that public television was supposed to honor. Moyers' response was a tortured invocation of public television's mission:

> What deeper understanding of our role in the world could we have come to by praising Oliver North yet again, when we had already gotten five full days before Congress, with wall-to-wall coverage on network, cable and public airwaves, to tell his side of the story? *In fact, it hardly seems consistent*

with "objectivity, balance and fairness" that
the other side of his story got only two 90-minute
documentaries on pubic television. (emphasis
added)

For anyone not steeped in Moyers' own political
mythology, this was an eccentric view of what had taken
place. North, of course, had not produced his own network documentary but was more realistically the target of
an attempted public hanging—hauled before a congressional
inquisition without the benefits of due process, prosecuted
and judged by political enemies themselves protected by
governmental immunity. None of these concerns was even a
potentially worthy issue for public television in Moyers'
insular view. What was worthy was the fact that North
seemed to have emerged from his ordeal with a positive approval rating. The commercial networks, true to their conformist reflexes, had been used to promote a conservative
icon. The mission of public television was not to present a
balance of views within its own schedule, as its enabling legislation required, but to provide a kind of affirmative-action
program for radical views that the body politic had itself
rejected. This would promote the balance that, in Moyers'
eyes, ought to exist.

But who outside the public television community
would maintain today that there are two and only two
perspectives on important national issues like Iran Contra:
that of the "establishment" and its adversaries on the left?
The cognitive dissonance provoked by Moyers' narrow conception of the varieties of America's political experience is
provoked equally by the PBS schedule itself. (Indeed, in one
week in April 1991, a major PBS station aired 10 hours of
Moyers' shows in a prime-time total of 13 hours of current-
affairs programming.) Public television has become a prisoner of the history that created it. Its present dilemma is
caused by the failure to redefine its "mission" to accord with
the changes of the times since. There was indeed once an establishment presiding over America's political culture that,
though divided on many issues, was united on one: the Cold
War with communism was a vital national priority. When
Fred Friendly resigned from CBS in protest over the networks'
refusal to air the anti-war testimony of George Kennan, it is

quite possible that the CBS judgment was made for political reasons. In such an atmosphere there may have been a "mission" for a public-television service, which, because it would act under different constraints, would be ready to air such views.

But a lot has changed in 20 years. The Cold War consensus that provided bipartisan support for administration policy has long since dissolved. Since Watergate, the press itself has adopted an adversarial posture towards all administrations, despite the "commercial constraints" it operates under. The Iran Contra hearings, which attempted to impugn the integrity and even legitimacy of the Reagan White House, were aired on all three networks, not to mention C-SPAN and CNN. The Democratic legislators interrogating North were not bi-partisan adherents of the Reagan policy but its bitter opponents.

In short, the mission that had originally inspired public-television professionals and made possible public-television's birth has been overtaken by events. Public television can no longer position itself as the channel necessary to create a national dialogue because the commercial channels have now incorporated that mission. *Nightline*, as Bruce Christensen testified to Congress in 1988, is a direct outgrowth of *MacNeil/Lehrer*, while *60 Minutes* was inspired by the Public Broadcast Laboratory of NET. Recognizing that their point on the spectrum has been occupied, public-television officials have sought a new space by allowing their political message to be pushed further and further to the left.

But it is a self-limiting solution. As the country itself has become increasingly conservative, this radical posture has alienated a major part of public television's audience of supporters as well as its Republican constituency in Congress. Indeed, it is only because Congress has remained stubbornly Democratic against the conservative tide that public television has not been in more financial trouble than it has been. But the current situation is inherently unstable and will remain so as long as public television fails to reflect the broad interests of the population that is being taxed to support it.

From a purely self-interested viewpoint, therefore, public television's romance with the left makes no economic sense. Public television is now a billion-dollar industry and its 300-odd stations are run by boards whose personnel are financial and social pillars of their local communities. Moreover, those public television executives, like Daniel Ledwig, whose concern is the financial future, are themselves mainly recruited from the corridors of industry and commerce. This is in marked contrast, of course, to its program staff. A recent study by Rothman and Lichter reveals that only 7 percent of public-television journalists consider themselves "conservative" and only another 18 percent consider themselves "moderate." The other 75 percent are to their left. Is this a healthy situation for public TV?

The division of labor between conservatives and liberals in public television has been compared by Midge Decter to the political economy of Malaysia, where the ethnic Chinese run the economy and the Malays run the politics. A great deal of public television's chronic penury stems from the fact that while the "Chinese" presidents of its stations are out soliciting corporate sponsors and planning business strategies to expand their empires, the "Malay" programmers are busily at work undermining their own corporate environment.

In fact, public television's self-destructive tilt is more readily explained as a case of bad conscience than bad judgment. This bad conscience comes from the fact that in the last two decades, not only has PBS become increasingly commercial in its search for funds, it has become increasingly indistinguishable in its non-political programming from commercial TV.

The first of these developments began, in earnest, during the Nixon fracas. Between 1973 and 1978, corporate "underwriting" of public television went up nearly 500 percent. Worse yet, for the liberal conscience, the leaders in this trend, contributing more than half the total support, were big oil companies like Mobil, Exxon, and Gulf. The oil companies had a predilection for underwriting the British programs (*Masterpiece Theater*, etc.,) that in the '70s began to make public television a viable channel. (So dominant was this oil-fueled British invasion in the PBS schedule, that critics began referring to it as the Petroleum British System.)

By the 1980s, corporate sponsorship accounted for almost as much of the public-television budget as its entire federal subsidy. The staid underwriting announcements at the top of its programs have come more and more to look and sound like the advertisements on its competitor stations. And the programming has as well. First, because public-television stations have begun buying syndicated shows from commercial TV (including *The Wonderful World of Disney*, *I Spy*, and *Lou Grant*). But far more significant is the fact that with the advent of cable, commercial stations have begun to compete directly with PBS.

The Arts & Entertainment network was started by the head of PBS's cultural programming, and its schedule—whether showing European movies, or serious drama, or biographies of historical figures—is comparable to anything PBS can offer. Another cable channel, Bravo, features drama from Aeschylus to O'Neill, film from Olivier to Bunuel, and music from Monteverdi to Messiaen to suit the most esoteric tastes. The Discovery Channel now repeats the nature shows that made PBS's early career, while C-SPAN provides round-the-clock political interviews and discussions at the most serious level, including live sessions of Congress and political conventions and meetings.

The one PBS signature that these channels don't, in fact, feature is the monotonously served offering of left-wing politics. Indeed, by presenting the entire range of the political spectrum from Maoist Left to movement Right, C-SPAN has shown that political controversy is perfectly acceptable when a fair shake is given all around.

In the final analysis, left-wing politics is PBS's ill-conceived solution to its identity crisis as well as the key to its financial unease. This unease is compounded by the political gravity that will not let it break fully into the commercial market but pulls it relentlessly back to the public trough. Like all the other socialist pockets in the American market, public television is bloated with redundant bureaucracy, burdened by legendary inefficiency, and bled by incomprehensible waste. Public broadcasting, former PBS president and NBC executive Lawrence Grossman told *TV Guide* a few years ago, "is so diffuse, duplicative, bureaucratic, confusing, frustrating and senseless, that it is a miracle [it] has survived at all." And yet, instead of looking to the market to invigorate its future, PBS executives compulsively return to the taxpayer's pocket.

"One of the great harms the Reagan administration did," former CPB chairman Sharon Rockefeller said recently, "was to tell anyone who would listen that public broadcasting is supposed to be self-supporting. It can't be." The question public television executives should be asking themselves is: Why not?

—*David Horowitz*

A Note On Sources: The principal sources for this chapter are John P. Witherspoon and Roselle Kovitz, "A Tribal Memory of Public Broadcasting Missions, Mandates, Assumptions, Structure," 1986, privately circulated typescript; Robert K. Avery and Robert Pepper, *The Politics of Interconnection: A History of Public Television at the National Level,* National Association of Educational Broadcasters, 1989; *A Public Trust, The Report of the Carnegie Commission on the Future of Public Broadcasting,* 1979; AIM Reports, 1975-1991; John W. Macy Jr., *To Irrigate A Wasteland,* 1974; interviews with Michael Hobbs, Bob Kotlowitz, Richard Brookhiser, James Day, and James Loper.

PERCEPTIONS OF INTEGRITY

Integrity is more than just a word in the public-broadcasting lexicon. It is its alpha and omega. If public television is to be identified with quality in broadcasting—indeed, if it is to have an identity at all—then integrity is necessarily its defining asset. Commercial television can afford to be merely entertainment. Its bottom line is clear. As long as it holds an audience, anything goes. But for public television, a high standard is a necessity. Otherwise *cui bono*? Why should it exist at all?

This truth is self-evident to public broadcasters and an article of faith throughout the public television system. Thus, the August 1990 edition of the *PBS Program Producer's Handbook* explains the need to protect the editorial integrity of programs bearing the PBS logo: "PBS's reputation for quality reflects the public's trust in the editorial integrity of PBS programs and the process by which they are selected."

To establish standards of integrity, PBS sends out a guide to program developers and station managers called

PBS National Program Funding Standards and Practices. These standards are considered so important that PBS in-sists not only that they be observed in fact, but that they also be perceived to be so by the viewing public. Thus, the memorandum:

Perception of Editorial Control

One of public television's objectives is to be accepted by the public as a free and independent broadcast enterprise....Only if so regarded can public television maintain the confidence of its viewers, a confidence which is essential if public television is to accomplish the goal of serving the public by a program service that is enriching and enlightening. Therefore, even if the public television professionals know that programs have not been inappropriately influenced by program funders...steps must be taken to avoid the public perception that pro-gram funders have influenced professional judgments.

In order to make absolutely sure there is no misunderstanding of intentions on the part of producers of PBS programs, the guidelines are specifically spelled out.

The following examples illustrating the perception test are provided in the memorandum:

☞ A series of documentaries, interviews, and commentaries on the subject of drug abuse would not be accepted if funded by a special-purpose nonprofit corporation whose primary purpose is to foster the understanding of drug-related programs, even if the program proposal suggests that the series will not deal with the more contro-versial aspects of drug abuse and its pro-posed solutions.

☞ A Jewish social-welfare organization

could not fund a documentary on a leading Nazi official. The controversial nature of the program combined with the organization's obvious direct interest and stake in the subject matter combine to make this underwriting arrangement unacceptable. Again, the public might easily conclude that the program was created to foster the views and objectives of the funder.

These are the PBS guidelines. Programs that do not adhere to their strictures are regularly barred from the PBS feed and denied an audience by station managers who invoke them. Thus is the integrity of the system maintained. Or is it? A study of the PBS programs listed in the back of the very same *Producer's Handbook* shows that these standards are ignored with alarming regularity:

> 1. *Legacy of the Hollywood Blacklist* (KCET, 10/21/87)
> Funder: Writers Guild Foundation
> [In other words, a critical history of the Hollywood blacklist by an organization of past and potential victims of Hollywood blacklists. This case is exactly analogous to the example offered above in the PBS memo on standards that refers to a Jewish welfare organization as a potential funder of a film on Nazis.]

> 2. *Witness to Revolution: The Story of Anna Louise Strong* (KCTS, 1/10/88)
> Funder: U. S./China People 's Friendship Association
> [A paean to a noted propagandist for Communist China funded by an organization seeking closer ties to that Communist state.]

> 3. *Sanctuary* (PBS, 6/3/85)
> Funder: World Council of Churches
> [A documentary on a highly controversial organization funded by one of the chief

sponsors of that organization.]
4. *Peter, Paul and Mary in Central America*
(Heartstrings, Margery Tabanken, 11/13/87)
Funder: Youth Project Benchmark Fund
[A documentary with strong political over-
tones produced by a noted left-wing activist
with views on U.S. policy in Central America
similar to those of Peter, Paul, and Mary.
Tabanken was head of the Youth Project at
the time this documentary was made.]

And this is just a tiny sample. In the December 1990 issue of
the PBS newspaper, *Current,* one can find, for example, the
following announcement of a project undertaken by Greater
Dayton Public Television that conforms almost to the letter to
the first example of impermissible funding cited previously
from *Standards and Practices*:

> Greater Dayton Public Television, licensee of
> WPTD in Dayton, Ohio, and WPTO in Ox-
> ford, Ohio, received $15,750 from a county
> agency for a program about women alco-
> holics and drug addicts. The Montgomery
> County Alcohol, Drug Addiction and
> Mental Health Services Board awarded the
> station the grant for *Women in Crisis,* a pro-
> gram the station is developing for broadcast
> next May.

Here is another item from the same issue of *Current*:

> Texaco gave WNET up to $300,000 for pro-
> duction and education outreach for a 30-
> minute special about energy conservation.

A common thread connecting all the above programs
is that they conform to the well-known political and cultural
biases of PBS programmers. One need hardly speculate as to
what the reaction would be to a program proposal on the Jim
and Tammy Bakker affair if one of the funders happened to
be a fundamentalist organization (a parallel to example 1
above) or an anti-Communist program about China funded

by a Free China lobby (see 2, previous page)

Yet PBS's contempt for its own funding standards extends beyond the realm of political culture to the most sacrosanct area of all, viz., the line that separates its mission of non-commercialism from the crass materialism of network TV. Here are the PBS guidelines on "Commercialism" from *Standards and Practices* [caps in original]:

PUBLIC TELEVISION, COMPRISED OF FREE AND INDEPENDENT NON-COMMERCIAL BROADCASTING LICENSEES, LICENSED AS SUCH BY THE FCC AND EXPECTED TO BE SUCH BY THE PUBLIC, MUST VIGOROUSLY PROTECT ITS NON-COMMERCIAL CHARACTER.

One of public television's obligations to the FCC, the Congress and the public is to retain its non-commercial character. Because of its non-commercial status, public television has received special treatment from the FCC, special treatment from the various taxing authorities and funding from the federal government and state and local governments. It has also received special tariff provisions from the common carriers, and special rates from unions, talent and the like. Most important, public television, because of the character and quality of this program service, has received a special place in the public's mind. Therefore, in addition to the program funding principles already set forth, a commercialism test will be applied to determine whether certain proposed program funding arrangements are acceptable for the national program service.

The following is a further sample of PBS programs taken from the list at the back of the *Handbook* that violate these guidelines, with airing dates and funders:

1. *More Than the Music* (KCET, 2/20/85)

Funder: Yamaha International Corp.
2. *Legends of American Skiing* (Keystone Productions, 11/30/86)
Funders: Yosemite Park and Curry Company and Ski Industries America

3. *Storytellers: The PEN Celebration* (WHYY, 10/9/87)
Funder: Waldenbooks

4. *Money in America: The Business of Banking* (KQED, 1/8/89)
Funder: Wells Fargo Bank

5. *This Old House* (WGBH, 10/8/88)
Funder: Weyerhaeuser [a lumber company]

6. *America By Design* (WTTW, 9/28/87)
Funder: American Institute of Architects

7. *Air Force One: The Planes and the Presidents* (WGTE, 1/2/85)
Funder: The Boeing Company

8. *The Health Century* (9/21/87)
Funders: Bristol-Meyers; Ciba-Geigy Corporation; Merck and Co. Inc.; Pfizer Inc.; The Upjohn Company officials

Again, a very small sample of a very large problem. For years the Chubb group, a major theatrical and show-business insurer, underwrote *American Playhouse*. The most famous health programs on PBS—*The Brain*; *Health Care On The Critical List*; *The Health Century*; *Quest For The Killers*; *Who Lives, Who Dies*; etc.—are funded by the largest pharmaceutical corporations, while the popular science series *Nova* is sponsored by a cluster of high-tech companies.

So where are PBS's standards? Obviously standards that are inconsistently or intermittently applied are no standards at all. Because they are unfairly applied, they become instruments instead for hidden agendas and thus a threat to the cardinal principles of balance and fairness. Because this issue of standards and practices is so central to the identity, integrity, and mission of public television, the inconsistencies outlined above ought to be the cause of considerable concern for public television. Unfortunately, as the story of *Fire From The Sun* told next shows, they are not.

—*David Horowitz*

FIRE FROM THE SUN: A DOCUMENTARY PBS REFUSED TO AIR

In December 1990, as U.S. and allied forces were massing in the Persian Gulf to rescue the world's oil supply from Saddam Hussein, the *Los Angeles Times* ran a feature about a prize-winning documentary on a potential alternative energy source that PBS refused to air. Actually, *Fire From the Sun*, a Manifold Films production, had been shown on nearly 200 of the smaller public-television stations, but it had been rejected for the PBS feed and by major market stations like WGBH, WNET, WTTV, WETA, WQED, KCET, etc. According to the *Times* (Dec. 26, 1990), "Programmers who have declined to run the program say it violates PBS funding guidelines. They say viewers would perceive a conflict of interest in [Manifold's] decision to accept funding from organizations with an interest in fusion." Barbara Goen, spokeswoman for KCET, was quoted as saying, "It could definitely be perceived that the funders have an interest in the subject matter."

Of course, like PBS generally, KCET regularly ignores violations of the PBS funding guidelines. Even as Barbara Goen was explaining KCET's position, KCET vice president Blaine Baggett was putting the finishing touches on KCET's most ambitious production in nearly a decade, the $5.3-million series *The Astronomers*, which received 100 percent of its funding from the W.M. Keck Foundation. As the *Los Angeles Times* reported:

> The underwriting Keck Foundation, which was founded by the late oil baron William Myron Keck with proceeds from his Superior Oil Co., is building one of the largest telescopes in the world on the volcanic Mauna Kea in Hawaii. Also working on the telescope are scientists at Caltech and JPL, some of whom are involved with the series. The Keck telescope—called "the Mighty Keck" by a scientist in the series—is featured for about three minutes in the first episode, with a total of about 10 minutes devoted to Mauna Kea itself as a site for observing the heavens.

How concerned was KCET about the possible violation of PBS standards by its $5.3-million series?

"Baggett said that the question of whether it was appropriate to accept funding from Keck was never discussed at KCET" (Sharon Bernstein, *Los Angeles Times*, April 12, 1991). Apparently, when a program serves KCET's own interests, or does not offend the cultural and/or political sensibilities of its program executives, PBS standards need no longer apply.

Unlike *The Astronomers*, *Fire From the Sun* received no more than 20 percent of its funding from any single source. Moreover, as the *Times* reported, programmers at public-television station KOCE in nearby Huntington Beach, which aired *Fire From the Sun*, pointed out that "there is no conflict [of interest] because the funders did not exercise any control over [the program's] content." In fact, *Fire From the Sun* is a straightforward educational film about fusion energy with an editorial message: More funds should be devoted to the development of this relatively safe (there is no nuclear waste problem) and remarkably efficient energy source.

When COMINT became aware of the fusion documentary, it decided to see if reason could persuade the major public-television stations to lift their ban on *Fire From the Sun* and permit the public to be educated on what was obviously a very important and topical subject. We therefore sent letters to the station managers of 30 major-market public-television stations. There were four replies.

Four replies is not a good percentage. What other institution (government or private) would so readily ignore a respectful request for information from a public interest organization? Particularly when the inquiry was about the reasons for a decision with such public ramifications?

This was not the only disturbing response (or non-response) we got from the public-television authorities. As noted, four wrote back to say they had rejected *Fire From the Sun* because it violated PBS funding guidelines. But when we sent a second letter, describing the way in which PBS consistently ignored the same guidelines, the response was a uniform silence. In other words, if you can't answer an argument, pretend it doesn't exist.

Undaunted, we appealed directly to PBS programming chief Jennifer Lawson. (In our correspondence, we referred to *Fire From the Sun* as Documentary X, just to make the points a little more objective.)

> Dear Ms. Lawson,
> ...In the last year, we have been engaged in a dialogue with several public television stations over the articulation and application of guidelines affecting objectivity, fairness, and balance in current affairs programming....
> Our organization has made inquiries to several PBS stations about an award-winning documentary, which I will call *Documentary X*. *Documentary X* was actually shown on nearly 200 of the smaller PBS stations but was rejected by all but one of the major markets on the grounds that it allegedly violated PBS guidelines governing the funding of documentaries. Thus, one Assistant Director of Broadcasting wrote to us:
> "We rejected Documentary X because, at its center, the documentary pleads for increased federal funds for fusion research, while being underwritten by corporations

which would directly benefit from federal funding for such activities."

A program manager for another station wrote us essentially the same thing: "PBS underwriting guidelines, to which XYTV adheres, specify that underwriters may not have any real or apparent input into a program that they have helped fund."

Yet, not only do 200 other PBS stations ignore these guidelines but, as the following item from the last issue of *Current* shows, a major-market public-television station can violate the very standard it has already used to reject *Documentary X*: "WTTW-TV in Chicago received $40,000 from the Great Lakes Protection Fund, a multi-state water quality endowment, to develop programming about environmental issues in the Great Lakes region."

I could cite such contradictory applications (or nonapplications) of the PBS guidelines all day. The most famous health programs aired on PBS have been funded by pharmaceutical companies with no apparent sense of conflict by the same stations that refuse to air programs like *Documentary X*.

Nor are these the only guidelines that suffer from confusion in conception and inconsistency in application. A documentary challenging the "global warming" thesis, produced by British Independent Television and called *The Greenhouse Conspiracy*, was recently rejected by PBS on the grounds that it was "too one-sided." Yet, at the same time, PBS aired a two-hour program called *After the Warming*, presenting the other side of the case. How can a program that assumes the truth of a theory be considered less one-sided than a program that argues the theory?

I think you will agree that this is not a healthy state of affairs for a publicly funded medium that has to navigate the mine fields between corporate influence and governmental oversight into its affairs. Our organization has given a great deal of thought to these matters. We are interested in the health and prosperity of public television. But we are convinced that these are not served by an ostrich strategy that ignores problem areas until they become highly charged political issues. I would very much like the opportunity to discuss our ideas and experiences in these matters with you. I would be happy to come to Alexandria at your earliest convenience.

Sincerely, etc.

It took Jennifer Lawson nearly a month to respond, although her letter, when it did arrive, seemed more like an evasion of the points we had raised than a reply. We print it in full:

Dear Mr. Horowitz,

Thank you for your recent letter. I appreciate the opportunity to respond. Fairness and balance are important elements of news and public affairs programming and apply to all journalistic endeavors.

They are important elements of public television programming as well. Let me assure you that there are indeed clearly defined and well articulated PBS guidelines for decision-making in terms of balance and fairness. These are qualities we seek to fulfill over the course of our broadcast schedule. PBS seeks to be ideologically diverse as one would expect from a system that has no central news division, more than 300 independent stations, a wide range of funding sources and one which showcases the work of more than 200 producers a year.

PBS makes every effort to distribute the best public affairs programs on timely relevant topics. PBS may reject a program because it does not meet PBS journalistic standards or simply because another program does a better job of telling the same story. But there is no PBS political agenda and no program is rejected because it favors one viewpoint over another. Public television programs are judged individually, on the merits of the information they provide and on the quality of their production. Within that context, we seek to provide to the American people the widest range of quality programming possible on important issues.

On environmental programs, for example, which you mentioned in your letter, PBS is proud of its record. In 1990 alone, public TV's *Operation Earth* brought to the home and classroom series such as *Race to Save the Planet, Decade of Destruction, The Miracle Planet, Icewalk,* and specials such as *Profit the Earth, For Earth's Sake: The Life and Times of David Brower, One Second Before Sunrise* and *Arctic Haze* among others. Also, programs such as *Nova, Nature,* National *Geographic* specials and even *Sesame Street* devoted themselves extensively to environmental topics. These programs covered a wide range of viewpoints on a broad spectrum of environmental issues.

In terms of specific PBS policy on balance and fairness, I refer you to the enclosed excerpt from our *Report of the Special Committee on Program Policies and Procedures.* Balance, it says, is to be sought over the course of PBS's entire program. Like an Op-Ed page in a newspaper, this allows many voices to be heard and—having heard those voices—viewers can make up their own minds on important issues based on complete information.

Also, every effort is made to ensure public television programs are free from political influence or editorial interference from funders. Public television's editorial integrity and its reputation for fairness are its most important assets and the very reasons that it is the most respected source of information on television today.

Sincerely,
Jennifer Lawson
Executive Vice President
National Programming and
Promotion Services

Unfortunately, this mixture of boilerplate and eyewash is the end of the story to date. Thus, from top to bottom, public-television executives speak with a single voice. They are either aware that the very standards that justify the existence of their medium are regularly ignored and inequitably applied and just don't care, or they are unable to recognize the unpleasant reality of their own arbitrary, one-sided and capricious governance, which would be more unfortunate still.

—*David Horowitz*

Addendum to Jennifer Lawson's
Letter to COMINT:

PBS Balance Guidelines: This balance is derived from the original standard in the Journalism Guidelines that states: "We pledge to strive for balanced programming." Consistent with that earlier standard, the new document does not require balance within every PBS program but, like the FCC's fairness doctrine, recognizes that balance is to be sought over the course of PBS's entire program schedule.

The new standard affirms that PBS may also consider a program's internal balance in deciding whether to accept it. Because PBS does not produce programs itself, often lacks the resources to commission program production, and does not control program content, it is not always clear whether future programs can be counted upon to provide appropriate balance. Especially in those circumstances, it is important that PBS be able to condition its decision to accept a program on the addition or deletion of program material.

By making explicit PBS's authority to condition its acceptance on the addition or deletion of program material, this standard recognizes established PBS practice. Over the years, the types of additional program material required have ranged from introductory comments, to follow up discussions, to an additional segment or program. Sometimes PBS has sought such balancing material from the original producer, but on other occasions PBS has sought such material elsewhere. Inasmuch as it is PBS that is responsible for the overall balance of the PBS program schedule, PBS must retain discretion to decide when balancing material is required, what type of material is required, and who should produce it.

—Excerpt from *Report of the Special Committee on Program Policies and Procedures*

THE FAR SIDE OF THE '60S

On page 41 of this volume we print a letter from Jennifer Lawson, the national programming chief of PBS now presiding over a $100-million CPB-PBS fund for future programs. In her letter to the Committee on Media Integrity, Lawson writes, "Let me assure you that there are indeed clearly defined and well articulated PBS guidelines for decision making in terms of balance and fairness."

There are no such guidelines. A perusal of the official PBS statement on guidelines, supplied by Ms. Lawson, will serve to convince any reasonable person of this. Instead of clearly defined guidelines there is (1) a pious pledge by PBS "to strive for balanced programs," (2) a caveat to the effect that the "internal balancing" of particular programs will not be required, followed by (3) a catch-all loophole that states that "since PBS does not produce programs itself,...it is not always clear whether future programs can be counted upon to provide appropriate balance." In other words, don't expect to hold PBS to anything.

Of course, even the catchall loophole is disingenuous. For, as everyone involved in public television is aware, PBS has both the resources and the means to bring programs and series it chooses into existence. And to shape them in the process. In the past, these means were informal but real. Now, as a result of the pact signed on Feb. 26, 1991, between CPB president Donald Ledwig and PBS president Bruce Christensen, they are both formal and real. And Jennifer Lawson holds the levers of control.

[As a result of the pact] Jennifer Lawson, executive vice president of national programming and promotion services at PBS, will disburse approximately $100 million in program funds to producers beginning in fiscal year 1992, which begins July 1.
—*Current*, March 4, 1991

We at COMINT wish to submit a proposal to Jennifer Lawson for one of the first disbursements of her $100-million fund. This grant would rectify a bald affront to the principles of fairness, objectivity, and balance, which PBS claims to hold in such high regard. We ask her to reserve $2.3 million of the program fund and six hours of PBS air time for a six-part series to balance *Making Sense of the 60s*, an indefensibly one-sided perspective on the most controversial decade of this century, aired on most PBS stations the last week of January 1991.

Just how one-sided was *Making Sense of the 60s?* Here is the way *New York Times* critic Walter Goodman reviewed its premiere episode (*New York Times*, Jan. 21, 1991):

> *Making Sense of the 60s*, the latest PBS opus, tells the story of that "most tumultuous, confusing and controversial decade" through the recollections of some of its participants. These middle-aged folk seem generally pleased with their youthful activities, and they cannot complain of unkindness from the producers of this six-hour series.... The first hour, *Seeds of the 60s*, offers a picture of the 1950s that is straight out of the New Left canon. Writers and others, most of whom seem to have been chosen for their congenial opinions, comment on scenes from

Ozzie and Harriet and other easily put down television shows....The sociological and political simplisms of the narration and the parade of self-flattering reminiscences do not make for a fascinating hour. The program's pleasures are mainly in the glimpses of old television shows, but it's not easy to decide which is sappier, the narration or *Ozzie and Harriet*.

Seeds of the 60s takes the youth rebellion pretty much at its own assessment....

This result should hardly have come as a surprise to PBS and CPB, which provided $2.3 million in funding for the series. *Making Sense of the 60s* was the brainchild of Ricki Green, then vice president of news and public affairs for WETA in Washington, D.C. By her own account, Ricki Green was a Berkeley student radical during the 1960s and a leader of the women's movement. Like many '60s radicals, she had difficulty justifying her actions to others, and sometimes even to herself: "The series really grew out of my own need to come to terms with my own experience of the '60s. It was important in setting the future course of my life, but I had trouble putting the pieces together to see what they meant, and I had a similar problem trying to talk to my kids. It's easy to talk about the symbols of the '60s, but I wished I could explain to them what the '60s really meant to me" (*Maine Times*, Jan. 25, 1991).

This is an unobjectionable ambition, but what is the rationale for spending $2.3 million of public monies to calm the narcissistic angst of one Berkeley radical, or even a dozen? In shaping the film, Green assembled panels of "experts" at public television's expense. These experts—no surprise again—represented mainly unrepentant veterans of the '60s left (the members of the panels are listed in the closing credits). She also found a producer, David Hoffman, and his partner, Kirk Wolfinger, of Varied Directions, whom she could trust not to trouble her radical conscience too greatly in putting the pieces of the decade together while bringing the film to fruition. Wolfinger, who personally directed the first and third segments of the PBS film, is also the director of a two-hour television program, *Portrait of Castro's Cuba*, about one of the last remaining Communist gulags in the world. Wolfinger's documentary was described by *The Village Voice* as "the mother of all puff pieces" (April 9, 1991).

As fate would have it, while *Making Sense of the 60s* was still in its formative stages, COMINT was engaged in a dialogue about program fairness and balance with the chief executives of station KCET in Los Angeles, William H. Kobin and Stephen Kulczycki. In lodging our complaints about the imbalance in PBS's current-affairs programming, we pointed to the politically weighted pre-production process for *Making Sense of the 60s*, which had come to our attention. We had some expertise in this area, having co-edited the leading New Left journal *Ramparts* and having co-authored the most well-known book about the '60s, *Destructive Generation*. In our view, the fact that our opinion on this topic was critical explained why no one connected with the film had contacted us for our expertise. Yet both Kobin and Kulczycki pooh-poohed the idea that we might have been excluded because of our views. They assured us that the producer David Hoffman was "no ideologue," hinting that he was actually conservative and that he might even produce a series we would find congenial. If we were concerned about any possible imbalance in this series, they encouraged us to contact Hoffman directly. So we did:

April 3, 1990

Dear David Hoffman,

I am writing at the suggestion of William H. Kobin and Steven Kulczycki (president and program director of KCET, Los Angeles, respectively). I understand that you are producing a documentary series called *Making Sense of the 60s*. As you probably are aware, Peter Collier and I are the authors of *Destructive Generation*, the main critical account yet published of the '60s. *Destructive Generation* challenges the nostalgic orthodoxy purveyed in books by Todd Gitlin, Tom Hayden, Maurice Isserman, and others; its accounts of the Black Panther Party and the Weather Underground, based on first-hand interviews with the participants, are the definitive histories of those organizations to date. We are also the co-organizers of the "Second Thoughts Conference," which was held in Washington, D.C., in October 1987 and which brought together two dozen former movement leaders and activists, who were also reflectively critical of the '60s. (The conference papers were subsequently published as *Second Thoughts* by Madison Books, Lanham, Md., 1989.) On May 3, 1990, we will hold a follow-up conference in Washington, D.C., called "Second Thoughts About Race in America," which will look at the legacy of the civil rights movement and its derailment by the "black power" left and which is bound to generate comparable publicity and interest.

Because of the quality and stature of the participants in the original Second Thoughts Conference, and as a result of the national publicity it generated, the term "second thoughts" has now entered the language of cultural discourse. Any serious effort to "make sense of the '60s," would as a matter of course be concerned to confront the perspective with which the term "second thoughts" has become identified. It is difficult for me to understand, therefore, the failure of the producers of your series to contact Peter or myself, or the dozens of former '60s activists associated with our project, for the purpose of script consultation and on-camera interviews. This group represents more than a widely recognized perspective on the '60s. Its members are active participants in the cultural struggle over the legacy of that decade (the subject of the sixth segment of your series). I hope the omission of members of the Second Thoughts project in your preliminary research was an oversight, and I look forward to your reply to this letter.

Sincerely, etc.

The letter was faxed to Mr. Hoffman and he replied the next day:

April 4, 1990

Dear David:

I thank you for your interest and concern for our series, *Making Sense of the 60s*.

Of course we are aware of your work and the work of your associates. We read your book with interest and enthusiasm.

Our concept from the start has been to avoid all well-known characters (stars, heroes, experts, personalities, etc.) and ideas. Six one-hour shows is of course not enough time to deal with the 1960's, particularly when the first hour is on the 1950's and the last hour is on the present. So we selected 100 what we call "extraordinary, ordinary people." Among them are people who represent your point of view as well as the points of view of those even more extreme in their criticism of the 1960's.

They include political conservatives and people like Governor Richard Lamm who were supporters of the general thrust of the anti-war movement of the 1960's and now consider it to be the most nihilistic decade in modern history.

We are attempting to make a program that gives people a sense of why the 1960's went the way it did without spending any time debating political issues.

In fact, you may enjoy the program because it is more a study of popular culture of the period than it is a study of the political movements and forces that were active.

We received an audio copy of the Second Thoughts Conference held in Washington, D.C. in October, 1987 and found the material provocative and interesting.

You'll have to wait for the finished series

to see how we approach it, but rest assured that the point of view you present in the book and at the conference is one of several points of view presented, albeit not in a political sense.

Thanks again for your interest in the series. We look forward to your comments on the series once it is aired.

Sincerely,
David Hoffman

"In fact you may enjoy the program because it is more a study of popular culture of the period than it is a study of the political movements and forces that were active."
—David Hoffman, director, *Making Sense of the 60s*

"Tonight we're going to examine separately two rebellions, first the cultural, then the political."
—Narrator, *Making Sense of the 60s*

It would be superfluous to deconstruct the manipulative prose of this letter. Suffice it to say that the resulting series produced by Hoffman was a highly political view of the '60s. One interminable hour-long segment was devoted to a litany of "liberation" movements—black, female, Native American, gay, differently abled, etc.—that sprang up like mushrooms out of its fertile political soil, without any critical perspective on their impact. Moreover, "famous" people did appear, including former SDS president Carl Oglesby and *New Republic* editor Rick Hertzberg, a former presidential speech writer for Jimmy Carter. Hertzberg, who had written one of the most vitriolic attacks on *Destructive Generation*, even joined Hoffman for the promotional tour for the series. On this tour, in a Hollywood press stop in early January 1991, Hoffman let the final cat out of the bag. It was no accident, it turned out, that Hertzberg and others sharing similar views were picked to serve as promotional spokesmen for the series. For in advertising himself to the press in Los Angeles, and by way of explaining his production, Hoffman said: "This is our answer to *Destructive Generation*."

—*David Horowitz*

THE BLACK PANTHERS
AND PBS

The Black Panthers were one of the emblematic movements of the '60s. Regarded as heroes by the New Left, SDS designated them the "vanguard of the revolution"; Tom Hayden called them "America's VietCong." On the other hand, they were feared and reviled by the silent majority, who saw them as street hoodlums made doubly dangerous by their adoption of a revolutionary rhetoric that brought legions of white radicals and lawyers to their defense. These white radicals viewed the Panthers as passive victims of a racist power structure, when they were not being seen as the active agents of revolutionary revenge. History has not proved kind to the leftist embrace of the Panthers. An investigative *New Yorker* article by Edward Jay Epstein exploded the myth of police conspiracy and Panther victimhood, while a *New Times* report by left-wing journalist Kate Coleman documented the brutal felonies, including murder, arson, and rape, that the Panthers themselves committed against other ghetto blacks. In the end, the Panthers proved to have been just another criminal gang, albeit a colorful one.

But if investigative research by journalists and historians has killed the heroic myth of the Panthers, public television has done its best to revive the corpse. In the PBS series *Eyes on the Prize II*, in *Making Sense of the 60s*, and especially in *Black Power, Black Panthers*, a one-hour KQED-produced documentary, the Panthers are back in all their radical innocence and revolutionary glory.

At a time when even the Kremlin fabulators are making efforts to restore respect for historical truth, is it too much to ask PBS to take steps to rectify its own abuse of the historical record? On August 20, 1990, COMINT appealed to the management of KQED-TV in San Francisco to look into the matter of *Black Power, Black Panthers*. While purporting to be a documentary history of the Black Panther Party, the program suppressed widely known facts about the Panthers' criminality, including the murders of at least a dozen Bay Area residents, and presented the Panthers as victims of a governmental conspiracy to eliminate black civil rights activists. In making their "documentary," the producers ignored half a dozen Bay Area reporters who had covered the story, in some cases risking their lives to do so. (Pearl Stewart, a black reporter for the *Oakland Tribune*, had had her car firebombed after breaking the first story about the Panthers' criminal operations.)

As events soon showed, the "documentary" was little more than a promotional film for a group of Panther veterans, led by ex-felon David Hilliard, who were busily reviving the party's apparatus and newspaper.

The first issue of the new *Black Panthers* appeared in early 1991, recalling that in the '60s it had been "an uncompromising voice for exposing attacks on the 'Afrikan Amerikkkan' community and for advocating an implacable stand to redress them....History once again demands that we take action."

The letter COMINT sent to KQED president Anthony S. Tiano called the film "a disgrace to KQED and a public outrage." It noted that the distortions of the film

> serve to feed the racial paranoia that has done so much to poison the public atmosphere of late. Thus the clear message of the tendentious "history" recorded in *Black Power, Black Panthers*, is that white America, and white American law enforcement agencies in particular, conducted a campaign of "assassination" against the leaders of the Black Panther Party and a war of extermination against its members. [But] in the light of historical evidence, the reverse is closer to the truth.

The letter concluded by demanding that KQED remove its name from the film, conduct an inquiry into how such a travesty could have occurred, and provide funding for a film that would be "corrective" to the distorted version of events it had sponsored.

KQED's response to this appeal was written by station manager David H. Hosely, who ignored or simply glossed over its charges and defended both the filmmaker and the Panthers themselves. "We believe that, by adding to the body of information on this historic political movement, we encourage multi-dimensional analysis, and ultimately, understanding," he wrote. "We are proud of this contribution and our association with it."

Having been rebuffed by KQED staff, COMINT turned to the KQED board, requesting an opportunity to present its concerns. An invitation was duly extended and on Dec. 6, 1990, with PBS programming chief Jennifer Lawson in attendance, I spoke to the KQED Board. What follows is the text of my remarks:

"I am here to discuss the KQED-produced film *Black Power, Black Panthers*. This film portrays the Black Panther Party as an idealistic organization of ghetto youth, driven to violent but essentially innocent posturing and rhetoric by brutal police forces in the '60s. According to the film, as the party's influence grew among the oppressed, its leaders were targeted by the FBI and other law-enforcement agencies for assassination and were murdered, jailed, and, in the case of their founder, Huey P. Newton, driven to desperate, drug-influenced courses of action that ended in sordid and violent death. Thus, even Newton, whom the film criticizes for creating a "cult of the individual," is presented as a victim of assassination (albeit psychological) by the powers that be.

"I understand the seductive appeal of this image of the Panthers (which is, after all, their self-image) as victims of a white racist society bent on destroying any black person who dared to challenge its oppressive order. It was this image that brought me into close association with Huey Newton and the Black Panther Party in the early '70s. I did not especially like their violent rhetoric. I was suspicious of their gang-like behavior. But I basically believed the radical and liberal apologists for the Panthers who, like the KQED filmmakers, assured us all that they were really the well-intentioned victims of racist authorities, vicious police agencies, and a hostile media.

"Influenced by these deceptive images, I agreed to work with the Panthers. I raised over $100,000 and created the Oakland Community Learning Center, which is improbably featured in the KQED film as "an internationally recognized school" that provided free meals for children and which was, in fact, the party's showpiece and base of operations throughout the '70s. It was for embezzling money from this school that Newton was finally convicted and was about to be sent to jail when he was killed. The school was real, but it was also a front for a criminal gang attempting to control the illegal traffic of the East Oakland ghetto. My association with the Panthers terminated in 1974 when they kidnapped and murdered the woman I had engaged to do bookkeeping for the school, Betty Van Patter, a well-known member of the radical community and the mother of three children. Huey Newton, the only Panther the KQED film finds fault with, was in Cuba when Betty was kidnapped and murdered. Ericka Huggins, who is featured in the film as an idealistic Panther leader, was the head of the Panther school at the time. (Elaine Brown, who is celebrated in Eyes on the Prize II, was the head of the Party.) Betty's death is not mentioned.

"In the years after Betty's murder, partly because of the horror that many working Bay Area journalists felt over her death, reporting on the Panthers began to change. A number of journalists—Lance Williams, Pearl Stewart, and Kate Coleman among them—despite considerable risks to their personal safety, gradually uncovered the true story of the Black Panther Party, its origins as a criminal gang, its assumption of a political personality, its continuing criminal activity, and the reign of terror it conducted mainly in the Bay Area's black community. During its brutal career, more than a dozen people were killed. The positive effect of these stories was to warn others not to make the mistake that I, and so many like me, had made in responding to the Panthers' idealistic image a decade earlier. Under the impact of this adverse publicity, the Panther Party ceased to exist.

"Recently, however, some Panther veterans led by David Hilliard, a convicted felon and the principal on-camera "authority" in KQED's film, have begun to organize a revival of the party in the Bay Area, appearing at demonstrations and promoting the same hate-filled rhetoric as in the past. KQED has produced the perfect vehicle to make this revival a success: A film posing as history that covers up as much of the truth that has been discovered about the Panthers as possible, while refurbishing their image as the idealistic victims of a white racist society that ruthlessly set out to destroy them.

"How could KQED finance and produce such an obscene rewrite of contemporary history? How could the KQED producers systematically ignore the well-known Bay Area reporters responsible for uncovering the truth about the Panthers in the past? Pearl Stewart, a black journalist who reported this story and whose life was threatened by the Panthers, has appeared on many programs on KQED. How could her testimony be ignored? How could this whole travesty have slipped by the KQED executives responsible for controlling the quality of the KQED product? What measures is KQED prepared to take to limit and/or repair the damage done by this film? What measures will it consider to prevent a repetition of this experience in the future?

"The present position of the KQED staff is that it is "proud" of this film and stands by its producers. KQED management seems to have no interest in answering the troubling questions posed by the making of this film or in confronting the issues they raise. We are therefore placing our case before the KQED board. We would like to ask you first to set up a committee of inquiry to look into this matter and to provide us with a point of contact for our concerns. It has taken four months just to get to where this presentation could be made, a situation that is frustrating enough to actively discourage inquiries like ours. The reaction of KQED management to date says, in effect, that KQED has no interest in the fairness, objectivity, or integrity of its programming, something I am sure its board does not ascribe to.

"The committee of inquiry we are proposing should, in our view, be the prelude to the setting up of a permanent committee to handle questions of fairness, objectivity, and balance in KQED's programming. As you know, KQED is a taxpayer-funded institution with a responsibility to the public for fairness, balance, and objectivity that necessarily exceeds the responsibility of commercial stations that do not enjoy the benefits of governmental support. This is a trust that PBS and KQED officials have affirmed on numerous occasions and that is written into the law governing the Corporation for Public Broadcasting which funds KQED. This law, Title 47, U.S. Code Section 396(g)(1)(A), specifies that the funds provided by the public will be used to: 'Facilitate the full development of telecommunications in which programs of high quality, diversity, creativity, excellence, and innovation, which are obtained from diverse sources will be made available to public telecommunications entities with strict adherence to objectivity and balance in all programs or series of programs of a controversial nature.'

"Presently, KQED has no institutional mechanism or corporate officer responsible for enforcing this policy. If there were such an office or officer, they would have been in touch with us four months ago. It is cause for concern that such a lacuna still exists, but it does, and this is as good a time as any to begin to remedy the situation.

"The critical role of media and the problem of media responsibility in the functioning of a democracy is universally acknowledged. Even a private media corporation like *The Washington Post* recognizes its public responsibility in establishing principles of fairness and balance in reporting. It has appointed an "ombudsman" to receive complaints and make periodical reports and recommendations to the staff of the paper in order to correct existing imbalances and redress grievances that its readers and the subjects of its coverage may raise. The existence of an ombudsman provides both a court of appeal for the complaints of the public and a disinterested perspective on the functioning of the organization which can guide the staff towards better performance. We believe that in the case of publicly funded institutions like KQED, which enjoys the special privileges of a publicly supported medium and is therefore mandated by law to promote both fairness and balance, this ombudsman function should be the responsibility of a committee of the board, and not merely an individual.

"We would like to discuss these matters further, and hope to hear from your representatives soon. Thank you."

This appeal was made in December 1990. Four months afterwards, there has not been a single word out of the KQED board, not a letter of inquiry, not an invitation to appear, not even a courtesy note. Meanwhile, *Eyes on the Prize II* is a constant re-run on PBS, especially during pledge-week; *Making Sense of the 60s* will be aired again this fall; and *Berkeley in the 60s*, another tendentious self-celebration by the radical left complete with ritual glorification of the Black Panther Party, will be on PBS soon. Just in case we didn't get the point.

—*David Horowitz*

PANTHER OUTRAGE

"Well brother man you just keep passin' it on—passin' it on Lumumba, Dhoruba, Assata Shakur..."

In the '60s, Martin Kenner was a New Left activist at Columbia University and supporter of the Black Panthers. In 1969, he organized the famous fundraiser for the Panthers at Leonard Bernstein's, which gave a new phrase to the language after it was satirized by Tom Wolfe in *Radical Chic*. Kenner is still a Panther stalwart and with his friend, writer Lewis Cole, helped Panther leader David Hilliard write his memoir, *This Side of Glory*. In Hilliard's book, Kenner is quoted at length about a murder committed by a dissident Panther faction in New York:

> Nothing ever shook me up in my political life as much as the murder of Sam Napier....It was so unjust. Sam had never been involved in the military aspect of the Party. He only worked on distribution [of the Panther newspaper]. He was defenseless and his murder was unspeakably brutal. He was caught unarmed and unprotected in the newspaper distribution office in Queens, tied to a bed, tortured, shot to death, then burned. The murder was fratricide. The assassins grabbed the two-year-old child Sam was taking care of in the office and literally threw him out the door, giving him lasting injuries, and two young neighborhood kids who happened to be in the office at the time were locked in a closet and left in the fire.

One of the dissident Panthers arrested for this crime was Richard Moore, a.k.a. Dhoruba Bin Wahad. Dhoruba Bin Wahad is familiar to PBS viewers as a panelist-expert on the two-hour show *A Question of Race*, hosted by Phil Donahue, and as the subject of a celebratory one-hour PBS film *Passin' It On*, produced by ITVS and shown on *POV*, in which he is portrayed as a victim of police conspiracies, a champion of the oppressed, and a friend of Nelson Mandela.

Dhoruba, whose criminal career by his own account began when he was eight, was tried with three other New York Panthers for the murder of Sam Napier. The trial ended in a hung jury, and the defendants then pled guilty in exchange for sentences of time served.

Dhoruba was the leader of an East Coast faction of the Panthers that broke from the party over Huey Newton's decision to "put down the gun" and turn away from "armed struggle." Newton was accused by Eldridge Cleaver, Dhoruba, and others of betraying George Jackson, a San Quentin prisoner who had murdered a prison guard and whose brother Jonathan had been killed attempting to take hostages from a Marin County courtroom. Jackson, a judge, and two other people were killed in the attempt.

Dhoruba was also charged with killing two New York policemen in an ambush similar to the ambush of police that Eldridge Cleaver had arranged in San Francisco as part of the "armed struggle." After his conviction, Dhoruba served 19 years in prison before being released on a technicality. Dhoruba was linked to the ambush of the policemen because the machine gun used in the attack was found in his possession when he was arrested after holding up an after-hours club where he robbed the patrons of their drugs, jewelry, and cash. In the PBS/POV/ITVS film, Dhoruba explains the robbery as a revolutionary attempt to "take drugs off the streets." In the context of the film, which is a political infomercial for Dhoruba and his agendas and which portrays local police forces as occupying armies in America's ghettos, even so transparent an alibi might seem to make sense to the uninformed viewer.

The title *Passin' It On* is from a poem read at the beginning of the show that seeks to establish a link to the generational chain of Panther dissidents who lined up on the Cleaver-Dhoruba side of the Panther conflict. The Dhoruba faction formed the Black Liberation Army in the '70s and defined its armed struggle as a quest to liberate "New Afrika," a territorial enclave in America with majority black populations. The Black Liberation Army, led by Lumumba and Assata Shakur (a.k.a. Joanne Chesimard), who are invoked in the poem as guiding spirits for Dhoruba and his followers, conducted an ambush of police officers in New Jersey similar to those led by Cleaver and Dhoruba. The Shakurs shot and killed two New Jersey state troopers with machine guns. Assata Shakur fled to Cuba and is still wanted for the crime. The same military sect of black liberationists, led by Metula Shakur and aided by Weatherman Kathy Boudin and others calling themselves the "May 19 Communist Movement," attempted to rob a Brinks armored car in Nyack, New York, in 1982, killing three officers, including the only black policeman on the Nyack police force. The rantings of Metula Shakur and followers of George Jackson were recently featured on Pacifica public-radio station KPFK in Los Angeles.

Passin' It On is only the latest in a series of PBS films promoting the political gang called the Black Panther Party, which committed hundreds of felonies in the '60s and '70s, murdered more than a dozen people, mainly black, and extorted the inner-city black populations of New York, Chicago, and Oakland, committing rape, arson, armed robbery, and other crimes. These crimes have been documented by black journalist Hugh Pearson, a reporter for Pacific News Service and well-known figure on the left in the San Francisco Bay Area left. Pearson's new book, The Shadow of the Panther, was not reviewed on NPR's Fresh Air. When contacted by Pearson's publisher, host Terry Gross said she would not review the book unless she could get a Panther to come on the program to defend the party. This is a curious attitude for a book reviewer to take. Similarly, All Things Considered and Morning Edition, which mention new books and interview authors on a regular basis, rejected repeated requests that they bring Pearson's book to the attention of the public-radio audience. The Panther story is so explosive and so close to the interests of large sections of the public-radio audience that this can hardly be attributed to oversight or simple editorial misjudgment.

Just as PBS has made no effort to balance its fawning service to the Panther cause with more responsible accounts, NPR has refused to conduct a journalistic investigation into the Panther story. This is in striking contrast to NPR's readiness to investigate claims of injustice presented by leftist groups, such as Joseph Lowery's SCLC, which accused Mississippi prison officials of murdering black prisoners and making the racist murders look like suicides. NPR sent a team to Mississippi to investigate the charges, which it found to be baseless. (Most of the reported suicides, for example, turned out to be white prisoners.) *All Things Considered* editor Ellen Weiss, while refusing to assign reporters to interview Pearson, offered a paid monthly commentary to a Black Panther on death row for murdering a policeman. Only public outcries prompted wiser heads to reconsider the decision. The Panther in question was part of the same political network as Dhoruba and the Shakurs. His show can be heard regularly on the Pacifica network, which annually receives $1 million from the Corporation for Public Broadcasting.

The extreme left has established a pipeline into the PBS and NPR systems through friendly agencies like ITVS, *POV*, and Pacifica, which provide it with greater access to public-broadcasting outlets than the underrepresented voices in the political mainstream. The editorial standards that should guard against this abuse are ignored, despite a congressional directive to put them in place. The unchallenged proliferation of propaganda over taxpayer-supported airwaves in behalf of violent and extremist groups like the Panthers is a disservice to the American public, which pays for public broadcasting, and a violation of the laws that make public radio and television possible.

—*David Horowitz*

MARLON RIGGS' COLOR ADJUSTMENT

Marlon Riggs made no bones about his politically correct view of how blacks have been portrayed in the media. He wrote that public television and commercial television share the same perspective: "Like most of mainstream American media, it serves merely to consolidate the myths, power and authority of the majority: 'minorities' might be granted the right to speak and be heard, but only if we abide by the 'master codes' of courteous speech, proper subject matter, conventional aesthetics and 'mainstream' appeal. Disobey this often unquestioned rule and you risk banishment into cultural oblivion."

Riggs' own career revealed the emptiness of his claim. PBS aired the controversial POV program, *Tongues Untied*, which he produced and directed. Its graphic depiction of black homosexuality (interspersed with sophomoric poetry recited into the camera) provoked viewers across the country and became part of a national controversy over the use of tax dollars to fund subjects offensive to significant publics. Dozens of PBS stations refused to air the program. Yet rather than consigning Riggs to cultural oblivion, as his overwrought thesis would predict, his tactics catapulted him into the cultural limelight, winning him festival awards, critical kudos, and new funding (including $245,000 as one of the first recipients of an ITVS grant).

Riggs, the outlaw, taught at UC-Berkeley. He first made his name with a film called *Ethnic Notions*, broadcast as a PBS special in 1988 during Black History Month. Riggs' distributor, California Newsreel, advertises the film thus: "Loyal Toms, carefree Sambos, faithful Mammies, grinning Coons, savage Brutes and wide-eyed Pickanninies roll across the screen....Situating each stereotype historically in white society's need to justify racist oppression from slavery to the present, *Ethnic Notions* reveals how popular culture both shapes and reflects public attitudes." In other words, Riggs' indictment of racist exploitation could also be seen as a not so subtle exploitation of sensational racist images.

To those blacks who did not find their image in *Tongues Untied* uplifting, Riggs had this to say: "Equally predictable in this so-called 'obscenity' controversy was the collusion by silence of mainstream black America in this nakedly homophobic and covertly racial assault. Black heterosexuals...passively, silently acquiesced as political bedmates with the likes of Rev. Wildmon, James Kilpatrick and the rabidly anti-gay, race-baiting Senator Jesse Helms." It would be difficult to imagine even Sen. Helms expressing such bilious contempt for the morality of America's mainstream black communities in this way.

Riggs' penalty for this attack on black America was to be given the opportunity to repeat the argument in a two-part PBS film called *Color Adjustment: Blacks in Primetime*. Naturally the film is funded (through CPB and NEH grants) by the very taxpayers toward whom Riggs has expressed such pathological feelings.

Color Adjustment was about the depiction of blacks on American television. Its text is apparently drawn from J. Fred MacDonald's book, *Blacks in White TV*, which traces in a scholarly way the influence of minstrel shows on American television. But in the NEH-CPB production, Riggs changed the book to fit his extremist agenda. In order to hew to his signature thesis, Riggs omitted all references to actual depictions of blacks that contradict the point he was so determined to make. In a Brechtian style complete with agit-prop slogans and large blocks of text, the portentous commentary zeroed in on what Riggs regarded as negative portrayals of blacks in shows like *Amos and Andy*, *Beaulah*, *All In the Family*, *The Jeffersons*, *Roots*(!), *I Spy*, *The Cosby Show*(!), *Julia*, and *Frank's Place*. He contrasted this "drivel" with sound bites of civil rights protests and urban riots (the latter being his own preferred form of black authenticity). The film argued that the television fare was made in order to tranquilize public opinion. The tendentiousness of the whole exercise is emphasized by the omission of shows like *The Mod Squad*, *Room 222*, *The White Shadow*, *Amen*, and *A Different World*, not to mention *Arsenio* and *Oprah*, where black hosts define their own reality. ABC anchor Max Robinson and the *Today Show*'s Bryant Gumbel, like PBS's Charlayne Hunter-Gault, are of course not acknowledged.

To complete his circular logic, Riggs argued that depictions of successful middle class blacks in programs like *The Cosby Show* are "myths." But to make this logic stick he has to misrepresent his own on-camera authorities. When Professors Henry Louis Gates Jr., Patricia Turner, and Herman Gray were interviewed in *Color Adjustment*, they were not identified as faculty members at Harvard, University of California at Davis, and Northeastern University. The fact that Gates is perhaps the highest paid humanities academic in American history was also averted. Instead, Riggs made his own "color adjustment" and presented these very successful, very establishment authorities under the heading "cultural critics," as though they were on the outside of the academy looking in, rather than its reigning powers. To admit that his "critics" had a great deal in common with Bill Cosby (who himself has a doctorate in education from the University of Massachusetts) would have unhinged his entire case.

The NEH guidelines for media projects under which this dishonest film was funded require that controversial subjects be treated in a fair-minded manner and from a balanced perspective. Yet at a November screening of the film sponsored by the American Studies Association, Professor Turner told the audience that Riggs had decided to present a one-sided point of view, without balance, in order to counteract what Turner called the "dominant images" in the media. (Thus is ideology a self-fulfilling prophecy.) The other panelists, Henry Louis Gates Jr. and Herman Gray, agreed. Gray, employing the fashionable Marxist argot of today's university, went on to say that the only way to have balance would be to "transform society" and "the means of production."

Color Adjustment was cheap and uninteresting propaganda. It provides a clear example of how the public-television funding system is easily abused by an irresponsible and extremist fringe. If fairness means anything to CPB officials, they would have commissioned a documentary to balance the distortions of Riggs' production. Perhaps Bill Cosby should be invited to host, making up for the fact that Riggs didn't include an interview with Cosby in his show.

—*Laurence Jarvik*

PBS AND ISRAEL

Over the last decade the Public Broadcasting Service, supported by tax dollars, viewer contributions, and, increasingly, private corporations and foundations, has aired at least 15 documentaries on the Arab-Israeli conflict. No more than three of these can reasonably be described as balanced, a standard that federal statute mandates in "all programs or series of programs of a controversial nature." The remainder have projected a clear anti-Israel bias.

Struggle for Peace: Israelis and Palestinians, an hourlong documentary aired in early March 1992, is the latest addition to the list. The broadcast marks the first phase of an ambitious PBS venture, *Perspectives on Peace*, in which the network is promoting study guides, a book of essays by "noted scholars," and copies of a satellite-facilitated video conference featuring audience participation from multiple academic sites. A promotional pamphlet distributed by PBS describes these spin-off "educational products" as suitable for academic, community and religious groups as well as for "peace studies" programs.

The entire project is directed by Elizabeth Warnock Fernea, a professor of English and Middle Eastern studies at the University of Texas whose credentials include the controversial 1983 film, *Women Under Siege*. Funded in part by the National Endowment for the Humanities, the film elicited sharp criticism from NEH chairman William J. Bennett for its stridently pro-PLO tilt. Bennett termed the work "propaganda" and a "political tract" that should never have received federal money. Nevertheless, Fernea's record of tendentiousness has not deterred PBS from sponsoring her new documentary.

A veteran activist promoting Arab views to American audiences, Fernea, along with George Ball and Gary Sick, is a member of the board of governors of the Middle East Institute, a quasi-academic, pro-Arab group heavily drawn from State Department retirees and former oil-company executives. The institute, which has displayed a particular interest in American schools, helped finance the study guide for Fernea's *Perspectives on Peace* with a $23,000 grant. The documentary itself was underwritten in part by the Arabian American Oil Company.

True to type, the documentary features interviews with a wholly unrepresentative set of Israelis and Palestinians, whose views are proffered as the truest and sincerest representation of the conflict and, as well, the foundation of any hope for peace. *Struggle For Peace* erases or distorts any and all historical facts that contradict the premise that Israel bears total responsibility for the plight of the Palestinians and the absence of peace, omits all reference to the virulent anti-Semitism of Arab governments and the PLO and the campaigns waged by these parties to annihilate the state of Israel, ignores current military threats to Israel, excludes mention of the historical obligations of all parties under international mandates, focuses narrowly on Israel's allegedly brutal response to civil rebellion and on the resentments of Palestinian Arabs under Israeli control, and reiterates ceaselessly that the route to peace lies through Israel's relinquishing the West Bank and Gaza.

In pursuit of her candidly stated agenda, "to give a

mass [American] television audience images of people with whom they can identify," Fernea freely mangles the Middle East landscape. Thus, most egregiously, her spokesmen for the Palestinian cause are not Muslims but Christians: a priest from Jerusalem, a principal at a Friends School, and a "civic leader" whose long ancestral claim reaches back to the "shepherds' field when they got the first good news from the angels about the birth of our lord Jesus Christ." (Is the viewer therefore to understand that the man's ancestors were Jews? Somehow one doubts it.)

Reliance on these Palestinian "spokesmen" is deceptive in the extreme. Christians comprise only 5 percent of the Palestinian population, and their status within the Palestinian Arab community has long been a tenuous one. Today, in all Muslim-dominated territories, Christians (along with other minorities) exist under threat from the forces of Islamic fundamentalism; an attack in April 1992 on a Christian village and school in Egypt left 14 dead.

If the dominant Muslim voice is generally omitted, even more thoroughly expunged are any Palestinian voices that contradict the portrayal of the Palestinians as oppressed peace-seekers. No mention is made, for example, of the Grand Mufti of Jerusalem, the spiritual leader of the Palestinian Muslim majority who, in the summer of 1989, offered his own vivid opinion on the subject of the Arab quest for peace: "Kill the Jews until the stone shall cry, 'Oh, Muslim, this Jew is hiding beneath me, come and kill him.'" Similarly, Fernea advances her thesis of Arab innocence by avoiding any focus on Hamas, the violent and virulently anti-Semitic Islamic fundamentalist movement that claims the support of up to 40 percent of the population of Gaza and the West Bank. She devotes half a sentence to them.

Israelis interviewed in the film are as false a measure of the Israeli public. Ostensibly "ordinary," they are, in fact, among a tiny minority—men who agree to fulfill their military service only if assigned to areas outside the occupied territories and women who demonstrate weekly for Israeli withdrawal from those territories. The concerns of truly ordinary Israelis, that majority who continue to express a willingness to compromise with the Arabs but harbor very concrete fears about the military threat posed by surrounding Arab states and the continuing terrorist attacks of the PLO and kindred

Arab groups, are ridiculed. Viewers are told of the seemingly absurd actions of the Israeli government preventing Palestinian Arabs from planting trees and vegetables or acquiring a dairy herd—as if these were the sorts of dangers the Israeli public and military truly fear. Needless to say, no Israeli government voice is permitted at any time to provide an explanation or response to any of the charges leveled.

Sweeping historical falsehoods promoted by the film are actually surpassed by those in the companion "study guide." Therein can be found a version of the Middle East past lifted whole from Arab propaganda. A three-and-a-half page chronology enumerating events in the period 1850-1991 reiterates the fraudulent theme that modern-day Israel is an artificial creation of European Jews collaborating with the British against native Arabs, omitting any reference to the millennia-long ties of the Jewish people to the cities and towns of the region; omits any mention of the Holocaust; fails to note a single act of terror perpetrated by the Arab states, the PLO, the Muslim fundamentalist Hamas organization, or any Arab group against Jews, including the myriad instances of hijacking, hostage-taking, and murder of children, athletes, tourists, commuters, and worshippers; notes the creation of the PLO in 1964 without reference to the PLO Covenant, which stresses the illegitimacy of Israel and the determination of the PLO to destroy it; describes the Six-Day War in terms that, like the film, evade entirely the issue of the declared Arab intention to annihilate Israel; suppresses reference to the dramatic concessions—including the entire Sinai, with its oil fields, settlements, and air bases—made by Israel in exchange for a peace treaty with Egypt under the Camp David accords; and omits any reference to Syria's takeover of Lebanon.

One can only speculate at the ultimate damage to public understanding and discourse when poisonous materials such as these penetrate mainstream school and community groups, promoted under the prestigious imprimatur of the Public Broadcasting Service. Yet concerned Americans retain a means of self-defense against PBS's biased films and appalling "educational" materials; they can refuse to underwrite the defamation of Israel by withholding financial support from the network. Perhaps that, finally, will focus the thinking of network officials on issues of truth and public trust.

—*Andrea Levin*

JOURNEY TO THE
OCCUPIED LANDS

In response to the Public Broadcasting Service's history of airing inaccurate and biased documentaries about Israel, the Committee for Accuracy in Middle East Reporting in America has launched a wide-ranging campaign to improve journalistic standards at PBS and thus prevent such abuses from recurring. As part of the effort, a new detailed report entitled *PBS and Israel: The Case of Journey to the Occupied Lands* has been sent to members of Congress and the media, and CAMERA representatives have met in Washington, D.C., with congressmen, with Richard Carlson, president of the Corporation for Public Broadcasting, and with Ervin Duggan, president of PBS.

In the meetings, CAMERA has urged PBS to create a separate fact-checking department that will review all documentaries for accuracy and fairness prior to broadcast, just as CBS, NBC, and ABC have done for years. PBS's practice of relying solely on the integrity of the producer has produced a notable lack of integrity in the network's more than 20 documentaries concerning the Arab-Israeli conflict, with false charges maligning Israel the rule rather than the exception.

CAMERA is also urging that PBS publicly withdraw its most recent major documentary on the Arab-Israeli conflict, the error-ridden *Frontline* production *Journey to the Occupied Lands*. That PBS continues to endorse the accuracy of *Journey to the Occupied Lands* despite proof to the contrary published by CAMERA and continues to sell the videotape that it promotes as an educational tool to students and educators is a violation of its own program policies requiring fairness, accuracy, objectivity, and balance.

Among the journalistic breaches in *Journey to the Occupied Lands* that have been documented by CAMERA are:

☛ Doctored satellite images meant to illustrate the alleged crowding out of West Bank Arab towns by Israeli settlements;

☛ False charges that Israel has changed the population balance in Jerusalem to ensure a Jewish majority, when the fact is that Jews have been the majority in Jerusalem since 1870, and that from 1972 to 1992 the Muslim population of Jerusalem grew by 96 percent while the Jewish population grew by only 74 percent;

☛ False charges that the Israeli town of Givon Hachadasha stole land from an Arab farmer named Sabri Gharib, when, in fact, the Israeli High Court's 1986 ruling found that it was Gharib who was attempting to steal land. (Subsequently, Gharib has been fined for bringing yet more frivolous claims before the courts.);

☛ False charges that Israeli policies are turning Arab West Bank towns into ghetto communities by restricting their growth. On the contrary, a recent academic text reports...uncontrolled expansion of Arab villages and...irregular village sprawl.

After receiving CAMERA's initial written critique one year ago, PBS refused to study the matter independently and instead adopted a response written by Michael Ambrosino, the producer, and Marty Rosenbluth, the film's senior researcher. PBS thus allowed the filmmaker to investigate himself—a clear conflict of interest and violation of PBS guidelines. The network also repeatedly refused, without explanation, to send CAMERA a copy of Ambrosino's response. This was apparently an attempt by PBS to distance itself from Ambrosino while still publicly maintaining that *Journey to the Occupied Lands* was accurate.

CAMERA's reply to Ambrosino is a more than 150-page monograph that includes almost 100 pages of exhibits. Much of the text and many of the exhibits prove in detail the validity of CAMERA's original findings and the shocking lack of veracity displayed by Mr. Ambrosino in both his film and his response.

Typical is Ambrosino's claim that since 1967 Israel has oppressed Gaza citrus farmers by not allowing them to export directly to Western Europe. Not only is this claim untrue—for example, a typical *Financial Times* headline is "Surge in EC Trade with Palestinians" (July 11, 1990)—documents leaked to CAMERA prove that when Ambrosino made the claim, he knew it was untrue. Still, in his film Ambrosino claims that Israel forbids Gazan farmers from exporting citrus to the EC: "Since the occupation, the only direct exports allowed go east to the Arab world via Jordan..."

The filmmaker gratuitously repeats this false claim in his response: "As we say in the film, after 1967 Israel barred Palestinians from exporting directly to the European markets."

But in a 1993 memo to *Frontline* chief David Fanning, Ambrosino tells a radically different tale: "It was only after the EEC [now the EC] countries imposed economic sanctions on Israel in 1987 that the prohibition on direct export was lifted." So Mr. Ambrosino's claim that Israel prohibits Gaza citrus farmers from exporting is not just untrue, it is actually an intentional lie. In the face of such unethical conduct by one of its handpicked producers, PBS's obdurate defense of the film's accuracy is in violation of its own guidelines requiring that producers "adhere to the highest professional standards" and warning that "PBS may reject and withhold the PBS logo from a program if PBS has reason to believe that a producer has violated basic standards."

PBS must publicly withdraw *Journey to the Occupied Lands,* cease selling the videotape, and must forthrightly address the serious institutional shortcomings that allowed such a program to be made at taxpayer expense in the first place.

—*Alex Safian*

*A*BSENCE OF *S*TANDARDS:
*T*HE *R*EAL *L*IBERATORS

Perhaps the most distressing case of the cavalier attitude of PBS towards the standards that govern most journalistic media is that of *The Liberators*, produced by William Miles and Nina Rosenblum for *The American Experience*. Among its many falsehoods, the film claimed that the black 761st Tank Battalion (the "Black Panthers") liberated Buchenwald on April 11, 1945.

The program had been revealed as phony before broadcast. Melvin Rappaport, a captain in the division that actually liberated Buchenwald, called WNET three weeks beforehand to protest, to no avail. Some ten days before the air date, Colonel James Moncrief (Ret.), the senior surviving officer of the division, wrote to WNET to urge them not to show the film because of its fabrications. He sent another letter a week later, again fruitlessly.

The Liberators was shown on PBS on Veteran's Day, Nov. 11, 1992. Afterwards, despite the station's claim that the show had been withdrawn, the film and its companion book continued to circulate on college campuses and to be sold in Washington's Holocaust Memorial Museum and New York's Jewish Museum bookshops.

The filmmakers, who have never admitted their errors, hired the high-powered public-relations firm Clein and White to argue their case in an attempt to garner an Academy Award; they succeeded in winning a nomination. Nor has PBS ever made any on-air correction. The Corporation for Public Broadcasting has declined to investigate the issue or commission its own production to set the record straight as required by Congress. Needless to say, no PBS, CPB, WGBH, or WNET official has been publicly chastised or held accountable for the errors and omissions of the program.

The Liberators is perhaps the most appalling case of CPB's failure to protect the integrity of the public broadcasting system, because it was a widely publicized scandal in which not a single step has been taken to fulfill the congressional mandate for objectivity and balance in areas of public controversy. Perhaps no area is more controversial than the depiction of the Holocaust, and perhaps no documentary has been more lacking in objectivity and balance than The Liberators.

Shortly after the film's broadcast, articles appeared in the press questioning the film's claim that the 761st Tank Battalion had liberated Buchenwald and Dachau and citing the absence of documentation in military archives. The first reporter to expose the hoax was Chris Ruddy of The Guardian (now with the New York Post). His December 1992 article carried the headline "PBS Documentary Lies About Liberation of Concentration Camps: 'Black Vets, Jewish Survivors Angry with PBS: Black Units Did Not Liberate Buchenwald and Dachau.'" Ruddy's reporting was confirmed by Pacifica station WBAI's Jim Dingeman, who hosted a radio discussion of the errors of the film with veterans and survivors, and Jeffrey Goldberg of *The Forward*, who published an expose in the widely-respected Jewish weekly.

In the face of the initial journalistic onslaught, WNET, New York, issued a press release on February 2, 1993, signed by executive Karen Salerno, that read: "Thirteen/WNET, WGBH, and *The American Experience* have absolute confidence in the veracity of this outstanding film. Scrupulously researched and based on unimpeachable eyewitness testimony, it vividly recounts an unjustly ignored part of our country's history. It is because historical accuracy is so essential, that we believe films like *The Liberators: Fighting on Two Fronts in World War II* must be made and broadcast." Producer Nina Rosenblum accused critics of being racists and revisionists.

On February 8, *The New Republic* carried Jeffrey Goldberg's *The Exaggerators*, which quoted E.G. McConnell, one of the black soldiers featured in the film, saying, "It's a lie. We were nowhere near these camps when they were liberated." Nina Rosenblum responded that McConnell, a central spokesman in her film, was "severely brain-damaged."

Two days later, on February 10, the American Jewish Committee released a report by Kenneth Stern called *Liberators: A Background Report*. The document charged that the program made the "factually erroneous" claim, among other mistakes, that the all-black 761st Tank Battalion had liberated Buchenwald. The next day WNET announced the station and The American Experience had withdrawn the film pending its own investigation. They added, however, "Thirteen and the producers of *The American Experience* make absolutely no retreat from the essential thesis of the documentary that black American soldiers played a role in the liberation." This weasel-worded statement was again signed by WNET executive Karen Salerno. It did not point out that the film was not being withdrawn from the home-video market or that the Harcourt Brace Jovanovich companion book was not being withdrawn from stores.

Six months later, on Aug. 19, 1993, came a report by Morton Silverstein, Diane Wilson, and Nancy Ramsey called "Findings of the Review Team: An Examination of *Liberators: Fighting on Two Fronts in World War II*." The three investigators concluded that "the review team cannot substantiate the presence of the 761st Tank Battalion at Buchenwald on its day of liberation, April 11, 1945, nor during the 48 hour period [following its discovery by Allied troops]." The report concluded that the Third Army's Sixth Armored Division, Fourth Armored Division, and 80th Infantry Division deserve credit for the liberation of the camps.

Three weeks later, on September 7, Karen Salerno issued another press release about the film from WNET, concluding that Silverstein's study "confirmed allegations that some portions of the film contain factual inaccuracies. Thirteen/WNET has determined that research for this documentary was not as diligent and comprehensive as basic documentary practice would require, and that the producers' panel of expert advisers was inadequately utilized to monitor the factual content of the film. Thirteen/WNET will continue to withhold public television station broadcasts until the documentary is corrected." The statement added that the New York station had asked that the production company remove the channel's name from the production credits. However, the station did not ask for its money back and did not insist that the videocassettes be withdrawn from schools, libraries, and museums.

That same day, producers Miles and Rosenblum issued a statement blasting WNET's report. "We do not feel that WNET has conducted an independent assessment of the program," they charged, adding, "we continue to object to PBS censorship. We feel it is dangerous to limit historical inquiry, especially in light of recent revelations concerning the role of black troops in the military. A continuation of this dialogue is counter productive and only serves to denigrate the courageous concentration camp survivors and their heroic liberators."

That was over a year ago. Since then, Colonel Moncrief and the surviving members of his division have continued their lonely quest to set the record straight. "PBS has reflected deceit, insincerity, and a lack of forthrightness in its actions since the film's airing," says Moncrief. "If they can lie about history in my lifetime, what can they do when I'm gone?"

Asked why he persists in his Quixotic struggle against the public-broadcasting bureaucracy, Mel Rappaport, who served with Moncrief as an army captain, notes, "It was a sea of blood. We still owe something to the guys who didn't come back."

The real liberators of Buchenwald have continued their efforts to preserve the history of what actually happened. The 9th Armored Infantry Battalion of the Sixth Armored Division of General George Patton's Third Army reached Buchenwald on April 11th, 1945. Captain Fred Keffer, later head of the physics department at the University of Pittsburgh, led the patrol that first reached the camp in the late morning. A second team of soldiers, led by Sergeant Milt Harrison, himself Jewish, set an explosive charge on the camp's gate and entered at approximately the same time. Additional troops shortly arrived from the 80th Infantry Division and the Fourth Armored Division. Rappaport, also Jewish, who was present at the liberation of Buchenwald, said in the *New York Times* that he told producer William Miles, "We liberated Buchenwald. I was there. I saw no black troops."

In every issue of the division newsletter, *The Super Sixer*, published since the broadcast of the phony documentary, there has appeared an article by Colonel Moncrief demanding a correction of what he calls PBS's "Big Lie," giving his comrades-in-arms details of the stonewalling by public broadcasters at all levels, expressing "displeasure at the manner in which PBS has betrayed the public trust (and therefore does not deserve federal funding)" and asking fellow veterans to write their congressmen and senators. Moncrief has written numerous letters complaining to CPB president Richard Carlson, PBS president Ervin Duggan, PBS programming executive Jennifer Lawson, and other public-broadcasting officials. He says that while he has gotten polite letters back, they have not responded to the specific complaints about the film's falsehoods or the actions of PBS since its airing.

Among those who have responded to Colonel Moncrief and his comrades, however, has been Rep. Gregg Laughlin (D-Tex.), who made a passionate speech on the House floor this summer denouncing *The Liberators* as "a grave injustice to the millions of veterans of our great nation." Moncrief also submitted testimony to Rep. Ed Markey's Subcommittee on Telecommunications, urging that "federal funds for PBS's use be eliminated or reduced considerably" because the network "has not been honest and forthright with the American people."

The fight to correct the historical record has become the

last mission for these veterans. This year's annual reunion of the Sixth Armored Division drew some 300 survivors to Minneapolis in September and was called "The Last Battle of World War II" in the *Minneapolis Star-Tribune* account of the proceedings. Writer Chuck Haga noted, "The longest battle the Sixth Armored Division fought wasn't the siege of Brest, the relief of Bastogne, or the run-and-gun race across Germany at the end of World War II. That all took less than a year. The Sixth Armored's battle with the Public Broadcasting Service started almost two years ago, and the shells are still flying."

—*Lawrence Jarvik*

TALES OF THE CITY

After a 15-year wait and controversy over the inclusion of foul language, nudity, and homosexual characters, Armistead Maupin's *Tales of the City* was finally broadcast nationwide on PBS in early January 1994. While pundits from the right and left have been squabbling over questions of "pro-gay" or "liberal" bias, they seem to have missed the real point of the show. Finding love and companionship has always been a difficult proposition; the freedoms reaped from the post-'60s era of sexual liberation and cultural relativism have only made this more terrifying and dangerous.

Tales of the City is the enjoyable story of a diverse group of people struggling with their garbled identities and looking for love in the often bizarre world of 1976 San Francisco. The miniseries, say the show's producers, is set during a time "when our hearts were young and our mood rings were blue." The miniseries is based upon Maupin's novel of the same title, itself inspired by the daily column Maupin wrote for the *San Francisco Chronicle* from 1976 to 1987.

The show's producers have assembled an extremely talented group of actors for *Tales*. Academy Award winner Olympia Dukakis stars as the eccentric Anna Madrigal, the owner of the Barbary Lane apartment complex. Donald Moffat plays Edgar Halcyon, a conservative businessman with six months to live. The womanizing lawyer turned waiter named

Brian Hawkins is played by Paul Gross. Chloe Webb is compelling as Mona Ramsey, a bisexual, Quaalude-popping, bohemian with a longing for love. Mona's best friend is a sweet gay man named Michael Tolliver, played by Marcus D'Amico. Laura Linney rounds out the main cast, playing Mary Ann Singleton, the innocent recently arrived in San Francisco.

Reviewers of *Tales* describe the '70s as a "golden age" or "Paradise Lost." To Frank Rich it was a time of "live-and-let-live innocence which looks a lot like democracy." To the *Post*'s Tom Shales, the '70s was "a time when people still basked in what seemed the refracted enlightened glow of the Sixties." Armistead Maupin, the author, agrees: "The '70s were a golden age to me. I knew it at the time, and I know it now. It was a golden age for a lot of people....I regret nothing. I had a wonderful time. I discovered more about myself and more about humanity at that time than I had ever learned before. And I am thrilled to be celebrating this in film." This feeling of nostalgia is evident in the miniseries, in the music, in the dress, and in the devil-may-care attitude some of the characters have with regard to sex and drugs.

But to someone who was five years old in 1976 and is herself the child of flower children of the era, the '70s of *Tales* seem an aesthetically and morally revolting time. The sexual liberation and freedom often appears more as a source of pain and anxiety than joy. Was life then really laden with casual sex? Were the streets really crawling with sexually predatory hetero- and homosexuals? Much like *Looking for Mr. Goodbar* and *Urban Cowboy*, *Tales* seems to have captured the desperation and anxiety of a bygone era.

In one telling sub-drama, the prolifically promiscuous Brian picks up a middle-aged waitress in a diner, returning to her trailer park dwelling in a tense silence. Upon entering, Brian is overcome with a momentarily terrifying sense of *deja vu*. He had been there before, after all, when he bedded the woman's daughter. After a quickie amidst the white-trash kitsch of her trailer, the woman pathetically asks Brian if she is as "good" and "pretty" as her daughter. To those of us who grew up in the comparatively chaste '80s, the thought of a woman seeking affirmation from a strange man she just slept with is more than mildly revolting. For a movie supposed to be offensive for its homosexual content, this is one scene that really made my skin crawl.

In *Tales*, however, that's basically par for the course. All of the characters have sex with relative strangers in the quest for love, companionship, or affirmation (or merely to relieve momentary boredom). All are left instead with loneliness, though interestingly, not guilt. This impression is only reinforced by the myriad images of leisure-suited swingers looking for love in gay bars, discos, bath houses, supermarkets, and even the coin-operated laundry.

Maupin wittily portrays some of the other disturbing aspects of the '70s. Several minor characters mourn the passing of the '60s, and in fact seem permanently crippled by them. Vincent, who runs a suicide-crisis hotline, kills himself because his wife left him to join the Israeli army. It seems that after Vietnam, her life lost its meaning. She tried protesting the killing of whales, injustice to Native Americans, and impending nuclear holocaust, but nothing could eclipse her nostalgia for good old 'Nam.

Maupin also cleverly depicts the birth of the "trendy left." In an amusing moment, wealthy debutantes gather for a "consciousness-raising session." The guest speaker is a Native American woman who escaped a gang rape by a group of bikers. After deep exploration of the psychic pain of being violated by a pack of insensitive easy riders, they decide what "cause" they are going to support by charity. DeDe decides on whales, because "you don't have to hug whales like you would handicapped children."

The most pervasive element to *Tales*, however, is the notion that our postmodern, urban world has a noticeable lack of true meaning. People are alienated and alone without any visible means of spiritual or moral support, despite casual sex and trendy spiritual movements like Transcendental Meditation or Existential Survival Training. But *Tales* also depicts the honest quest for meaning and the search for connection with others that, of course, has nothing to do with the '70s or being gay.

Perhaps this lack of meaning is so evident in Maupin's story because his characters are never who they seem to be. Anna Madrigal turns out to have been a man who underwent a sex-change operation. Mona's black lesbian lover is really white. Beauchamp Day, the adulterous married man, frequents gay bath houses for homosexual trysts. Norman, the repressed neighbor, is really a child pornographer and a blackmailer.

The world of *Tales* is a cultural relativist's Utopia. All the characters are treated with respect regardless of their diverse lifestyles and values. The philosophy and politics of this proposition aside, the theme makes for some of the program's more hilarious and heartwarming moments. In one of these, the heterosexual Brian and the homosexual Michael get stoned and then sexually aroused. Fearing the worst, one is relieved when they decide to go "cruising" together, in a bar with both straight women and gay men.

Tales of the City is touching in that it attempts to transcend the differences that divide people and reveal that which all people share—the search for love and a place to call home. Whether the characters are homosexual or heterosexual, rich or poor, black or white, all of them have the same basic experience of being alone and not liking it. Issues that are so divisive in the politically correct '90s are treated with a refreshing lightness, without the preaching and moral grandstanding to which we now have become accustomed.

The controversy surrounding *Tales of the City* reveals the state of our cultural discourse on "gay issues." It is ironic that Hollywood, the city famous for self-righteous preaching of politically correct social mores, optioned but never produced the book as either a miniseries or a movie. Maupin has said that Hollywood producers wanted to reduce the gay characters to "cameo walk-ons; the witty gay neighbor down the hall, not a person who has a life of his or her own." It seems progressive social causes are only something to hold parties for—not to risk corporate sponsors for.

PBS finally decided to run the British-produced miniseries. PBS offered the show to affiliates in two versions: the original and a cut version without the blunt language and with the nudity blurred. The Washington, D.C., affiliate ran the unedited version. In a rather sad statement on our popular culture, one hardly notices the "strong" language. As for the nudity, it is rather noticeable and could easily be seen as offensive or gratuitous. After all, it is slightly shocking to see gay men giving each other deep, wet kisses and naked people romping in bed on the same channel that runs *Nova* documentaries about arctic foxes and frozen cavemen.

The combination of nudity, strong language, and the explicit presentation of homosexuality has caused some groups to deem *Tales of the City* inappropriate for airing on PBS, a public corporation funded by the taxpayer. Conservative groups such as Accuracy In Media and The Family Research Council point to *Tales* as just another example of PBS's pro-gay and liberal bias.

Robert H. Knight of The Family Research Council argues that *Tales of the City* "nostalgically celebrates life in the gay bars and bath houses" and is "a slick piece of gay propaganda that presents 1970s gay life in San Francisco as superior to marriage and family, with few apparent consequences from promiscuous sex or illicit drugs."

It seems either naive or slightly paranoid to assume that *Tales* is mere propaganda or will elicit an acceptance of homosexuality from an unsympathetic audience. Ironically, there is much in the miniseries that could serve only as confirmation of the decadence of the gay lifestyle. The scene of a man entering a cubicle in an all-male bathhouse to have anonymous sex is the quintessential metaphor of the gay lifestyle—and the precursor of the present AIDS epidemic. The portrayal of a cabal of snobby and pretentious "queens" who sadistically ridicule working-class gays gives credence to the stereotype of the "bitchy fag." Further, one of the most distasteful of all Maupin's characters is a married male bisexual. This is not a miniseries that sees all homosexuals through rose-colored glasses.

Gregory King of The Human Rights Campaign Fund, an organization that advocates gay rights, was delighted that Maupin's gay characters were not presented as simple "cardboard saints." He sees the show as "an accurate depiction of a particular time and place," representing the bittersweet diversity of the gay community.

It's unfortunate that activists like Knight and King spent the six hours of *Tales* looking for affirmation for their political ideology. But it is more enlightening to approach *Tales of the City* as a social history of a certain time and place in America's past. For a person who did not live through the '60s and '70s but must endure the era's consequences, the lesson of *Tales* is simple. Anna Madrigal, the mother figure of 26 Barbary Lane, tells her newest resident, "Honey, I don't object to anything." When as a society we refuse to object to anything, the social and moral fabric of our culture is destroyed.

Living without rules and afforded the boundless freedom to reinvent ourselves at will is no doubt seductive. Hedonism provides many sensual pleasures. But the logical outcomes of living without moral structure are alienation, anxiety, and ultimately either physical or spiritual death. It is inevitable that at least some of the characters in *Tales* will get AIDS, hepatitis, or other venereal diseases. If they are somehow fortunate enough to avoid disease, they will suffer from drug or alcohol dependency or some variety of psychological illness. We all know the consequences of the lifestyles portrayed in *Tales of the City*. This knowledge imbues *Tales* with several levels of ironic meaning that cannot simply be dismissed.

—*Alyson Todd*

COLORADO'S JIHAD

In *The New Holy War* segment of *Bill Moyers' Journal*, Moyers travels to Colorado to hear the "voices" of the Proposition Two debate. Proposition Two, designed to stop legislation making discrimination against homosexuals in housing, employment, and public accommodations illegal, was passed by Colorado voters last year. *The New Holy War* presents the conflict over Proposition Two as a culture war between homosexuals and evangelical Christians. At first glance, *The New Holy War* appears to be an objective documentary, for members of both the Christian and the homosexual communities are interviewed extensively. Yet the two communities are approached and portrayed in very different ways.

Opening with a majestic view of an American bald eagle soaring over the Rocky Mountains, the soundtrack to this quintessential American image is *America the Beautiful*. As the music fades, a chorus of individual voices denounces homosexuality as immoral. Then Moyers begins his narration. He says that the beauty of Colorado Springs inspired Katherine Lee Bates to write *America the Beautiful*...and that Ms. Bates is suspected to be a lesbian.

From the outset, homosexuals and the advocates for homosexual rights are presented as patriotic and more true to American ideals than those who denounce homosexuality, whose voices and words mar the beautiful image of the bald eagle soaring over mountains. Moyers says Colorado Springs is a "conservative town" by virtue of being home to the Air Force Academy, missile tracking systems, and Christian churches. He ignores the facts that Colorado College is located in Colorado Springs and numerous former hippies live in the vicinity.

Subtly presenting himself as an objective journalist, Moyers claims that because he is a former newspaper reporter, he decided to go first to the "conservative" *Colorado Springs Gazette* for information. There he interviews reporters who tell him that the evangelical Christian community was the main political force behind Proposition Two. He is told to talk to Tim Daggart of the New Life Church and Will Perkins, a car dealer and founder of Colorado for Family Values.

The next 15 minutes of the segment are devoted to the Christian perspective. Leaders of some of the Christian churches and political groups are interviewed extensively. The Christian view is presented fairly and accurately. Most of those interviewed argue that they do not hate homosexuals but feel homosexuality is immoral. As one Christian says, "Love the sinner, hate the sin." Christian parents interviewed say that the sexual practices of homosexuals are disgusting and express concern that "pro-homosexual" teaching is going on in public schools. They feel that homosexual-rights legislation would be an attempt by the government to make them endorse and condone homosexuality. Therefore, they argue that Proposition Two was designed not to grab control of the government but to protect them from the government. They also mention *The Gay Agenda*, a video produced by the Christian group Focus on the Family.

Moyers shows clips of a gay-rights march taken from this video. The march is a parade of half naked homosexuals lasciviously grinding and grabbing their buttocks. There are cross-dressers, S&M practitioners, women with strap-on dildos and more. One scene shows a male couple "deep kissing." In another, a member of the parade is holding a sign declaring "God Is Gay." Other images include a doctor discussing the sex practices of the gay male, such as "rimming" and "golden showers." The narrator of *The Gay Agenda* states that male homosexuals have an average of 20 to 106 partners per year. The sequence features a page of gay male personal ads.

Moyers then investigates Focus on the Family, which

produced *The Gay Agenda*. He finds the group to be extremely efficient and effective. Because 12 other states have amendments similar to Proposition Two on the ballot, Focus on the Family put together a "How-to Workbook" that teaches in great detail how to start an anti-gay rights organization. Members of Focus on the Family claim that it is not a religious organization. Moyers juxtaposes this claim with the ex-director's statement that "Christ is the King of kings and Lord of lords."

Moyers asks a gay rights activist to analyze *The Gay Agenda*. She denounces the tape as crude propaganda and claims that the "so-called experts" were "homophobics." Another member of a gay activist organization tells Moyers that the Christians want Biblical law to be American law and are "a very dangerous group."

Moyers loses all pretense at objectivity during the second half of *The New Holy War*. Although Moyers does an in-depth critical look at Focus on the Family, he neglects to research the various gay activist organizations that played a considerable role on the other side of the Proposition Two debate. Moyers interviews homosexuals not so much for their opinions on Proposition Two and the evangelical Christians, but to contradict the Christians' portrayal of homosexuals.

Here we meet Lynn B. and her partner. Lynn B. is a former nun. Her partner is a church-attending Christian. Both are politically moderate without any expressed desires to restructure the system of the "patriarchy" and "compulsory heterosexuality." They both say they were born lesbians and had no choice in the matter. The relationship is presented as full of family values—love, compassion, mutual respect, religion, and a lifelong commitment of fidelity. Lynn's partner is even shown putting on mascara.

The gay male couple Moyers introduces the viewer to is equally stable. They have been together in a monogamous relationship for six years. One man is a former United States Marine and the other is a geology professor, and both are church-going Christians. They are shown working in the garden, walking their dog, and doing dishes together. The only stated political concern they have is violence against gays. Moyers states there have been 1,900 hate crimes against homosexuals, 12 of which resulted in death.

Both couples express shock at *The Gay Agenda* video. They complain about the "constant negative images of gays." One of the lesbians asks, "How can they say this about me?" All express hurt and pain. But what the homosexuals are saying is less im-portant in the mind of the viewers than who they are. Moyers discredits the Christian argument against homo-sexuality not by confronting or attacking the Christian arguments but by presenting homosexuals who are Christian, monogamous, and politically moderate as representative of most homosexuals.

There are other problems with Moyers' presentation of the Proposition Two debate. The viewer is never informed what the vote totals were or the percentage of evangelical Christians in the state of Colorado. Moyers never mentions that many evangelicals do not describe themselves as political conservatives or as Republicans. He never interviews the nonevangelicals who voted for Proposition Two. The film does not present any factual data with which to assess Moyers' framing of the debate as being strictly between homosexuals and fundamentalist Christians. Most importantly, Moyers neglects to represent the homosexual community fairly and accurately.

The New Holy War would have been more thought-provoking if Moyers had searched for a diversity of opinions and lifestyles within both the Christian and homosexual communities. Instead the film is based upon stereotypes and, as such, neglects many of the more complex and interesting questions provoked by the Proposition Two debate.

—*Alyson Todd*

MOYERS ON THE
POWER OF MONEY

Bill Moyers devoted his January 21, 1994, *Bill Moyers' Journal* to the topics of how money corrupts politics and the need for campaign finance reform. The program's lineup was completely one-sided, with every one of the nine guests opposed to corporate influence on politics and in favor of campaign finance "reform." Moyers began with an interview designed to suggest balance with Republican expatriate Kevin Phillips, author of *The Politics of Rich and Poor* and a favorite Democratic pundit, and left-wing populist William Greider, author of *Who Will Tell the People?* Both predictably lamented the influence of money on politics and expressed no hope for reform in the coming year.

Moyers then did a segment with Ellen Miller of the Center for Responsive Politics, a liberal think tank that investigates election contributions with an eye for corporate malfeasance. Interestingly, while Miller's outfit bemoaned the influence of corporate interests on debates like the North American Free Trade Agreement, it did not proclaim its own dependence on textile interests for funding and has not acknowledged that it does work at the request of funders just like everyone else. Unsurprisingly, Moyers did not explore this line of investigation.

The last third of the show was devoted to a panel of six activists for campaign finance "reform." To suggest balance, Moyers included Jim Boutelle, a former Reagan-Bush supporter now with Ross Perot's "United We Stand." The other five were left-wing activists who supported the elimination of private contributions to campaigns, leaving only the government as a source of campaign funds.

Some panel members were so fervent about the poison of money that they thought campaigns shouldn't spend any money to reach the voters. When Moyers pointed out that polls regularly show majorities against public financing of elections, Maine activist Betsy Sweet replied: "When you package that with...[the idea that] people are going to take $5,000 to run and that's it—they're going to get this money and that's it—and you really do take everything out of it, then the numbers [favoring government-funded campaigns] actually go up." How does Sweet expect any citizen outside of Ross Perot to run for federal office with a treasury of $5,000? Moyers didn't ask.

Massachusetts activist Randall Kehler was still expressing 10-year-old gripes about the unsuccessful nuclear freeze movement, "whose wishes for a halt to the nuclear arms race between the U.S. and the Soviet Union were thwarted because the big money interests, weapons manufacturers and their allies in Washington, had the ear of our representatives in a way that the majority of American people, who supported the freeze, did not." It mattered little to Kehler that if the freeze had been successful there would still be a thousand nuclear tipped ICBMs in Central Europe or that his goal—withdrawal of the missiles and an end to the U.S.-Soviet arms competition—was actually accomplished by Ronald Reagan's zero-zero option, the policy that the freeze activists said would lead to World War III. Moyers, of course, did not raise this point. To Moyers and his panel, whenever the political system failed to enact a left-wing initiative like disarmament or tax increases, it was not simply a loss for the left, but a loss for the concept of democracy itself. When the right prevailed on an issue, it was the result of moneyed interests triumphing over the will of the people. For Moyers and his panelists there could never be a triumph of moneyed interests on the left—unions, foundations, the AARP. Left-wing victories were always democracy in its purest form. That the side opposing publicly financed elections was favored by a majority, as Moyers noted, seemed to be no impediment to claiming the truest interests of democracy were represented by whatever the left proposed.

Moyers concluded the show with a lecture:

> As a football fan, I admire the referees who keep the game honest. They do their work in public to keep the playing field level. If it were okay for players, coaches or owners to contribute to referees on the side, I'd stop trusting the game or watching the game. Supposedly, government is the arbiter between the competing claims of citizens. No one, no one should get a leg up from putting money in the umpire's pocket. When political donations lead to the selective enforcement of the rules, we can't trust government any more. Representation becomes determined by a clever form of bribery.

He then lobbied for the left-wing activists: "You can work to challenge the system locally, as these folks have, and you can start by finding out who has bid what for whom. If you want to know where your members of Congress get their campaign funds, call this toll-free number for Project Vote Smart."

One thing the show failed to mention is that the Moyers family itself isn't so disgusted by the campaign fundraising process that they actually abstain from it. Federal Election Commission records show that Moyers' wife, Judith Davidson Moyers, who is also co-executive producer of *Bill Moyers' Journal*, made two donations in the 1991-92 cycle: $1,000 to Democratic Sen. Harris Wofford and $250 to Emily's List, the pro-choice Democratic women's political action committee. In September 1990, Mrs. Moyers toured Texas in a "dog and pony" caravan for Democratic Gov. Ann Richards. According to Celia Morris' book *Storming the Statehouse*, Mrs. Moyers and Mrs. Lloyd Bentsen "were also women who had grown up in Texas and were fiercely loyal both to their state and to Ann Richards."

Morris added:

> Judith Moyers' two-minute spiel was a classic piece of political persuasion. She gave her qualifications (her roots went back to the Stephen F. Austin colony and the Fredonia rebellion), sounded the alarm (there was an emergency in Texas), startled the audience by citing the evidence ("The murder rate is higher in my hometown of Dallas than it is in the place where I live: New York....A national study recently rated the Texas air quality among the worst in the nation"), and proposed the solution ("There are two candidates, but one has no experience in government, a questionable reputation in business, and in my opinion he is unfit to be governor").

The show's condemnation of using political pull for private profit also did not extend to Moyers' own company, Public Affairs Television, which makes millions of dollars each year off PBS Home Video without ever having to disclose a penny or provide a return to the taxpayers who fund the production and broadcasting of his shows. It also avoided the question: If corporate money is an evil influence on what it funds, why is this public-television series underwritten by Mutual of America, a private insurance company?

In any case, Moyers' football analogy is wrong. The judicial branch of government is not analogous to referees in a football game. The president and Congress are hardly arbiters. They are advocates. Politicians represent ideologies and constituencies, and that's exactly the way the Constitution envisions it. Nowhere in the show was a politician allowed to object that they aren't bid for like items in an auction, that special interests often cancel each other out, that a corporation lobbying to stay in business is also lobbying on behalf of its employees and customers. If Moyers were sincere about his concern that political donations lead to selective enforcement of the rules, we might expect a *Bill Moyers' Journal* on Whitewater Development and Madison Guaranty Savings and Loan.

—*Tim Graham*

PART II

PBS ELECTIONEERING:
THE PRESIDENTIAL ELECTION OF 1992

LEFT FROM THE BEGINNING

In August 1991, PBS announced its plans for covering the 1992 presidential elections. This included a collaboration with NBC News to cover the party conventions, live coverage of the three-day National Issues Convention, a follow-up to the 1988 program *The Choice*, which examined the candidates' public lives, and a three-part *Frontline* series by left-wing journalist William Greider. Of these five projected programs, only the Greider series seemed to offer wide editorial latitude to the producers. On Aug. 21, 1991, we therefore wrote the following letter to PBS programming chief Jennifer Lawson:

> Dear Jennifer Lawson,
> In previous correspondence you stressed the importance of observing the principles of fairness, objectivity and balance in accord with the terms of the Public Broadcasting Act of 1967. This is a presidential election year, and I am writing you on behalf of the Committee on Media Integrity because of our concern about the announced plans for PBS election coverage. We wish to know what steps you are taking to ensure that this coverage will be fair and balanced, what guidelines you will observe, and who or what group will be responsible for ensuring that the guidelines are observed.
> We are particularly concerned about the announcement in the July 22 issue of *Current* that as part of PBS's 1992 election coverage

Frontline will air a three-part special by William Greider and producer Sherry Jones, based on Greider's forthcoming book *The State of Democracy*. There has been no announcement of any PBS project comparable to Mr. Greider's or any that will serve to balance the well-known biases of Mr. Greider's and Ms. Jones' previous work.

William Greider is a well-known left-wing journalist. His biases are so pronounced that a previous *Frontline* report by Greider and producer Jones, *The War on Nicaragua,* was rated one of the worst programs of the year by the liberal San Francisco *Chronicle* television critic John Carman (Dec. 30, 1987). In his review of the program (April 21, 1987), Carman criticized Greider for "shoddy, unfair and manipulative journalism."

I quote from his columns:

"*Frontline: The War on Nicaragua.* Someone should have examined the show in advance and cried foul. Underhanded and biased against U.S. policy in Central America, the program never bothered to label itself as opinion. Heaven knows it's all right to challenge the U.S. role in the region. But *Frontline* disguised its broadside as objective journalism.

"Yet the reporting and editing are anything but objective. One example: While Lieutenant General Wallace Nutting says in an interview that bringing U.S. troops to neighboring Honduras educated the Americans and contributed to their world understanding, his words are illustrated by scenes of U.S. servicemen throwing grenades and shooting up the countryside.

"That might be clever, but it's also shoddy, unfair and manipulative journalism. Viewers are supposed to draw their own conclusions based on an unbiased presentation of facts on *Frontline* without a condescending shove from Greider and producer Sherry

Jones. We might hear more about *War on Nica-ragua*. For once, PBS has handed its right-wing critics some real fodder for controversy."

It should be clear from these comments and from Mr. Greider's published political commentaries in *Rolling Stone* (where he has been Washington editor) that his work contains an extreme political bias, which would locate him somewhere on the left wing of the Democratic Party. Has PBS asked the directors of *Frontline* to ensure that there will be a comparable series of programs representing the center and right of the political spectrum to balance Mr. Greider's efforts? Is PBS planning any series at all that might reflect the centrist politics of the Democratic Party or the conservative politics of the Republican Party in a manner similar to the left-wing series that *Frontline is* evidently planning?

The issue is one of fairness and equal time for opposing points of view on issues of public policy. As the election year is rapidly approaching and the time required to conceive and produce television programs is considerable, I would appreciate an answer to these questions at your earliest convenience.

Sincerely, etc.

On September 9, we got our reply, or, more accurately, non-reply from Jennifer Lawson:

Thank you for your August 21 letter concerning the 1992 election coverage on public television. As the 1992 presidential race approaches, public television is preparing an extensive array of programs exploring the issues and individuals at the heart of the elections. These programs—and others yet to be announced—will provide the American electorate with what we believe to be television's most insightful, useful and varied coverage. And, like other public TV news

and public affairs programming, it will provide balance through the utilization of a
broad range of journalists in front of and behind the scenes.

Having delivered this boilerplate, Ms. Lawson then
listed the programs that had already been announced, which,
we had already pointed out in our letter, were not comparable
to the Greider series. She then concluded:

Through these and other programs in
the months ahead, viewers will be well
served with an engaging presentation of a
multiplicity of views on the important issues
facing all Americans. Thank you for your interest in public television.
Sincerely,
Jennifer Lawson

Two weeks after Ms. Lawson's letter arrived, Bill
Moyers announced that he was about to launch a new PBS
series that would deal with issues facing the nation during
the election year, further tilting the PBS coverage to the left.
Perhaps, in the interest of balance, some of the "other programs" Jennifer Lawson alluded to will include a series by
Parliament of Whores author P.J. O'Rourke, a *Rolling Stone* editor with a different perspective on politics than Mr. Greider
or Mr. Moyers. Perhaps Mr. O'Rourke will write his next book
on public television.

—*David Horowitz*

PBS ELECTIONS '92

On January 5, 1992, PBS officials held their annual "press
tour" at the Ritz-Carlton Hotel in Marina Del Rey, California. At a session where PBS executives met the press, the
following exchange took place between COMINT editor
David Horowitz and PBS vice president John Grant. Grant
had previously presented the PBS plans for covering the 1992

presidential elections:

HOROWITZ: You've announced two editorial series on the elections this year, one by William Greider, the other by Bill Moyers, both of whom are left-wing Democrats. You're planning to rerun LBJ, which is a four-hour pitch for Great Society liberalism. You've announced a two-hour special on health care, which is the Democrats' primary domestic issue. You're going to run a four-part series on the Kennedys. You have run three *Frontline* series programs this year—one accusing Ronald Reagan of treason, a second accusing George Bush of being responsible for all the suffering in post-war Iraq, and a third promoting the spurious "October Surprise" theory that accuses the Reagan-Bush team of stealing the 1980 elections by cutting a deal with Iran to delay the release of American hostages.

As you know, the appropriations for the Corporation for Public Broadcasting are on a personal senatorial hold now. I suspect one reason for the hold is PBS's consistent failure to observe the balance provisions of the Public Broadcasting Act. I want to know if you have any plans to respect those provisions. Are you going to provide any programs produced by identifiable Republicans or conservatives? In short, what do you propose to do to respect the provisions of the 1967 act?

GRANT: Well, I think all of the programming we do respects the provisions of that act. The balance of programming, the fairness within programming, I think speaks for itself. The health-care issue, for example, I'm not sure necessarily has to be defined as a Democratic issue. I don't think the producers of the program and most Americans necessarily define that as a purely Democratic issue. So I think the fairness and balance throughout the course of our election coverage will speak for itself and it will be there.

I always find it difficult to label people or programs such as Bill Moyers. I forget what your label was, a "left-wing something or other," but we have, which will cover election issues. Bill Buckley will have several debates. I'm not trying to characterize them, but I think they do offer a different perspective. So I think the balance and the fairness across all of the programs that you'll see during the election year on public TV will speak for itself.

Frontline's
October Surprise

When Democrats on the Senate Judiciary Committee wanted to undermine the confirmation chances of President Bush's Supreme Court nominee Clarence Thomas, they selectively leaked unsubstantiated rumors found in a committee file to NPR reporter Nina Totenberg. There is evidence that Democrats in the House may have used the PBS program *Frontline* in a similar way in order to build public pressure for an investigation of the so-called October Surprise. According to conspiracy theorists, the October Surprise was an attempt by the Reagan '80 election campaign to delay the release of the American hostages in Iran and thus ensure a Reagan victory.

"By any measure of honest reporting, the October Surprise theory should have died long ago," wrote investigative journalist Steve Emerson in the December 1, 1991 issue of *The New Republic*. But, as Emerson also observed, there were other factors at work in the story's promotion: "An October Surprise cult emerged, fueled by entrepreneurial journalists who had made the allegations into a lucrative cottage industry." On April 16, 1991, PBS's *Frontline* series joined the chorus with a $255,000 effort whose title captured the partisan agenda of the conspiracy theorists: *Election Held Hostage*.

According to a senior staff member in the office of Rep. Henry Hyde (R-Ill.), much of the information that went into the *Frontline* program originated with Congressman John Conyers (D-MI), the House Democrats' chief proponent of the October Surprise theory. As chairman of the Government Operations Committee, Conyers had secretly ordered the government's General Accounting Office to probe the October Surprise allegations. In the words of a report of the House Rules Committee, "The request was made without the approval, knowledge, or participation of any other members of the Government Operations Committee or the subcommittee directly involved."

The subsequent GAO investigation of the "October Surprise" conspiracy theory, in the words of its general counsel, "found nothing to corroborate those allegations." But this didn't stop Conyers or *Frontline*. As an internal clash between Republicans and Democrats on the House Government Operations Committee revealed in June 1991, Conyers selectively passed information that the GAO had obtained to *Frontline* producers Martin Smith and Robert Ross. This information related to individuals who claimed to have knowledge of the October conspiracy.

Frontline then uncritically accepted the testimony of these sources, even when there was compelling evidence that their stories did not make sense. These sources have been found guilty of serious crimes, have been proven liars, and have publicly changed their stories several times, even to the *Frontline* team. In some instances, even the most basic details about where alleged meetings between Reagan campaign officials and Iranian representatives were supposed to have taken place were blurred when different sources noted different meeting locations for the same rendezvous.

Among the discredited sources used by *Frontline* were:

BARBARA HONEGGER, a former minor Reagan White House employee. Honegger was one of the original proponents of the conspiracy theory. *Frontline* relied heavily on her testimony but never mentioned, for example, her strong belief in "paranormal events." When she left the White House, Honegger told one reporter that her political instincts came from "channel led information...as if it were from the future." Even *Nation* columnist Christopher Hitchens described her claims as "diffuse and naive." No questions about Honegger's credibility, however, were allowed to leak into the *Frontline* presentation.

HENRICH RUPP, an operator and con artist, once convicted of bank fraud. *Frontline* touted Rupp as an "eyewitness" to the alleged meeting that was supposed to have taken place between William Casey, George Bush, and Iranian emissaries in Paris on October 18, 1980. Rupp claimed to be Casey's favorite pilot, who flew Casey to Paris for the meeting with the Iranians. *Frontline* never checked Rupp's passport (which shows no evidence of entering France or leaving the United States) or the logs for the aircraft he said he piloted (the plane's logs and airport records show it was parked in California at the time).

RICHARD BRENNEKE, an Oregon businessman who claimed to have worked for the CIA and FBI as well as for French, Italian, and Israeli intelligence. Brenneke claimed he flew along with Rupp to Paris on October 18, 1980. *Frontline* said Brenneke was a credible source and that the government had tried and failed to prove that William Casey was not in Paris. But *Frontline* never checked to see whether Brenneke himself was in Paris on the date he claimed. A reporter for *The Village Voice* who asked to see Brenneke's personal records disclosed that Brenneke had used a credit card to stay in a Seattle Hotel on October 18 and had dined at a local restaurant. Jack Blum, a counsel to Sen. John Kerry (D-Mass.), has publicly called Brenneke a liar and a fraud.

ARI BEN-MENASHE, whom *Frontline* described as a "former Israeli intelligence officer." Ben-Menashe claimed that he acted as a go-between for the Reagan campaign and the Iranian representatives. *Frontline*'s producers apparently never checked on what Ben-Menashe told them. But as Steve Emerson discovered quite easily, Ben Menashe was no Israeli intelligence officer but a low-level translator for the Israel Defense Forces External Relations Department, a largely irrelevant division of the Israeli military. *Frontline* never confronted Ben-Menashe regarding the wild claims he had made in the international press only a few weeks before *Frontline* interviewed him: Ben-Menashe once claimed that Israel shipped more than $82 billion in arms to Iran in the 1980s— *more than 35 times Israel's total imports and domestic weapons production! Frontline* producers also never questioned him on the changing location of the alleged meeting. At one point he claimed it was the Hotel Ritz, then the George V. *Frontline* cleverly blurred the fact that, while Ben-Menashe put the meeting at these two hotels, Brenneke pointed to two others: the Raphael and the Crillon.

Along with their uncritical acceptance of what the sources claimed, *Frontline* producers and researchers never attempted an independent check on the whereabouts of Casey and Bush during the time they were supposed to be meeting the Iranians in Paris. A cursory scanning of the public record, including press accounts and Secret Service logs, indicates that Bush was in the United States campaigning. Nor did *Frontline* apparently attempt to contact anyone who might know where Casey, then a senior Reagan campaign official, might have been. Subsequent research by Steven Emerson and others revealed that Casey was in London at the time for a conference, and his off-time was almost entirely accounted for.

Despite its abysmally unprofessional journalistic methods, *Election Held Hostage* had an important impact on Rep. Conyers' partisan crusade, prompting requests from newspaper editorialists across the country, as well as from President Jimmy Carter, for a "blue-ribbon panel" to be established by Congress to investigate its charges. When, on November 7, the Democrat-controlled House Rules Committee voted to formally set up a task force to investigate the October Surprise allegations, the decision was based largely on what Congressman Lee Hamilton (D-IN) called "independent press accounts," including the "serious investigation" conducted by *Frontline*.

Thus is the prestige of public television used to legitimize shabby, partisan journalism and to influence the political process.

—*Peter Schweizer*

Listening to America *or to the* Democrats?

The first two segments of Bill Moyers' election-year series, based on a *Philadelphia Inquirer* report *America: What Went Wrong?*, have already tilted in a predictable direction. The original *Inquirer* series, by reporters Donald Barlett and James Steele, ran in nine parts last fall to the delight of Democrats, who waved the newspapers from the House floor and proclaimed the report proof of their indictment of the economic policies of the Reagan years. Bill Clinton held up the paperback book of the *Inquirer* series during a recent speech at the Wharton School of Business to illustrate the same claim.

The bias that permeates the *Inquirer* series is first evident in its focus on laid-off blue-collar workers, a bias the Moyers' program faithfully repeats. The most urgent question for Barlett and Steele, by their own account, is "What happens to the people who lost their jobs?" This is a question that is old hat for Moyers, who loaded a one-sided CBS documentary called *People Like Us,* full of Reagan budget victims, back in 1982, the year before the Reagan boom took off.

"Asking a laid-off factory worker what's wrong with America is like asking a typhoon victim how he feels about nature," observed *Philadelphia* magazine writer Paul Keegan in one of the rare critiques of the *Inquirer* approach. "The unstated theme of the series is that the market, left unfettered by the government, does horrible things to people."

But the problem with both the *Inquirer* and Moyers' series goes much deeper than the angle of entry. In between the unemployment vignettes, Moyers reprises statistics from the *Inquirer* that have sent many professional economists climbing the walls. For example: "During the 1980s, the combined salaries of people in the $20,000 to $50,000 income group increased 44 percent, and the combined salaries of people earning $1 million or more a year increased 2,184 percent."

How did Moyers and his sources arrive at that enormous 2,184 percent gain? By ignoring the textbook rules for compiling statistics. First, no adjustment is made for inflation. Second, there is no mention that the number of people making more than $1 million increased from 3,000 in 1980 to 51,000 in 1990. Now, clearly, if you add 48,000 millionaires to the pool, the total amount of money made by millionaires is going to rise a little. But the chart misleads people by making them think that a static number of millionaires made an enormous killing.

Third, Barlett and Steele claimed that this pool of money came only from salaries not other forms of taxable income, like interest, dividends, or capital gains. But to arrive at their pool of 51,000 millionaires, they did count all adjusted gross income, making the chart statistically shoddy.

In the first Moyers program, Barlett explained their method: "I think one of the things that we do, which even a lot of economists don't do, is that we base so many of the statistics, so much of the data we used in the series, on tax data not, in fact, census data." This admission defines the liberal bias of the reporters and thus of the Moyers program. The Democrat-appointed Congressional Budget Office prefers IRS tax data over census data because they provide a more stilted look at the differences between rich and poor. How? For tax purposes, the IRS currently does not index capital gains for inflation and does not count any capital loss of more than $3,000. Both practices inaccurately inflate the income of the richest Americans, providing statistics to fuel the politics of envy.

Barlett went on to tell Moyers: "To our way of thinking, so much of the tax data is more accurate than the census data, because when you're filling out your tax return, you're much more likely...to be accurate on that." Would the average American believe that everyone strives to be accurate on their tax forms? At least when you fill out census forms, there isn't money in it for you. One of the reasons the IRS data shows an explosion of millionaires is that the 1981 and 1986 tax reforms made it more profitable to simply pay taxes than pay accountants to avoid taxes. But neither Moyers nor Barlett and Steele mention inconvenient facts like the increase in total taxes and tax burden paid by the rich in the last decade.

Of course statistics, however arrived at, appear to be facts, especially when "backed up" by photographic images. TV critics, like the *Boston Globe's* Ed Siegel, were duly impressed: "Moyers and his colleagues throw statistic after example after interview to back up claims that become nearly irrefutable by the weight of the evidence."

Sometimes Moyers didn't even rely on faulty statistics, substituting unsubstantiated assertions instead. At one point, he acknowledged that "there were a lot of new jobs created in the 1980s" but found a way to make that seem like nothing. "One of the last things President Reagan did in office was to send a letter to Congress reporting that nearly 19 million non-agricultural jobs were created during his administration, that over 90 percent of them were full-time jobs and over 85 percent of those were in occupations in which average annual salaries exceeded $20,000. Fact is, the job growth was centered in the retail and service sectors, which pay the lowest wages."

In other words, "The sky is blue. Fact is, it's green." Fact is, the White House was using official Department of Labor statistics in establishing the number of new jobs. Moyers was simply asserting an interpretation of the statistic without bothering to link it to any evidence.

We may fruitlessly wait for more balance to appear in the *Listening to America* series as the election year winds on, but like nearly every other Moyers project, there's merchandising to be done. The paperback version of *America: What Went Wrong?* is currently at the top of the best-seller list, despite the occasional critic like Paul Keegan, who wrote: "Their series is so fundamentally flawed, its intellectual underpinnings so weak, that it actually says little about what went wrong with America, and everything about what went wrong with Barlett and Steele." That goes double for the Moyers series, which only takes a maudlin, mostly anecdotal newspaper report and adds television's power of pathos and illusion of reality to make its case. Moyers isn't listening to America, he's talking at America, and giving them only one side of the story.

—*Tim Graham*

Election Special: A Disturbing Episode

Last October Sen. Bob Dole (R-Kan.) noticed an article in *USA Today* describing plans for *The Finish Line*, a PBS election-night special that would feature Hodding Carter, Ken Walker, Daniel Schorr, Ellen Goodman, Anthony Lewis, and Roger Wilkins. He was incensed that, after months of Senate debate and new legislation requiring balance and objectivity, PBS would schedule a program so obviously one-sided. Dole issued a press release. In it, he wisecracked that in its choice of commentators the program "tilts so far to the left, your TV may fall over." He called PBS's decision to air the WGBH special on its National Program Service "another poke in the eye for Republicans and taxpayers" and recalled the one-sided history that had led to the Senate debate over public broadcasting:

> First, PBS gave prominent election year roles to liberal commentators Bill Moyers and William Greider. Then they hired two prominent Democrats, Barbara Jordan and Henry Cisneros, to host election-year specials. Now, we hear about another election special. When it comes to *The Finish Line*, it looks like balance and objectivity were never invited to the starting line...It's clear PBS has absolutely no intention or interest in ever making an effort to give the taxpayers balanced reporting.

At least two major stations, Chicago and St. Louis, decided not to broadcast the program. Theirs was not the typical PBS reaction, however. PBS went ahead with the decision to feed the show on its National Program Service. And, in response to Dole's charges, PBS and WGBH denied everything. Both institutions maintained publicly that *The Finish Line* would be produced according to the highest journalistic standards. Ken Walker, one of the scheduled hosts, objected to being considered a liberal, although given Walker's public views this would seem to be an idiosyncratic complaint at best. Journalists were told by public-broadcasting officials that the show would be fair and balanced.

In fact, when it was aired, *The Finish Line* had the appearance of a satellite hookup from a Democratic National Committee victory party. The camera work looked as if the crews had already uncorked the champagne bottles: Pictures were jiggly, shots panned and zoomed with abandon, hosts were caught unawares, and scenes shifted without warning. Technically, the program seemed more like a local cable-access show than a prestige program on a service that sells itself as synonymous with quality.

In the background guests milled around with drinks in their hands, and an animated and expectant chatter from the crowd was part of the continuous soundtrack. At one point, Kate Clinton, identified as a lesbian comedian (and a star of *In the Life*, a gay-themed public-television variety show previously criticized by Sen. Dole on the Senate floor), told predictably mean-spirited jokes about Ronald Reagan and Dan Quayle and (just as predictably) none with Democrats as the butt. Although one or two Republicans were trotted out briefly, they were always vastly outnumbered by the crowd of Clinton Democrats and supporters. And when Clinton went over the top, the room simply exploded. At this point the show ended, and PBS coverage switched to the far more sober and professional MacNeil-Lehrer team.

At first, there was little reaction in the press. But on Nov. 16, *The Washington Post* carried an item in John Carmody's TV column that began: "Those off-camera cheers on election night during the WGBH production of *The Finish Line* are still echoing around public television.... Discomfiting officials at both PBS and the Corporation for Public Broadcasting is the long shadow of Sen. Bob Dole (R-Kan.) who has been waging what many in public TV consider a vendetta."

PBS executives were indeed saying they thought Dole had a vendetta. It is attitudes like this that are part of public television's problem. No doubt, such views led PBS executives to ignore Sen. Dole's valid criticism of their planned show. In fact, Dole turned out to be correct as to the bias that could have been expected if no corrective steps were taken. None were, and the result was more like a PBS vendetta against Republicans.

This was emphasized by the silence of PBS president Bruce Christensen after the fact. By contrast, CPB president Richard Carlson was concerned. "It was like handing a gift to our critics," he told *The Washington Post*. "The WGBH production that night was biased, unbalanced, unprofessional, and boring. The camera work was awful, and the cheering for Clinton was pronounced and sustained." As an indication of his concern, Carlson showed clips from the show at the CPB board retreat, which resulted in the "Open to the Public" policy.

While Christensen and PBS stuck their heads in the sand, WGBH came out swinging. Judith Stoia, WGBH's executive producer, defended *The Finish Line* in its entirety. She told *The Washington Post*: "The notion of the program was that we were going to do something other than what the networks were going to do; our concept [was] that we would

watch the results with an interesting collection of people."
Stoia maintained that the broadcast had the highest level of
journalistic integrity and responded to the criticism that it
was ama-teurish with a dismissal, telling the *Post*: "They're
entitled to their opinion. When you try to do something new,
it's not going to be smooth sailing. If public TV is to try alternative programming, we have to be willing to experiment; the
form was rocky but the content was solid." In other words:
We're all right, Jack.

No one can assess at this point the damage that
Stoia's arrogance and inept production may have done, but
this fiasco reveals the problem created by the vacuum at
the top of PBS. Without a firm leadership hand to steer PBS
in a clear direction, the system is headed for trouble. A clear
mandate has been handed down by Congress. Under the
leadership of Carlson and Tate, the Corporation for Public
Broadcasting has shown that that mandate is intelligible and
that steps can be taken to strengthen the system, without
sacrificing its independence, by working constantly to maintain its integrity. If Bruce Christensen continues to sit on the
fence, the elements of the system will continue to lock horns
not only with CPB, but with the viewing public and—this
should be obvious to everyone by now—with Sen. Dole and
the U.S. Congress.

—Laurence Jarvik

PART III
PROPAGANDA DOCUMENTARIES

THE MYTH OF INDEPENDENT FILM

I used to believe in what is called independent film and to call myself an "independent filmmaker." I belonged to the Association of Independent Video and Film, personally recruited by radical filmmaker Emile de Antonio (*Point of Order, In the Year of the Pig, Millhouse*). I showed my film *Who Shall Live And Who Shall Die* at one of the early Independent Feature Markets in New York, paying $100 or so for the privilege. I was one of the first filmmakers interviewed for the "Independents" section of *Cineaste* magazine. I traveled with my picture to showings on the festival circuit: places like the Berlin Film Festival, the Pompidou Center in Paris, and so forth. I had my film shown in American theaters, on college campuses, and even on PBS stations. I had been lured into the life by Werner Herzog's visit to Berkeley's Pacific Film Archive. At the time he had said to just go out and make movies, steal a camera if you have to, you can do it all by yourself. Like P.J. O'Rourke, I believed.

What I believed was one of the enduring myths of so-called independent film: that it reflects the visions of individual filmmakers, unlike Hollywood movies, which are the result of an impersonal and corporate studio system. I *believed* that the world I had entered was different, yet in making my film I was, in fact, dependent on an equally complex and more demanding (in a political sense) network of support: a private sponsor, the cooperation of numerous interview subjects who often had agendas they wanted me to serve, archival institutions, and a distribution system that was itself dependent on an organized (and, again, political) community to deliver an audience.

Of course, I learned later that Herzog was himself hardly independent. He had enjoyed being part of the German government's official plans to better his homeland's cultural public relations; he had been lavishly subsidized by the German state; and when he deviated from the politically correct party line by championing the cause of the Miskito Indians persecuted by the Sandinista government, his films were no longer supported by the supposedly independent "Independent Filmmaking Community." In short, he was cut off from his audience. A similar fate befell Nestor Almendros when he exposed the dreadful conditions in Castro's political prisons in *Nobody Listened*.

There is no reason to presume film production could or should be independent. Making films is phenomenally expensive, labor intensive, and time consuming. The scale of even the smallest film is beyond the resources of most individuals. As I learned after completing my film, the so-called independent film world I had entered was in fact among the most dependent universes in existence. So-called independent filmmakers depend upon the approval of critics, receipt of awards, and cash subsidies to an extent unimaginable in commercial filmmaking, precisely because the enterprise is not economically viable. (Put another way, commercial films are attractive to a much more democratic audience than "independent" films, which have to rely on the favors of elites.)

Some so-called American independents were, I discovered, in fact totally dependent on German, British, or French television for financing their pictures. Others were dependent on the support of political or social movements or religious or educational organizations. In my own experience, I discovered that I had very little independence after all. After completing my film, I had to go begging with project proposals to public broadcasting stations, government agencies, foundations, and foreign television companies.

The critics who cover independent film give good reviews to certain films—sometimes out of charity, sometimes out of conviction. These reviews, in turn, convince libraries and institutions to purchase prints. Awards serve the same function. Those who position themselves as "gatekeepers" to these institutions are extremely important, and their favor is curried constantly. Often these gatekeepers are supporters of political and social causes. As I grew more familiar with its environment, it became clear to me that independent film was, in fact, institutional film designed for classroom and library showing. The role PBS plays in giving a "good housekeeping seal of approval" to these pictures cannot be overestimated. Of course, a PBS showing also exposes the films to audiences of millions—small in television terms, but far larger than the audiences of dozing schoolchildren and political camp followers they would otherwise attract.

I learned quickly that the term "Independent Film" was a marketing label designed for librarians, schoolteachers, museum curators, and political organizers as well as PBS executives and congressmen. It came about as a way of trying to make the "educational film" more sexy and less square and of justifying federal funding. In fact, most of the films were excruciatingly dull or aggressively didactic.

There are very few people who would voluntarily stand in the rain to pay money to see an independent film. Many of those who see these sorts of films are either required to do so as part of a course of instruction, paid to do so as critics or curators, or subsidized to do so by various grants to "media arts centers." This is actually admitted by pillars of the so-called "community." The brochure published by the Rockefeller Foundation's National Video Resources Project says: "We emphasized independent work because public libraries are the only resource most people have for these films. Because librarians receive practically no education in this area, filling this gap became the primary goal of the project." Translation: Very few patrons request that libraries stock "independent films." Therefore the Rockefeller Foundation provides money for the filmmakers to propagandize librarians and promote their productions. The John D. and Catherine T. MacArthur Foundation co-sponsors *Videoforum: A Videography for Libraries* with National Video Resources. This list features "affordable non-Hollywood videos." It is "a curated collection for librarians, who often have little time for previewing films." Needless to say, both the Rockefeller and MacArthur Foundations have political and social agendas that the films serve. So the propaganda cuts two ways.

The deformation that this structure creates in the character of the product is obvious. If the audience is going to be compelled to see the picture, or if those buying the picture need not see it beforehand, the standards are not going to include the need to hold the attention of the audience, let alone the standards of journalistic ethics like fairness and objectivity.

The output of so-called independent filmmakers is far more monotonous, far more standard, and far less individual than that of the Hollywood studio system that is dominated by the individual personalities of stars, writers, directors, producers, etc. Of course, no critic ever killed a commercial Hollywood film or television show. And no one cares what schoolteachers or librarians think of them.

"Independent" films can be broken down into two basic types: agitprop and avant-garde. These are two sides of the same coin, as they are supposedly in opposition to capitalist Hollywood. The agitprop film contains revolutionary content, and the avant-garde film has a revolutionary form. Yet each of these conventionalized types are far less independent as *genres* than the despised Hollywood fare.

Agitprop films are often dependent on politically correct ideology—depicting union struggles or revolutionary events according to the party line. They are as predictable as sunrises and sunsets. Perhaps the most famous of these is Paul Jarrico's production, *Salt of the Earth* (1953), written by blacklisted Hollywood screenwriter Michael Wilson. The film tells the story of a miner's strike in New Mexico—sympathetic to the strikers, antipathetic to the bosses. It was the spiritual forerunner of contemporary films like *Harlan County, Matewan, The Willmar Eight*, etc. The company that produced the picture was called, not surprisingly, Independent Productions Corporation. It was set up as a vehicle for blacklisted writers in 1951 by Jarrico, Herbert Biberman, and Simon Lazarus. Biberman had joined the Communist Party in 1934. The Independent Productions Corporation wasn't particularly independent when it came to financing. *Salt of the Earth* was paid for by the International Union of Mine, Mill and Smelter Workers. Barbara Kopple—who produced *Harlan County*, another film about a miner's strike and paid for by a miner's union—was instrumental in setting up the Independent Feature Project, which became a major "Independent" institution in the '70s.

Salt of the Earth tells the story of a strike that lasted for more than a year at a mine owned by New Jersey Zinc. It was shot in 1953 and opened in New York in 1954. The leader of the strike, Ramon, benefited from a "cleaning up" by the screenwriters, and his female comrade, Esperanza, was portrayed as a "Madonna figure," according to British film historian Brian Neve. And the screenplay wasn't particularly independent when it came to ideology, as Neve notes:

> The film is also unusual in that those who made it, unbeholden to any studio producers, shared a particular ideological view and were able to reflect this in the script. Writer and director saw the strike...from a perspective that emphasized the broad categories of Communist Party social analysis. Producer Paul Jarrico had, with Michael Wilson, become influential in the Hollywood Communist Party in the early fifties....Herbert Biberman had...joined the Communist Party on his arrival in Hollywood in 1934....The emphasis in official party thinking after the war was on class and the ills of capitalism.

In other words, *Salt of the Earth* was dependent on the Communist Party for its ideology and the Mine Worker's Union for its financing. Produced by party members for the purposes of propaganda and union organizing, *Salt of the Earth* was, in fact, far less independent than any Hollywood production. This point was noted at the time by critic Pauline Kael. She criticized the picture for following the Soviet party line regarding the mine workers and "arguing that although Hollywood would glamorize their lives, it would 'do justice to their dreams.'"

The avant garde, too, was hardly independent. Stan Brakhage admits, in the introduction to the 1982 edition of Lenny Lipton's *Independent Filmmaking*:

> It has been my experience, from earning a living often as a commercial filmmaker, that the success of even a professional is absolutely dependent upon his sense of himself as intrinsically independent: commerce, for him, is a means to an end; and, while its

limitations may trap him creatively in the end, the meantime of his rise to commercial recognition is, almost always, conditioned by his independence of attitude within a job limitation. Gertrude Stein wrote that there are only two kinds of people, "'independent dependents' and 'dependent independents.'"

In other words, no filmmaker is truly independent, and independence is a state of mind that can be shared by a commercial filmmaker. This rupture of the distinction between art and commerce enables one to call Frank Capra or Darryl Zanuck independent filmmakers. So, the avant garde must have something other than independence to distinguish it from commercial motion pictures. This is its revolutionary form. And Brakhage points out what that is, when he quotes Lipton saying: "...traditional concepts of best quality or good quality...is [sic], in fact, damaging to creative expression." So here is what makes the avant garde, per Brakhage: not independence, but a revolutionary rejection of traditional concepts of quality, which are in his view inimical to creativity.

These two categories then—the agitprop and the avant garde—provide capsule expressions of the nature of so-called "Independent Film." The agitprop picture is to be evaluated in political terms, the avant-garde in its rejection of traditional quality. Because they have little commercial appeal and tiny audiences, they are heavily dependent on sponsorship for their production and distribution.

A classic instance of this dependence is found in the career of Maya Deren, one of the icons of the independent film industry. Lauren Rabinowitz has written a fascinating chronicle of her artistic career that points out the chronic dependency on organizations Deren seems to have suffered. Deren was a champion networker. On November 25, 1953, she organized the Film Artists Society, enrolling some 40 members. In 1955, the group became known as the Independent Film Makers Association. Rabinowitz describes this group as "a monthly forum for a full-fledged social, intellectual, and professional community."

Rabinowitz makes clear Deren's link to the Communist film movement, noting that Deren was following in the footsteps of The Workers Film and Photo League. "The WFPL began in 1930 as an independent branch of the Worker's International Relief, a Communist party organization with cultural goals. It was the first American organization that understood the efficacy of coordinating production, distribution, exhibition, and education efforts to insure an alternative cinema system." Rabinowitz further comments: "Deren personally combined the theatrical outrageousness associated with the European avant-garde, the WFPL's commitment to Leftist political ideals, and the administrative acumen necessary to deploy a new film network. She represented the continuity of a film discourse begun in the 1920's in Europe and reconstituted in a series of alternative practices in Europe and the United States throughout the 1930's and 40's."

The film discourse was collectivist. Rabinowitz adds that Deren's vision of communal film was dependent on the college lecture circuit: "Deren presented her views at every opportunity, but especially when she appeared with her films across the United States, Canada and South America. She alone brought film theory and independent cinema to the Ivy League Schools as well as to state teacher colleges and film societies in the Midwest and far West."

According to Rabinowitz, after her divorce from Alexander Hammid, with whom she had made *Meshes of the Afternoon*, Deren spent more time organizing activities, writing articles, and giving speeches than she did making films. She was supported by funds from the John Simon Guggenheim Foundation, ostensibly to make a film about Haitian voodoo, which she never completed. Apparently, Deren was very sensitive to criticism of her own dance films—made without the help of Hammid, who had been a professional Hollywood filmmaker—as derivative and inept.

Deren founded the Creative Film Foundation in 1955. As Rabinowitz notes, "CFF was a nonprofit foundation that awarded filmmaking grants to independent filmmakers....CFF was the first American organization to award money grants and merit citations to independent filmmakers on a regular basis. Among its fellowship recipients from 1955 to 1961 were Stan Brakhage, Stan Vanderbeek, Robert Breer, Shirley Clarke, and Carmen D'Avino."

Yet like the Independent filmmakers Association, the Creative Film Foundation was dependent on the kindness of friends. As Rabinowitz observes:

Other than these occasional public activities, Deren's foundation was little more than a letterhead. She ran the entire organization out of the Greenwich Village apartment she shared with her third husband, composer and musician Teiji Ito. The grants were comprised from modest amounts of monies solicited from friends and other filmmakers. For example, Deren convinced Shirley Clarke that if Clarke's wealthy father contributed $1,000 he was going to give Clarke anyway, Deren would see that Clarke got a fellowship for $800. Deren netted a $200 cash contribution and the publicity attached to a substantial anonymous donation, while Clarke benefited from the attendant publicity as well as the status of receiving an artistic honor. Deren eventually repaid Clarke's generosity when she awarded her another $1,200.

Rabinowitz is being extremely charitable in her description of the transaction. If the issue were, say, a military contract and one party were Lockheed and the other the Japanese government, it would have been described as a bribery-kickback arrangement where Deren skimmed off a $200 commission in the initial transaction. Deren also engaged in Tammany Hall style politics. Again, according to Rabinowitz:

But perhaps more important than its awards and events was the way that Deren used the name of the organization to legitimize Independent Film's connections to the other fine art forms. When Deren began the CFF, she wrote to a number of celebrities and excerpted their responses in all subsequent CFF publicity as an indication of widespread artist support. Trading on the name recognition of such famous artists as playwright Arthur

Miller, architect Mies van der Rohe, aesthetician Sir Herbert Read, dancer-choreographer Martha Graham, and poet-filmmaker Jean Cocteau, Deren asserted that their personal endorsements of the CFF authorized independent cinema's rightful place among the postwar vanguard arts.

Deren was using an appeal to established authority, depending on the prestige of the celebrities and the power of peer pressure to build up her organization. Deren's effort, far from being independent, was intensely dependent on the trendy fashions of New York high society. And Deren went further than simply getting testimonials. Indeed, she turned over her organization to New York's artistic establishment. As Rabinowitz says:

> Deren lent credibility and respectability to the CFF by maintaining a full board of directors and officers who were nominally the fellowship committee. Although their positions on the board demanded little from them, the individual board members provided the prestige associated from their institutional affiliations within the New York arts community. Deren's board included film historian and scholar Lewis Jacobs, Cinema 16 director Amos Vogel, and film critics Parker Tyler and Arthur Knight. She also included anthropologist Joseph Campbell, the two art critics Clement Greenberg and James Johnson Sweeney who championed Abstract Expressionism, art historian Meyer Schapiro, artist Kurt Seligmann, poet James Merrill, and leading gestalt psychologist Rudolf Arnheim. The CFF may have been in practice a nominal apparatus of the independent cinema, but its discursive value obscured its limited economic function.

What Rabinowitz does not emphasize is that Deren's dependence on establishment figures and the inclusion of critics and scholars on the board of her presenting organization, institutionalized the Creative Film Foundation as an establishment organization. The so-called avant garde Deren claimed to represent was in fact made up of the pillars of New York society. Long before Tom Wolfe wrote of "Radical Chic," Deren was living it.

Deren peddled influence in other ways, using her network of establishment contacts to enforce politically correct perspectives for the independent filmmakers whom she organized. One supposed independent soon fell into line when New York's artistic mafia was brought to bear on his deviationism. As Rabinowitz points out, the victim of this re-education effort was none other than Jonas Mekas: "When Mekas wrote a blistering attack on the current experimental cinema as 'a conspiracy of homosexuality,' [in his new film magazine *Film Culture* in 1955] Deren called all her friends to meet collectively with Mekas. Soon thereafter, *Film Culture* began to respond less prejudicially and more seriously toward experimental cinema, and it regularly publicized experimental cinema activities and filmmakers."

One can only imagine what threats and imprecations were directed at Mekas during the collective meeting with Deren and her associates. Apparently, independent film could not withstand independent criticism. And in her so-called independence, Deren was dependent on the money, goodwill, and status of the most powerful and established forces in New York. Rabinowitz concludes: "[Thanks to Maya Deren] the overall structure that supported an independent cinema was firmly in place by 1961....Her work was no less than consolidating the first cohesive system of cinema as collective artistic activity and practices, thus defining an American avant-garde cinema."

The career of Shirley Clarke, whom Rabinowitz regards as a successor to Deren, shows how the structure of the independent film community, politically left and financially dependent on New York high society, was replicated in the successor generation. While Deren was the daughter of a well-to-do doctor, Clarke was the heir to a multimillion dollar fortune and grew up on Park Avenue surrounded by servants. Clarke pursued an abortive dance career, commuting to perform in Manhattan while servants cared for her daughter. She received bad reviews and soon became discouraged.

Her analyst suggested she try something else, and Clarke began using her home movie camera to make dance films with her husband Bert Clarke, whom she had married in 1944.

Her first film was called *Dance in the Sun* (1953), which Rabinowitz likens to Deren's *A Study in Choreography for the Camera*. Clarke then took a trip to Paris and made *In Paris Parks* (1954). Clarke enrolled at the City College of New York and joined Deren's Independent Film Makers Association with Jonas Mekas in 1955. She made a student film called *Bullfight*. With the help of her new friends, she submitted her films to festivals and won awards. Rabinowitz comments, "Such recognition, as well as the Manhattan film community's congenial, familial atmosphere, bolstered Clarke's ego and her commitment to film, and she made the transition to a life devoted to cinema."

One might pause here to note the bribery-kickback involved in Clarke's award from the Creative Film Foundation and further recall the circumstances under which she met Maya Deren. According to Rabinowitz, Clarke paid cash. "I learned that you paid to see her films and hear her speak, even in her own home," she quotes Clarke as saying of Deren. Realistically, one should not call such an atmosphere "congenial" or "familial."

In 1957, Clarke made *A Moment in Love* and met Willard Van Dyke, a principal in Frontier Films. Rabinowitz describes Frontier Films as the successor to the WFPL. Rabinowitz says that "members reorganized in 1937 as Frontier Films, uniting with a large number of other Popular Front groups to fight fascism. Throughout the latter half of the 1930's and early 1940's, Frontier Films advocated a 'serious theoretical goal of combining a profound personal sense of the human condition with political art.'"

When Clarke met Van Dyke, his agitprop abilities were being used in the American pavilion at the Brussels World's Fair. Van Dyke hired Clarke, Donn Alan Pennebaker, Richard Leacock, and fellow Independent Filmmakers Association members Francis Thompson and Wheaten Galentine to make two-and-a-half-minute film loops for the U.S. State Department. Rabinowitz notes: "Whereas the U.S. State Department was depending on the loops to sell America, the filmmakers inscribed richer, more ambiguous and ironic possibilities." The State Department rejected

Clarke's *Bridges Go Round*, which went on to win an award from the Creative Film Foundation and then was sent as the official U.S. entry to the Brussels International Experimental Film Festival in 1958. That same year, the *New York Times* named *A Moment in Love* among the top ten 16-mm films of the season. Clarke expressed her philosophy of avant-garde film as "one of the little stilettos we can put into the commercial world, so that eventually the kind of film we're talking about can get to bigger audiences."

In 1958 Clarke established Filmmakers Inc. with Van Dyke, Leacock, Albert Maysles, and Pennebaker. Rabinowitz describes it as "a cooperative film company...a symbolic site for communal activities." She quotes Clarke to the effect that it was "a major New York headquarters." Rabinowitz says Filmmakers Inc. "coalesced the origins of the new independent cinema....Like Deren, who was fond of historicizing events as illustration of group definition, socialist purpose, and solidarity, Clarke defines her participation in an organizational structure as the origins for an American counterpart to European movements."

Clarke made industrial films like *Skyscraper* and *A Scary Time*. Leacock, Pennebaker, and Maysles worked for Robert Drew sponsored by Time-Life and ABC Television, in Rabinowitz's words, with a new theme "of liberal reform." According to Rabinowitz, Clarke fought with Drew and his associates against cinema-verite and made *The Connection* in response. Apparently, Clarke wanted to take a more explicit advocacy position in her films.

The 1961 picture agitated for civil rights and called for "social activism" using a faked cinema verité film about drug addicts as a pretext. Breaking with Drew, Clarke then made *The Cool World*, also about the race issue, with Fred Wiseman in 1963. When the production ran out of money, Clarke put up $50,000 from her personal fortune. She fought with Wiseman and broke with him. Clarke entered a private mental hospital in 1965. On her release, she moved to the fashionable Chelsea Hotel. According to Rabinowitz, one artist said of Clarke's social circle, "We had a lot of close friends, a floating group of about 200 people." Clarke set up the Filmmakers Distribution Center in 1966 with Jonas Mekas and Louis Brigante, a non-profit co-operative to distribute films. They also established a Film Makers Lecture Bureau. The FDC distributed

Andy Warhol's 1967 *Chelsea Girls*, which became the organization's only hit. As soon as it was successful, Warhol pulled his film from the co-op, because, Rabinowitz says, "commercial distributors were promising better deals." Mekas issued an angry manifesto denouncing Warhol's decision in *The Village Voice* that called for "co-operative distribution as against private distribution."

Warhol's independent decision to distribute his film independently for his own independent profit had brought down the wrath of the independent film community. Without *Chelsea Girls*, Clarke's co-op was losing money. She traveled to film festivals and colleges promoting her organization and got cash from Hollywood directors, who also lent their names to the masthead. As Rabinowitz notes, "Clarke reproduced all the strategies that she had seen Deren use."

Meanwhile, like Warhol, Clarke was now the subject of abuse. She was denounced by Stan Brakhage and others. Rabinowitz says: "When filmmakers accused Clarke of being 'nothing more than a commercial filmmaker,' they were leveling their worst insult at her, articulating a pronounced ideological split regarding the definition of independent cinema itself." Rabinowitz says this split was due to the increasing dependence of independent film on the policies of the National Endowment for the Arts, which gave money to museums for screenings, and to the growing university circuit.

Rabinowitz notes a jump of 1,000 percent in the number of film classes from 1953 to 1965, when some 428 academic courses were offered. "Such institutions provided all the apparatus necessary for a self-contained economic base of production, exhibition, and promotion of independent cinema," writes Rabinowitz. That is, the independent film community now depended on this circuit for its existence. Apparently without irony, Rabinowitz goes on to say, "Brakhage, one of the most quickly valorized filmmakers within the new art institutional network, advocated an orientation to independent cinema that was consistent with museums and universities' redefined practices for supporting cinema activities as an artistic, noncommercial form." Clarke sent *The Connection* on the college circuit in 1967 and made *Portrait of Jason* (about a black male prostitute) for both theatrical and nontheatrical distribution. Clarke lost money in the New York theatrical run, but the film was successful on the college circuit.

Clarke closed the FDC in 1970 due to massive losses and spent her time protesting Nixon's invasion of Cambodia and being arrested. Mekas kept Clarke out of his new Anthology Film Archives and established himself as what Rabinowitz calls "privileged curatorship...within a united circle of political allies, the choices made by Mekas and others were inscribed...as *the* New York avant-garde cinema." In other words, Mekas—once disciplined by Maya Deren for deviationism—had assumed the directorate of the central committee, and Clarke had been purged. Clarke later joined the UCLA film school faculty, teaching film and video production. She moved back to New York in the mid-'80s.

The stories of Jarrico, Deren, and Clarke establish what might be called the recurring Stalinist pattern of the independent film community: extreme dependence on political correctness, social acceptance, and sponsorship by powerful individuals or institutions, with denunciation and purging as punishment for transgression. The established patterns of so-called independent film—dating from the Maya Deren and Shirley Clarke eras—were repeated again and again, with the establishment of groups having names like the Film Fund, the Independent Feature Project, the Independent Documentary Association, the Association of Independent Video and Film and the Foundation for Independent Video and Film. Like Maya Deren's outfits, they too are dependent on foundation funding, links to political activists, and support from prominent critics, academics, and socialites.

In the '60s, one major producer of such films was Newsreel (see "California Newsreel," page 128). Ten Newsreel operations located across the country produced agitprop accounts of anti-war agitation and Black Panther confrontations. After various factional infighting and a doctrinal split over Maoism, Third World Newsreel in New York and California Newsreel in San Francisco continued as major producers and distributors of political propaganda to the college circuit, libraries, and PBS.

With the establishment of the National Endowment for the Arts and PBS, so-called "Independent Filmmakers" immediately began to suck on the federal breast. Under Chloe Aaron, the NEA funded independent film. When she went to PBS, Aaron prided herself on support of independent filmmakers.

Meanwhile major foundations continued to support both types of independent film, the agitprop and the avant-garde. The Rockefeller Foundation threw major support behind the independent film community. In 1979, the Ford Foundation and the National Endowment for the Arts created the Independent Documentary Fund. This operation was based at WNET's Television Laboratory. The premiere season of the showcase series called *Non-Fiction Television* featured Saul Landau's *Paul Jacobs and the Nuclear Gang*, a work of anti-nuclear agitprop by a prominent New Leftist and crony of Fidel Castro. The second year it was home to Howard Dratch's *On Company Business*, an anti-CIA propaganda exercise based on the recollections of CIA defector and Castro admirer Philip Agee. During the 1981-82 season, they accused American industry of poisoning the Third World with Robert Richter's *Pesticides and Pills: For Export Only* and of poisoning American soldiers in Richard Schmiechen's *Nick Mazzuco: Biography of an Atomic Veteran*. During the 1984-85 season, they blamed the United States for starvation around the world with Richter's *Hungry for Profit* and promoted the gay left with Schmiechen's piece *The Life and Times of Harvey Milk*.

Robert Richter was the head of the Association of Independent Video and Film. This was the lobbying group for the establishment of ITVS, which secured congressional funding in 1988. Richard Schmiechen, who had been an AIVF board member, was a founding board member of ITVS.

Eight years before, CPB had established the program fund with a commitment to support independent filmmakers. It began a series called *Matters of Life and Death* to showcase independent films. In 1985, PBS began showing "Alive From Off Center," which featured avant-garde videos for seven seasons. While less obviously revolutionary in content, true to avant-garde tradition, the videos were revolutionary in form (by now somewhat of a 50-year-old tradition). Zbigniew Rybczynki's none-too-subtle *Discreet Charm of the Diplomacy* featured a parade of animals at a White House reception. Eric Bogosian's *Funhouse* portrayed the "haves and have-nots" and included a segment with "an agent good-naturedly leading a seminar on the techniques of torture." Stephen Oakes' *Bite and Smile* mocked television advertising. The series also featured broadcasts from The Kitchen, a New York avant-garde institution later to become infamous as the venue for Annie Sprinkle.

"Alive From Off-Center" was produced by John Schott for three years. Schott became the first head of ITVS.

In 1980, the NEA also began looking for cable outlets for independent films (which apparently were unsuitable even for PBS). After four years, in 1984 the MacArthur Foundation agreed to pay for The Learning Channel to run films by independent filmmakers in a series called *The Independents*. The first season had the politically correct title *Dis/Patches*. In 1987, it broadcast *Declarations of Independents*, a miniseries "curated" by Melinda Ward and John Schott. It featured the work of the usual suspects: Maya Deren, Robert Drew, Leacock and Pennebaker, Stan Brakhage, and Newsreel. Schott, apparently blessed with a short memory, has funded another yet to be aired series called *Declarations* for $1.25 million as one of his last acts at the helm of ITVS.

In 1983, the Rockefeller Foundation in cooperation with CPB sponsored a conference called "The Independent Documentary: The Implications of Diversity" at the American Film Institute in Washington, D.C. The keynote speech was given by Fred Friendly, long-time television mogul at the Ford Foundation. He told independent filmmakers to realize they were in fact "interdependent" and said: "You, the grant makers and you, the filmmakers need each other."

In 1987, the Rockefeller Foundation, the Massachusetts Council on the Arts and Humanities, and the New York State Council on the Arts joined together to fund "New Television," a series of "independent films" co-produced by WGBH and WNET. Again, the mixture was one of agitprop and avant-garde. Ngozi Onwurah's *Coffee Colored Children* was about racial identity while Beth B's *Belladonna* carried out the avant-garde precepts of New York "alphabet city" chic.

The MacArthur Foundation, the Benton Foundation, and the Corporation for Public Broadcasting joined forces in 1988 to fund *POV* as a franchise for independent film on PBS. The head of the operation was Marc N. Weiss, who had been active as a lobbyist for independents and in the Association of Independent Video and Film. He reported to David M. Davis, a former official of the Ford Foundation and assistant to Fred Friendly. The first season featured Deborah Shaffer's promotional film for Nicaraguan Sandinista police chief Oscar Cabezas, *Fire from the Mountain*, a whitewash of communist participation in the Spanish Civil War entitled *The Good*

Fight, and the by now obligatory chronicle of a politically correct disease, *Living With AIDS*. The series also added *Gates of Heaven*, Errol Morris' pet cemetery chronicle and Ira Wohl's academy-award winning film about his retarded brother, *Best Boy*, to round out the mix. Following seasons contained predictable attacks on American racism, *Who Killed Vincent Chin?*, on nuclear power and nuclear weapons, *Dark Circle*, narrated by NEA chairman Jane Alexander, and agitprop artist Leon Golub. *POV* is still on the air.

The scandal-wracked ITVS is scheduled to be a provider of programming to *POV*, although due to the disorganization to date only *For Better or Worse*—a program that promotes gay marriage—has aired on the series. As pointed out in the next two essays ("ITVS Pork-Barrel" and "Funding the Left: ITVS Grants"), ITVS has consistently shown the traditional independents' bias towards partisan productions connected to political movements with titles like *Endangered Species: The Toxic Poisoning of Communities of Color, Warrior: The Case of Leonard Peltier*, and *Citizen Dhoruba* (later retitled *Passin' It On*). No surprise with activists like Larry Daressa from Newsreel on its board of directors and producers like John Schott in its executive offices. What's more, the promises to Congress that ITVS would be "different" have consistently been broken. ITVS is funding series that are little different from *Frontline* (which also claims to be a venue for independent filmmakers) with titles like *HIV Weekly, Extended Play, Generations, TV Families*, and that old Schott chestnut, *Declarations*.

One can clearly see that the tradition of dependence on politically correct networking continues to this day with organizations like the so-called Independent Television Service, itself dependent on annual appropriations of taxpayer dollars from the federal Treasury. The dependence on revolving-door personnel also repeats itself. One of the architects of ITVS, Arthur Tsuchiya, is presently an official responsible for media grants at the National Endowment for the Arts.

"Independent film" is really just another name for politically correct filmmaking—what was called in the '30s "agitprop" and in the '60s "alternative" or "underground" media. It would be healthier to call its present incarnation just what it is—politically correct film—so that the taxpayers who pay for it would know what they're getting.

—*Laurence Jarvik*

ITVS PORK-BARREL

The intense lobbying effort that led Congress to establish ITVS in 1989 was spearheaded by complaints from independent producers that the PBS bureaucracy was slow, secretive, in-groupish, unresponsive to requests for information, and in violation of its congressional mandate to provide diverse sources of programming for public television. The ITVS advocates argued that there was an urgent need for new independent programming.

Prominent independent producers testified before the House and Senate committees to demand government funding. Sapadin's group and those who testified all promised that ITVS would be different from the old bureaucracies at CPB and PBS. Promoting the ITVS concept in Senate testimony, AIVF president Larry Sapadin asked rhetorically: "Won't this be likely to become just another inefficient bureaucracy superimposed on an existing one?" Sapadin answered his own question in the negative, promising the senators: "Our proposals will work; they have the overwhelming support of the independent producing community and many observers of the public broadcasting scene. The talent is there. All that is required is the creativity and resolve that will promote rather than frustrate the production for diverse and innovative programming for public broadcasting and the American public."

The ITVS proponents promised, in particular, to depart from the traditional ways of the PBS bureaucracy and its interminable delays. The articles of incorporation further promised to "commission, acquire, package (in a manner consistent with the antitrust laws of the United States), distribute and promote independently produced television programming."

But since ITVS filed its incorporation papers in 1989, it has not produced a single hour of television, issued a single grant to an independent producer, or begun production on any programming whatsoever. As of January 1995, ITVS had aired only nine hours of PBS's national feed after the expenditure of $38 million. This inaction is defended by ITVS apologists who point out that a contract with CPB was not finalized until June 1991. But ITVS received its first money for administration in 1989. In its first two years ITVS has spent $1,814,000 on administrative expenses.

When ITVS signed its contract with the Corporation for Public Broadcasting in April 1991, it was given an additional $12 million—$6 million for 1990 and $6 million for 1991—to fund independent productions. Yet, as of October 1991, not a single production has been funded. This, despite the testimony to the Senate and House committees that there was an urgent need for ITVS and that hungry talents and badly needed programs were waiting in the wings, desperately seeking funding.

Although no one else in the public-television community seemed to care, COMINT was curious as to why so much money had been spent without any visible effect. When COMINT asked ITVS spokesperson Ellen Schneider why it was taking so long to produce a product, she said that long lead times were in the nature of innovative media work: "People should be patient. These are things that have to evolve." Schneider said there were no official deadlines yet for the delivery of programs, if and when they were commissioned, "because of the nature of experimental programming."

YOUR ITVS TAX DOLLARS AT WORK		
YEAR	ITVS BUDGET	HOURS OF TV AIRED ON PBS
1989	$89,000	0
1990	$2,000,000	0
1991	$12,000,000	0
* * *		
1995	$38,000,000	9

Board member Larry Daressa, whom COMINT also approached, said ITVS will take its time, because it takes longer to make quality programming and Congress gave "no time gun" for ITVS. This was not correct. In fact, the language of the report written by Sen. Inouye to accompany the Public Telecommunications Act of 1988 said: "We expect that the [ITVS] will be in full service by the fall of 1989."

A truly democratic procedure would incorporate principles of professionalism, responsibility, accountability, informed decisionmaking, and the applicant's right to be heard. The net result of the panel process is that no one is responsible. No one is accountable. Weak programming decisions are made, and there is no appeal. The result is that quality, which should be the only criterion, is the least relevant consideration in programming. Personal politics, the buddy system, jealousy and pop ideology dominate the panel's deliberations.
—1988 congressional testimony of documentary film producer Fred Wiseman

It is now the fall of 1991 and for six months ITVS has had production money available to grant but has not done so. What has ITVS done with the money in the meantime? COMINT tried to find out. We tried to establish exactly where the money Congress appropriated to ITVS was located, but to no avail. No one knew whether the $12 million was still in the U.S. Treasury, at the Corporation for Public Broadcasting, or in a bank account belonging to the Independent Television Service earning interest. We called Ellen Schneider, ITVS spokesperson. She didn't know. We called Kathy Fulton at the Corporation for Public Broadcasting. She didn't know. We called Toni Cook, a lawyer on the staff of Sen. Inouye, who had sponsored the ITVS legislation in 1988. She didn't know. We called ITVS board member, *Current* publisher, and Central Educational Network head James Fellows. He didn't know. And when we called ITVS executive director John Schott at home and left a message on his machine asking him to call back, he didn't return the phone call.

What's the problem? Why does no one know—or care? And why can't we get a straight answer from ITVS? After all, its proponents promised it would be different from establishment bureaucracies like PBS. In the words of the official General Solicitation, signed by Schott himself: "ITVS will be an open organization." Our experience shows that this is far from the case. The names of the panelists who choose the grant recipients have been kept secret. There has been no explanation for the six-month delay in allocating production funds. There has been no explanation of the fact that 100 percent of the ITVS budget has been spent on administration during the last two years. Finally, there has been no indication of anything that would make ITVS different from any other PBS series, such as *POV, Alive From Off Center,* or *Frontline.*

In his testimony to Congress in 1988, Larry Sapadin specifically attacked *Frontline,* which used independent producers such as Ofira Bikel and William Cran to provide programs. Sapadin claimed that although the programs were made by independents, they were controlled by the *Frontline* staff producer and, therefore, were not truly independent. Sapadin claimed that CPB was misrepresenting the series as a venue for independent productions while using the series to keep truly independent productions off the air.

But the present ITVS setup shows that this, too, was just dust thrown into the eyes of the Senate and House committees to get them to come up with the funds. ITVS today has reserved a mere $2 million per year for its General Solicitation fund, which received more than 2,000 applications. While none of these has been funded to date, and while ITVS's spokesperson maintains that no announcements will be made until late October, twice that much ($4 million) has been set aside by ITVS for what executive director John Schott calls the "magazine" and "collaborative" modes of production—in short, programs which will be produced in much the way *Frontline* programs are produced, for these are series that will be produced in-house by ITVS staff. The January 21, 1991, issue of *Current* contained classified advertisements recruiting a senior staff producer and an associate staff producer for ITVS productions.

In a December 1990 statement, John Schott described such productions as more "directed" than those that fell under the general solicitation. The process here, to quote Schott, is "to focus and amplify program suggestions... [ITVS] will then announce the subject or theme to the field and invite proposals for works to be included in the series." In other words, the series will be run by John Schott. In other words, ITVS played a "bait and switch" game with Congress. The lobbyists promised an independent production service, and they delivered a series controlled by staff producers.

The pattern does not change when we consider the

General Solicitation process itself, which was allocated only one-third of its production funds by ITVS and which is supposed to be radically different from other public-television production setups. Schott called it "a spark plug for change: to prove that television can be different and to demonstrate that viewers [will] welcome it."

Yet the ITVS general solicitation is conducted through precisely the same sort of peer-panel process as used by the Corporation for Public Broadcasting's Open Solicitation. It was the perceived unfairness of this CPB Open Solicitation that led to the AIVF lobbying effort in the first place. At the time, supporters of ITVS argued that the CPB Open Solicitation process was the reason no truly independent productions could be mounted.

One of the witnesses lobbying for the establishment of ITVS was radical producer Pam Yates, who had made a career producing promotional films celebrating Marxist guerrilla fighters in Central America. In her testimony, to give Congress an idea of what the new service would look like, Yates held out the British Channel Four as a model. This was consistent with the official AIVF position as expressed in their house organ, *The Independent*.

But the English Channel Four is nothing like what ITVS has turned out to be. Channel Four has individual "commissioning editors" who choose the programs for broadcast. If programming decisions fail, the editors lose their jobs. It is a system of direct personal accountability. And the accountability comes from the fact that Channel Four is a privately owned, commercial television channel. There is no "peer review" at England's Channel Four, because it is a commercial service supported by advertising sales and owned by the ITV companies. Yates' testimony, while compelling to Congress, was misleading in the extreme. AIVF radicals like Pam Yates were not proposing an American version of Channel Four. They were proposing a mini-CPB that they would run.

If this sounds improbably self-serving, it is, in fact, the one area in which the creators of ITVS have been true to their word. The original legislation for ITVS called for its directors to be chosen by the AIVF lobbyists, through their sister organization, the National Coalition of Independent Broadcasting Producers—headed by Larry Hall and Larry Daressa. CPB could approve the choices, but could not make them. The board would pick the staff and have final approval over grants. Grants would be made by peer-panel review. The only difference between ITVS and the old CPB Open Solicitation process was who would be on the panels.

Like CPB, ITVS keeps the names of its panel members secret from the public, a blatantly unfair system permitting friends of the panelists to have the possibility of access that outsiders don't. Spokesperson Elizabeth Trumble told COMINT the names will be released only after the grant decision had been made, which is consistent with CPB policies.

In an article in *Current*, Al Vecchione, president of MacNeil Lehrer Productions, called the AIVF lobbyists "a vocal if obscure special interest" and accused Sapadin, Yates, and the other witnesses of using "a smokescreen" to obscure their real aims. They were, Vecchione warned, "a group of people who are simply seeking employment through the back door." Vecchione described ITVS as a pork-barrel project to reward a special-interest pressure group. He stands by his charges to this day.

Time has tested Vecchione's original claim and proved him correct. ITVS has provided employment to a familiar cast of characters, an old-boy inner circle of AIVF types and PBS regulars. The executive director of ITVS is John Schott, a Carleton College professor and PBS insider whose previous series, *Alive From Off Center*, was canceled after four years. Larry Sapadin is managing director of *POV.* Ellen Schneider, the public-relations spokesperson, formerly worked for *POV.* The board of ITVS contains several lobbyists who worked for passage of the legislation. The only money expended by ITVS, over three years, has been to pay its creators and set up their offices. In addition to Sapadin, lobbyists Larry Daressa and Larry Hall, a public broadcasting "advocate" and a director of Daressa's National Coalition of Independent Public Broadcasting Producers, are represented on the board. According to ITVS spokesperson Elizabeth Trumble, Larry Hall was personally responsible for selecting the board of ITVS. In that capacity, he appointed himself, through a selection procedure approved by the Corporation for Public Broadcasting.

The guidelines for the ITVS General Solicitation were written by consultant Arthur Tsuchiya, a "video artist" and "former visiting assistant professor" at Middlebury College, who then administered several application review panels.

Tsuchiya is also the new assistant director of the media arts division of the NEA. While serving on the NEA Inter-Arts peer panel in 1989, he approved the grant that supported Karen Finley's now famous "performance art." In the "Letter from the General Solicitation Policy Advisor" included with every application, Tsuchiya advocates television that "would serve a positive societal goal."

Not surprisingly, in addition to the lobbyists, the ITVS board consists primarily of public-television bureaucrats and arts administrators. Of the 11 board members, there is only one producer who is truly independent—that is, not a staff producer, a line producer, or a producer-for-hire. He is Richard Kurt Schmiechen, who produced *Nick Mazucco: Biography of an Atomic Vet*, an anti-military film; and *The Times of Harvey Milk*, which championed the gay rights movement through the life of the San Francisco councilman. Schmiechen was chairman of the board of Larry Sapadin's AIVF from 1980 to 1984.

ITVS has been guilty of shameless cronyism and deceptive politics. An opportunity to build a board of truly independent producers—professionals like Errol Morris, Ken Burns, and Frederick Wiseman—was passed by. Instead, ITVS is a politically correct pork-barrel, marked by the same secrecy, delays, and misrepresentation that its advocates charged CPB with in 1988.

—*Laurence Jarvik*

FUNDING THE LEFT: ITVS GRANTS

Following COMINT's report on ITVS (see preceding essay, "ITVS Pork-Barrel") and the ensuing controversy over ITVS's failure to fund any programs since its creation, the House and Senate oversight committees reminded CPB of its fiduciary responsibility for the use of tax dollars in such matters.

The Senate Report, for example, states: "The Committee does not, however, expect the CPB to provide increased funding in the event that ITVS does not disburse its funding allocations in a responsible manner. It is the responsibility of the CPB to ensure that funds expended on public telecommunications are expended in a manner that will result in the development of high-quality programs for and by public broadcasting."

On Dec. 12, 1991, ITVS finally announced its first grants. Of the 25 announced projects, 13 fell into the category of controversial and current affairs-related. These received $2 million or 80 percent of the $2.6-million grant total.

All 13 projects dealing with controversial subjects, without exception, appear to approach their subjects from a left perspective. Among them are *Endangered Species: The Toxic Poisoning of Communities of Color; Imagining Indians,* a film that "looks at how Native Americans have been 'imagined' in popular American media" (note: the use of quotation marks in ITVS descriptions is politically correct); *A Public Nuisance: Margaret Sanger and the Brownsville Clinic; Black is...Black Ain't,* yet another installment of the tendentious musings of Mar-lon Riggs on the meaning of blackness; *Post No Bills,* a portrait of leftist Robbie Conal's poster propaganda; *An Act of War: The Overthrow of the Hawaiian Nation,* which "portrays the 1893 American overthrow of Hawaii from a native Hawaiian perspective"; *Warrior: The Case of Leonard Peltier* (a celebrated leftist cause); *Memory of Fire,* "a stylistically rich narrative reassessing the 'discovery' of the New World by Columbus"; and *Passin' It On,* which "tells the story of a former Black Panther who was falsely accused of a crime and served 19 years until new evidence secured his recent release."

In point of fact, Dhoruba Bin Wahad, a.k.a. Richard Moore, was convicted of gunning down two New York policemen. He was released on a technicality two years ago and, at the time the ITVS grant was made, was facing a re-trial if his appeal was successful. His appeal has since been rejected. While Dhoruba was out on bail, he toured college campuses, where he revealed himself to be a voluble anti-Semite. In an interview with an Oberlin student magazine, Dhoruba claimed that American Jews were socialized into racism. "The first group they learned to be better than was Negroes," he claimed. "The first word they learned was *nigger.*" In an interview with a Jewish student magazine, Dhoruba claimed that if Hitler hadn't happened to have an anti-Semitic agenda, "it's very easy for me to imagine Jews singing *Deutschland Uber Alles* and fighting in behalf of European racist domination of people of color." This is the man the ITVS grantees propose to lionize.

Passin' It On received $149,758 from ITVS, *twice* the amount allotted to any single one of the 10 nonpolitical projects funded. This generosity makes *Passin' It On* the fifth PBS-CPB documentary project in the last few years to glorify the Black Panthers, with not a single critical (let alone accurate) portrayal to balance them.

The 13 ITVS awards, including *Citizen Dhoruba*, constitute a clear violation of the fairness and balance doctrine of the Public Broadcasting Act. They are politically partisan and thus a clear misuse of CPB funds. The question now is: When will CPB exercise its responsibility in this case?

—Laurence Jarvik

CALIFORNIA NEWSREEL: THE ART OF POLITICS IN FILM

California Newsreel, a documentary distributor, is perhaps the most important of the constellation of media groups that grew out of the '60s political culture and that play an influential role in the public-broadcasting system. Last year PBS stations aired Newsreel's *Teach the Children*, a film from the distributor's three-part *On Television* series during back-to-school week. PBS also showed Marlon Riggs' *Color Adjustment*, distributed by Newsreel, a biting critique of commercial media portrayals of blacks.

California Newsreel co-director Larry Daressa has

been on the board of ITVS from the day it was set up. Daressa helped coordinate lobbying efforts with the National Coalition of Public Broadcasting Producers and the Association of Independent Film and Video. He testified before Congress on behalf of ITVS in 1988. In an interview, Daressa said that he became involved with ITVS because he believed in independent production and "media reform." He said he wanted to create ITVS as a place where producers could make films where "pledge-driven programming was not a priority."

Daressa defends his dual role by observing that he helped "set up an organization from which we're prohibited by law from getting any money." On the other hand, Daressa does admit that California Newsreel is "not prohibited from distributing films ITVS funds" and, in fact, is currently distributing *A Question of Color*, an ITVS-funded production that PBS has declined to broadcast.

In his congressional testimony, Daressa called California Newsreel "one of the nation's oldest independent documentary production companies." Daressa spoke to Congress on behalf of all "independent producers" and said "our diverse voices reflecting the breadth of America's communities and opinions have no place in public television's plans to turn itself into an upscale version of the networks. We have found that insofar as we speak with an independent voice we have no place in public television, insofar as we address an audience beyond its paying members and corporate sponsors we will not be heard."

But how independent is the "independent voice" represented by Daressa's company? How accurately and fairly does it reflect the diversity of America's "communities and opinions?"

Daressa claims Newsreel's decisions to produce or distribute films are "market driven" by the needs of college and university courses. He says that 80 percent of his market is in higher education. While he says his operation is not ideological, commenting "my political agenda is to survive as a nonprofit," the history of California Newsreel shows its revolutionary origins have not been totally forgotten, even by its officers and directors. "I think we still definitely have a leftist tinge," Daressa admits, "but the board of directors doesn't sit around talking about politics."

According to Daressa, California Newsreel and New York-based Third World Newsreel are all that remain of a network of 10 Newsreel operations that grew out of the student protests of the '60s. Each was independently managed, and all shared prints of films documenting anti-Vietnam protests, Panther protests, and other political actions. By 1972, only two remained and stopped sharing prints.

Daressa maintains Third World Newsreel broke from San Francisco Newsreel (the progenitor of California Newsreel) in a "doctrinal split, something about Maoism, the comparative role of national liberation, color versus class." Third World Newsreel concentrated on issues of national liberation, California Newsreel on issues of class struggle. "It had to do with the 1972 SDS fragmentation, and the Revolutionary Communist Party. San Francisco Newsreel threw the RCP and the Revolutionary Union, out in 1971 or '72," he says.

Daressa says that all this occurred before his arrival in 1974 from Oxford, where he had been working with the Labor Party to organize car workers at British Leyland's Cowley Motor Works while pursuing graduate studies. He said he considered himself a "social democrat or a democratic socialist" at that point. Daressa says he was brought in when Resolution Inc., a nonprofit corporation producing a documentary called *Redevelopment* with Richard Smith and Andy Fahrenwald assumed the assets of California Newsreel to use the company for distribution of its picture.

"You know what a fictitious business name is," Daressa said. "California Newsreel had to give its assets to a nonprofit, Resolution Inc. Resolution Inc. is the corporate entity doing business as California Newsreel." According to Daressa, Resolution Inc. was never Maoist. Rather, it was "vaguely social democrat." He says that Resolution decided to keep the California Newsreel name because of the "quite remarkable demand on campuses" for its films: "When Newsreel started out, being left was the market. When the New Left ceased, from a marketing point of view, it was necessary to address people differently." He added, "We no longer feel comfortable with traditional left/right dichotomies." He says the apparent leftist reputation of California Newsreel is because his original "customer base was old New Leftists." He says of the New Left, "Now, nobody remembers it; it's not a liability."

But some clearly do remember. In February and March 1988, Michael Renov, a film professor at the University of Southern California who helped archive the California Newsreel collection, put together a 20-year retrospective of films distributed by the original Newsreels and its successors, Third World Newsreel and California Newsreel. This series was featured at UCLA's Film and Television Archive in an event called "In Celebration of Newsreel: The Alternative Media Conference."

The program notes are quite explicit. Newsreel— and its offspring, Third World Newsreel and California Newsreel—were founded as and continue to be political propaganda operations, according to Renov, who writes: "Newsreel's original mandate was the creation of a counter-cultural force capable of representing the Movement as insiders, as fellow activists...As the New Left coalition dissolved in the early 70's, Newsreel continued to function as an index of radical currents...Today, Third World Newsreel in New York and San Francisco's California Newsreel continue to produce and distribute work responsive to the requirements of political activism in the late 80's."

And what are the requirements of political activism? Renov continues: "Like the Movement of which it was a part, Newsreel was cognizant of pre-existent models of revolutionary practice. The Cubans had begun to document their own social transformation shortly after the 1959 revolution. The raw power and resourcefulness of their shoestring productions (among them a number of films which Newsreel continues to distribute in the U.S.) surely inspired the first flush of Newsreel filmmaking." In other words, Newsreel films are modeled on Cuban-style propaganda.

In his interview, Daressa discounted the film professor's views. Renov, he said, "exaggerates" the agitprop dimension of California Newsreel's productions: "If you make a film expecting to make a mass movement, you're making a mistake." In his view the process works in reverse: "We had a film called *Last Grave at Dimbaza*, which we got from the National Council of Churches. In 1975 we had the Soweto uprising, and there was interest in South Africa, so we started the Southern Africa media center."

Daressa describes his corporate credo as "a pragmatic relationship to reality." He says California Newsreel is simply in the business of "providing materials to movements" and supplying films about "social tendencies foundations are funding." Daressa says his company has received funding from the Ford, Rockefeller, and MacArthur foundations.

On the other hand, the catalog of films in the UCLA exhibit lends support to Renov's claims. Among the films distributed by California Newsreel and/or Third World Newsreel are the following titles: *Summer '68, Columbia Revolt, Yippie, Black Panther, Troublemakers, San Francisco State On Strike, El Pueblo Se Levanta, Only the Beginning, People's War, Controlling Interest, The Business of America, Hasta La Victoria Siempre, Hanoi, Tuesday the 13th, Seventy-Nine Springtimes* [a life of Ho Chi Minh], *Up Against the Wall, Miss America, The Woman's Film, Namibia: Independence Now,* and *Chronicle of Hope: Nicaragua.*

Daressa says that his company concentrates on distributing films about the economy and Africa, while Third World Newsreel focuses on Latin America and Asia. He adds that California Newsreel does not distribute gay-themed films, which are handled by another California distributor, San Francisco-based Frameline. For example, Marlon Riggs' *Ethnic Notions* and *Color Adjustment* are distributed through California Newsreel, while *Tongues Untied* is distributed through Frameline. He says the only goal of the films he distributes is to encourage viewers to think critically about the possibilities for social change.

With titles like those in the UCLA retrospective, it is hardly surprising that Renov should title an article on California Newsreel "The Imaging of Analysis: Newsreel's Re-Search for a Radical Film Practice" in a 1984 issue of *Wide Angle*. In contrast to Daressa's modest assessment of Newsreel's purpose, Renov calls Newsreel "the New Left's own camera-eye on the street and behind the barricades." He describes how skillfully Newsreel masks its radical agendas when dealing with PBS. In 1984, for example, PBS aired Newsreel's 45-minute film *The Business of America...* Writes Renov: "In contrast to the spray of machine gun fire that announced the Newsreel product of old and its agitprop intentions, a staid and simplifying identifying credit precedes *Business'* first image." The film was also screened at the 1984

Democratic National Convention.

In his discussion of *The Business of America...*, Renov applauds the agitprop approach, saying "the American Dream was, after all, but a cruel hoax. The film was conceived as a response to Reagan's ascendancy....California Newsreel set out to explore the potential for a mass movement aimed at insuring the public direction of economic decisionmaking in the area of industrial development."

Daressa discounts the possible impact of the screening of *The Business of America...* at the Democratic National Convention, saying it lasted "about five minutes." He maintains that most of the interest in the picture comes from business schools and that labor union leaders who were shown the film were uninterested. "It's hardly a radical film," says Daressa, who adds that the current Secretary of Labor Robert Reich called it "a compelling and insightful chronicle of America's deindustrialization." Reich also is a fan of California Newsreel's 1986 *Collision Course* about Eastern Airlines. According to Daressa, Reich said *Collision Course* should be widely screened.

When asked about Newsreel's apparent link to the left wing of the Democratic Party, Daressa says, "The Democrats certainly like those films. I have no problems with the Democrats liking those films. They were not just pro-labor, we wanted to come up with an industrial policy." Daressa says Newsreel's apparent advocacy of a planned economy is merely a call for "investing in human resources."

But Renov's article quotes a different Daressa when the question of Newsreel's politics comes up. "There's nothing that Newsreel has ever done than reflect the left in film," Daressa says. "By the mid-'70s," Renov comments, "Newsreel had begun to define its primary role as distributors of politically engaged films, channeling independently produced radical film projects from around the world to an audience in need of such instructional supplements and organizing tools."

Newsreel's political agendas naturally affect its journalistic output in other ways as well. "Newsreel has never bothered to assume a pose of objectivity in its documentary work," Renov notes: "Larry Daressa, in responding to charges of filmic manipulation, has argued that 'everything in film is manipulative...the very idea of documentary is preposterous. These things are totally fictive, totally constructed, and anybody who thinks any differently and doesn't acknowledge that fact is naive.'"

When confronted with this dismissal of journalistic standards and objective criteria, Daressa stands by his words, although he adds, "it sounds like something I said years ago." According to Daressa, "in making a documentary, you're making an argument. Reality isn't a story. You have to construct it, and put it in a narrative, which privileges certain events and not others." According to Daressa, this view is widespread in the field: "Even *National Geographic* documentaries are not objective. Why a beaver and not an otter? *National Geographic* anthropomorphizes animals when it talks about 'animal families.'"

This view differs strongly from the code of ethics issued by the journalistic fraternity Sigma Delta Chi, which calls upon reporters to be objective and to clearly label any editorial commentary. But what else could one expect from an outfit whose signature style is described by Renov as "The Newsreel touch, the pose of the un-abashed propagandist." According to Renov, "Newsreel is mixing pragmatism and radical advocacy and selling it to America." The question is, Should such agitprop activities be subsidized by the federal government and the Corporation for Public Broadcasting, and should they be featured as "documentaries" on PBS?

—*Laurence Jarvik*

MORE OF THE SAME AT *ITVS*

After five years, the first ITVS-funded program was finally shown on PBS in July. *For Better or Worse*, a cheap-looking videotape produced by David Collier and Betsy Thompson, was broadcast on the PBS series *POV*, whose new executive director, Ellen Schneider, was hired from a position as ITVS director of public affairs.

The hour-long film was presented as the story of five couples and set out to explore the "joys and sorrows" of long-term commitment. At first glance, the program appeared no different from those local news segments celebrating couples who have stuck together for 50 years. Stylistically, it had the trivial local-news feel of the "human interest story." But by including a gay couple among the heterosexual marrieds, without addressing the controversiality of such an inclusion, the film betrayed its hidden agenda: to establish by fiat what is actually the subject of intense debate in the culture at large.

The gay couple were actually gay rights activists who had been Grand Marshalls of New York City's 1985 Gay Pride Parade, and their relationship provided the frame for the portraits of all the other couples, whose narratives were intercut with theirs. They were also the only couple who talked explicitly about political issues or homosexuality, describing how they "came out" on the Bill Boggs television show and their public activities in support of gay rights.

Not surprisingly, the program contained credits acknowledging financing from a prominent gay activist organization, the Lambda fund. Where were Jennifer Lawson's guidelines police when this slipped through? And were the PBS executives who accepted *For Or For Worse* chastised? Was ITVS?

The other married couples—one apparently Jewish, one black, one ex-military, and one a minister and his wife—described their lives together without being asked to discuss politics or gay rights. One would be interested to know what Paul and Inez Jones, the jazz musicians, felt about gays invoking the language of the civil rights struggle, or how Christian minister Chet Loucks and his wife Vi felt about Biblical injunctions against homosexuality, or how Dan and Sophie Trupin might feel if one of their children declared themselves homosexual, or whether any of them, described as "breeders" by the gay community, would think of sharing their family tax breaks and other privileges with childless couples who have two earners. Or whether they thought a change in the law might impact long-term relationships.

Unfortunately, the makers of *For Better Or Worse* were no more interested in these questions than they were in long-term relationships as such. *For Better or Worse*— ITVS's first success—is a success for political correctness rather than quality television, a poor product made palatable by deceptive packaging.

ITVS supplied a list to COMINT of productions that have been aired or are scheduled to air on PBS stations (though not on the PBS National Program Service). Political correctness seems to be the common theme:

Greetings from Out Here, produced by Ellen Spiro and Kate Horsfield. According to ITVS, the film "offers a look at southern gay culture through the eyes of a southern expatriate, focusing on 'those gay people who don't flee, who stay at home and do the bravest thing of all...be who they are, where they are.' Her witty eye and spectacular footage capture the richness, vitality, and courage of 'out' gay southern life." The picture includes the Texas Gay Rodeo; a gay Mardi Gras ball; a rural faerie gathering; and the Rhythm Fest, a lesbian music festival. ITVS put up $78,604.

Warrior: The Life of Leonard Peltier, produced by Suzie Baer. This follows at least two Hollywood documentaries (and one *60 Minutes* segment), including one sponsored by Robert Redford, claiming that convicted murderer Leonard Peltier is innocent. According to ITVS, *Warrior* "is a disturbing factual accounting of the U.S. Government's disregard for the rights and traditions of America's native people as exemplified by the Peltier case...Was it murder? Self-defense? Or an inevitable tragedy arising from governmental subjugation of Native people?" These questions indicate a stacked deck. Not surprisingly, longtime defender of Third World drug dealers and murderers, William Kunstler, is a major element in this film. ITVS's contribution was $50,000.

White Homeland Commando, by the Wooster Group, directed by Elizabeth Le Compte, is billed as "an imaginative and intimate commentary on the rise of hate crimes, Klan-based electoral activity and white supremacist attitudes in this country. *White Homeland Commando* [note the not so subtle connotation of the title that America is South Africa— the only nation that has actual "homelands"] reveals that the reality of our troubled, violent society is as inescapable as the news headlines." (White racism is PC but black racism is not. In 1993, ITVS flatly rejected a proposal for a program on the subject by an Emmy-nominated filmmaker.) The ITVS description of *White Homeland Commando* concedes that its story is "fictional," since it is about an alleged New York City-based white supremacist organization. ITVS paid $55,669 for this.

Margaret Sanger: A Public Nuisance, produced by Barbara Abrash and Esther Katz. "Determined to right what she saw as a terrible social injustice, Sanger opened the first birth control clinic in a Brooklyn tenement neighborhood teeming with immigrant poor," notes the ITVS description of this film. The blurb does not point out that Sanger wanted to eliminate poverty by eliminating the poor—through birth control and sterilization. Again, a politically correct twist on the birth-control pioneer. ITVS put $16,500 into this production.

Post No Bills is Clay Walker's advertisement for leftist poster designer Robbie Conal, a vulgarian whose caricatures of Jesse Helms, George Bush, Ronald Reagan, Oliver North, and the Supreme Court conservatives have been plastered all over Los Angeles. Conal's poster of Clarence Thomas was titled "Long Dong Condom." Conal is clearly a candidate for ITVS canonization. This project received $92,155 from ITVS.

There are some notable politically correct items missing from the current list supplied by ITVS, representing much larger expenditures of ITVS cash over the past year. For example, where is Peter Miller's *Passin' It On*, which received $149,758 from ITVS to promote a Black Panther convicted of gunning down two New York policemen? Where is producer Marlon Riggs' *Black Is...Black Ain't*, which received $245,000 from ITVS? Where is Kathe Sandler's *A Question of Color*, which was given $100,000—and is distributed by ITVS director Lawrence Daressa's California Newsreel? Where is *Endangered Species: The Toxic Poisoning of Communities of Color*, which received $152,684?

The above films were given over half a million dollars by the American taxpayer, presumably for television broadcast. Yet they are not found in ITVS's listing of up-coming screenings or on the PBS schedule. Will anyone ask for an accounting? One ITVS series, *TV Families*, received $2,060,000 for five hours of drama and is not scheduled until Spring 1994, according to *Current*. *AIDS Films* received $1,450,000 for eight 30-minute episodes and an hour-long segment of a series with the working title *HIV/AIDS Project*. This too, is not scheduled until Spring 1994, according to *Current*. What is taking so long? An ITVS series not even listed in the ITVS press handout given to COMINT, called *Rights and Reactions*, received $1,530,000, according to *Current*. Produced by Louis

Massiah and *Passin' It On's* Sam Pollard for a company pro-
vocatively named *Testing the Limits*, this will consist of four
hours of "the struggle for lesbian and gay civil rights, illustrated through personal stories and political events." Why
isn't this listed? And what, by the way, is the politically correct allotment system that seems to assign ten times as much
money to gay issues as to anyone else's issues—blacks,
women, Jews, Armenians, etc.?

—*Laurence Jarvik*

CPB WHITEWASH
OF ITVS

One would have hoped that the Corporation for Public
Broadcasting—in its oversight capacity for ITVS—might
have investigated questions such as those raised in the previ-
ous essays in its 1992 report entitled *CPB Report to Congress:
Activities and Expenditures of the Independent Television Service
(ITVS) in Fiscal Years 1991 and 1992.*

Unfortunately, the report doesn't mention *any* problems with ITVS, even the obvious one of programs promised
but no longer mentioned. The report reflects poorly on CPB
management, since Congress specifically required the Corporation to submit a report "*evaluating* the performance of the independent production service in light of its mission to expand the
diversity and innovativeness of programming available to public broadcasting." In order to perform such an *evaluation*, CPB
would have had to analyze the programming ITVS produced
and/or failed to produce. This mandated task was one that
CPB simply failed to do in its report. CPB's investigator
merely repeated the ITVS descriptions of its programming
without evaluation. Moreover, it nowhere analyzed the dis-
bursement of program funds to determine whether ITVS
even attempted to fulfill its "mission to expand the diversity" of programming or whether it merely set out to serve a
narrow, partisan band of the diversity spectrum.

Some other obvious problems with the report:

☞ The report states CPB committed by contract to pay ITVS $6,967,000 for FY1990; $8 million for FY1992. ITVS had received $8,089,418 for FY1990-91, plus $1,636,300 for FY1992. Yet the report does not look at the contractual requirements incumbent upon ITVS, and does not mention the possible conditions for termination of its contract such as nonperformance, breach, etc. Is ITVS living up to all the clauses of its contracts with CPB? The inspector general's report does not even attempt to address this question.

☞ The report describes ITVS program funding grants incompletely. The report does not state the number of projects that have been completed, the number of productions funded, the number that are behind schedule, etc. It also does not explain how an "independent" television service can be funding *series* like the "focused programming initiatives" on teenagers, AIDS, and "new approaches to public affairs" without violating the premise of the ITVS enabling legislation: freedom from central control. Several million dollars are involved in these series projects. Series are not underrepresented in the current PBS schedule. They are not an innovative format for programs. A small number of series is not a diverse programming source.

☞ Solicitation procedures are described uncritically, as are the panel process and the selection of panel members. There is no description of the actual standards required to be a panel member, nor how suggested panelists are evaluated by ITVS. The report does not state how many panel applicants there were, how many were rejected, and if any procedure exists for protest or appeal. Are panelists chosen by competitive examination, or through a system of cronyism? Who are these panelists, and what qualifications do they have to judge *television* programming? Since some panelists are from PBS, in what sense are they independent?

☞ The report states that $3 million in grants for 25 TV programs were awarded in December 1991. According to the report, by September 1992 six programs had been delivered to ITVS. None had been scheduled for broadcast on PBS's National Program Service. Was this a satisfactory record? How much of the $3 million do these projects represent? What happened to the others? How fair were the selection procedures? What standards were enforced? What was the appeals process—since some 2,000 applied for 25 grants?

How are deadlines enforced?

☛ CPB states that in "an examination of thefirst productions funded by ITVS in December 1991, their carriage, and critical reception is not possible at this time, since the timeline for the completion of productions is at least 18 to 24 months." Since the law requires such an evaluation, why should Congress not withhold money until such a report is made? Did ITVS decide in bad faith to schedule such lengthy production periods? Why didn't ITVS decide to fund productions so they would be completed in time to be evaluated by CPB in compliance with the law? Is this satisfactory?

☛ CPB states that productions can be examined through their descriptions as provided by ITVS, while CPB has no independent knowledge regarding the accuracy of the descriptions. Why not? Is ITVS funding projects under inaccurate descriptions? Is this satisfactory?

☛ The ITVS audit found that ITVS had an adequate financial management system to monitor and identify expenditures incurred against CPB funds. Is this a positive evaluation?

☛ CPB certified that ITVS had adequate policies and procedures for selecting grantees to be funded with CPB funds. Yet earlier the report stated that CPB had no independent knowledge regarding the accuracy of the descriptions of the projects. Given the latter statement, on what basis is the CPB certification of procedures and policies being made?

☛ An Audit Report No. EA-92-60 by Lester Latney dated August 24,1992, states selection and evaluation procedures for panels "were not in writing." It says, "we informed management of the need and importance to have all applicable policies and procedures in writing and that such guidelines should be reviewed and updated periodically." If the procedures were not in writing, how could the auditor determine that proper procedures have been followed?

☛ It was reported in the journal *The Independent* that the series *Declarations* was funded outside of the panel process in the amount of $1.25 million. What procedures exist for funding programming outside the panel process? How was this series selected? Was this satisfactory?

How does CPB define "expand," "diversity," and "innovativeness?" In what sense has PBS programming been expanded since ITVS was established? In what sense has ITVS increased the diversity of PBS programming since it was established? In what sense are ITVS series increasing the "innovativeness" of PBS? If CPB cannot answer these questions, why is it continuing to fund ITVS?

☛ One ITVS-funded program, *Passin' It On*, was declined for PBS release by Jennifer Lawson, who cited its failure to meet minimal journalistic standards. *Passin' It On* cost the taxpayers $100,000. Why wasn't this mentioned in the report? How many other ITVS-funded projects fail to meet PBS's minimal journalistic standards?

☛ One form of diversity is geographic diversity. Sen. Dole complained on the Senate floor that most ITVS grants went to New York and California—not geographically diverse or innovative sources for PBS programming. Yet the report fails to include a geographic breakdown of ITVS grants. Where are ITVS recipients located?

☛ CPB's balance and objectivity provisions by law apply to all national programming. Since ITVS is producing national programming, is it in compliance with the balance and objectivity requirements?

Given CPB's failure to properly oversee ITVS, the obviously narrow political perspective of the programs it has funded, its problem with missing programs and, in at least one case, a censored program, Congress ought to reexamine whether ITVS should receive any more funds from American taxpayers.

—*Laurence Jarvik*

ITVS: THE PC
BOONDOGGLE GROWS...

It is a reflection of the incestuous world of public broadcasting that Globalvision's new series, *Rights and Wrongs*, has found a new funding partner at ITVS. ITVS was originally represented to Congress by founder Larry Sapadin as an attempt to provide a vehicle for independent producers and specifically as an alternative to the existing situation in which independents were forced to work for PBS series such as *Frontline*, with Sapadin promising ITVS would finance new and diverse producers not previously seen on PBS.

The funding of *Rights and Wrongs* shows how far ITVS has already strayed from its original mandate. *Rights and Wrongs* is hosted by an established PBS star, *MacNeil/ Lehrer NewsHour* anchorwoman Charlayne Hunter-Gault. The series is a presentation of PBS station WNET, New York, which also presents *MacNeil/Lehrer*. Producers Rory O'Connor and Danny Schechter are *Frontline* producers. Moreover, *Rights and Wrongs* is not even independent.

According to producer Rory O'Connor, the series is supervised directly by WNET executive Fred Noriega. The production agreement with WNET "includes editorial oversight," O'Connor told COMINT. We called ITVS to ask some questions about the recent funding decision, since it clearly is in contempt of congressional intent, but spokeswoman Robyn DeShields did not return our call.

However, a look at some upcoming ITVS programming reported in *Current* indicates that funding *Rights and Wrongs* fits a pattern of politically correct series, which seem to have been plucked from a pork barrel of special interest groups by ITVS executives with blithe contempt for their legal obligations to provide diversity, balance, and independent points of view. One five-hour series called *Television Families* was granted $1.9 million by ITVS. Producer James Schamus works for ITVS, directly supervising commissioned episodes as "supervising producer." This is a controlled series not the work of independents. And what has ITVS chosen to produce? According to the official ITVS newsletter *Buzzwords*, "tales of more or less dysfunctional families" that "all fall outside the mainstream."

Two examples give the flavor of the series. Todd Haynes' *Dottie Gets Spanked* is a camp deconstruction of '50s America from the producer of gay cult films *Superstar* and *Poison*. Jon Moritsugu's *Terminal USA* is described by ITVS as "wholly unwholesome folks" who "cram a lot of skeletons in their closet: drug abuse, homosexuality, teen pregnancy, elderly abuse, unemployment, and infidelity (with the pizza delivery boy)—all under one roof." Moritsugu says, "I just want people to see messed-up Asians on the screen." Just what Sen. Inouye no doubt intended as a wise use of scarce tax dollars when he championed ITVS against Sen. Dole's criticism in 1992. *Buzzwords* concludes, "unlike the absolute 'family values' of censorship-minded evangelicals, *TV Families* values all kinds of families."

Another ITVS series, *The Ride*, received $1.4 million. It has two producers: Shauna Garr, formerly of MTV, is series producer, and Lynne Kirby, an ITVS executive, is coordinating producer. This set of eight half-hour programs features four teenagers—selected by the producers—driving across the United States. And what do they find? "There was Julie, 17, a sexually active young woman living on her own and contemplating taking her first HIV test; Dominic, 15, a would-be transsexual struggling for understanding and acceptance; and Maria, 14, a street-smart teenager trying to decide whether to join a gang."

This voyeuristic exploitation of teen angst is presented as a public service by ITVS, which notes that the four teens chosen received counseling from "staff psychologist Stan Ziegler."

Other upcoming ITVS shows include the $1.4-million *HIV Public Television Project* about one of the most reported stories in the history of media and *AIDS and The Question of Equality*, promoting "the gay rights struggle" at $1.5 million, which lists an English filmmaker named Isaac Julien as one of the producers. (Recall that the special-interest lobby behind the creation of ITVS originally complained to Congress that PBS had too large a British component.) There is also the $1.4-million *Signal to Noise* about "how TV affects our lives." One of the producers here is Pat Aufderheide, an American University professor who, in an apparent conflict of interest, has covered public broadcasting for pub-lications like *In These Times, The Nation,* and the *Columbia Journalism Review.*

Of course, ITVS has consistently turned down worthwhile independent and innovative projects that do not meet its standards of political correctness—projects such as Gloria Borland's *The Business Owners.* ITVS has absorbed more than $38 million in public television funds since 1989 and has produced exactly nine broadcast hours on the PBS feed, which comes to $4 million per hour or about four times the cost of a commercial network show. It's time to shut it down.

—*Laurence Jarvik*

PART IV

FRONTLINE: A PROFILE

A comprehensive review of each *Frontline* show produced since the 1990-91 season reveals that the series' views on subjective issues such as domestic politics, foreign policy, race, and the environment are straight from the left-wing issue agenda. The evils of corporate greed, the alleged constitutional sins of Republican presidents, and the continuing oppression of a racist America were rehashed again and again. In 73 new programs produced since 1990 and 24 rebroadcasts from earlier seasons, only two had content that could be construed as conservative. Over the past three years (and on into the '93-'94 season), *Frontline* made shaky conspiracy charges against the usual suspects, bashed America as the evil empire, and gave famous-name liberal pundits a soapbox from which to preach their wares.

Conservative exclusion began in coverage of environmental issues. Out of seven programs dealing with ecological themes, none incorporated conservative or wise-use arguments. On this subject, "investigations" consisted of repeating the claims of the environmental left rather than questioning the bad science many of the claims rest upon. Last season Bill Moyers gave us *In Our Children's Food*, a *60 Minutes*-like attempt to scare mothers into thinking pesticides will give their kids cancer. Moyers neglected key information in his dire warning, such as the Center for Global Food Issues' finding that 99.9 percent of cancer risk comes from food itself not chemical additives. Moyers chose to ignore this and other arguments against the supposed benefits of organic farming. Similar programs included *To The Last Fish*, a charge that the oceans will soon be depleted of sea life from overfishing; *The Decade of Destruction*, a 10-year chronicle of South American deforestation; and *Global Dumping Ground*, another Moyers warning that the United States is turning the Third World into a pit for its hazardous waste.

Racial matters were covered in eight programs. Out of the eight broadcasts examining various facets of race relations, not one conservative voice appeared. In 1990, in *Throwaway People*, Roger Wilkins expounded on the decline of the inner city. His reason for urban decay? Ronald Reagan, of course. In Wilkins' extreme view, every opponent of the bankrupt welfare system was suspect as a racist: "In the '80s it became even harder. [Inner city] communities like Shaw absorbed two more hammer blows. The old racist libel about moral inferiority that used to be leveled at blacks was now focused on the poor. It justified crippling the only programs that provided any ladder at all. The Reagan Revolution slashed $51 billion in social spending."

Other programs have stated that the reason black teenagers are murdered more often than their white counterparts is lack of gun control, supported questionable NAACP claims that banks deny loans to black applicants, and charged that a racial double standard exists in the armed forces. During the Gulf War, Anita Hill confidant Charles Ogletree moderated a one-sided panel discussion with Hodding Carter, Jesse Jackson, and *Newsweek*'s Joe Klein (then with *New York Magazine*) titled *Black America's War*. A lead-in documentary set the tone for the discussion to come: "The disengagement of the rich, the growing divide between black and white: the arguments seemed a metaphor for what this country had become in the 1980s. One writer, looking at how differently the war was received by whites and blacks, dubbed it the Reagan-Bush gap." *Frontline* narrator Will Lyman went on to label Colin Powell an Uncle Tom and even attacked the chairman of the Joint Chiefs for conducting a successful military campaign: "Domestic programs were being cut, civil rights leaders protested loudly. [General Colin] Powell remained loyal to Weinberger and Reagan. They, in turn, were loyal to him. This man would go on to orchestrate in the Persian Gulf one of the most punishing bombing campaigns ever unleashed on this planet. Iraqi casualties are estimated at 100,000 or more. Yet few have chosen to criticize Powell for that."

Coverage of domestic politics would seem to have provided producers a chance to redeem themselves, since the Democrat-dominated House and the misdeeds of bloated regulatory agencies provided ample fodder indeed. But apparently *Frontline* didn't see much worth investigating. Of the 15 broadcasts on political topics, a few were bipartisan attacks on the political process itself, but only one directly scrutinized a Democrat. Then-candidate Bill Clinton's effort to capitalize politically on a newly-adopted Arkansas child-welfare program met with criticism in April 1992. Yet even in this case, the critique came from the left, accusing Clinton of not implementing a big-government solution fast enough.

The programs included a critical biographical look at David Duke but no corresponding investigation of, say, Louis Farrakhan, a far more potent national force; an hour-long complaint that America does not have a "national energy strategy" primarily because of Bush Chief of Staff John Sununu; and *Springfield Goes to War*, a Moyers pre-Desert Storm morale booster proclaiming "Springfield, Massachusetts right now is a town divided. The President of the United States is sending its sons and daughters off to the Persian Gulf, but he has not explained what America's interests are there, or if there is a moral imperative to fight."

Frontline also went after conservatives directly in *The Resurrection of Reverend Moon*, a program alleging that the conservative movement is partially controlled by the "Moonies." Reagan and Bush election landslides were belittled by former *Washington Post* reporter William Greider in a rambling and disjointed two-hour essay that aired in April 1992. "The Republican Party's artful election strategy has been accomplished not by addressing the real economic concerns of the disaffected working class but by broadcasting messages attuned to their resentments," he sermonized. "They concocted a rancid populism, perfectly attuned to the age of political decay. The party of money won national elections mainly by posing as the party of the alienated." Speaking of money, Greider's two-hour soliloquy aired just as his current book, *Who Will Tell The People*, hit the stands. It wasn't the first time Greider used taxpayer air time to fill his pockets. In 1986, *Frontline* gave him an hour to describe *The Disillusionment of David Stockman*, a subject about which he had also just written a book.

But *Frontline*'s favorite topic by far is foreign policy, or more precisely, Republican foreign policy crimes and conspiracies. In three years, *Frontline* devoted 25 programs to U.S. policies abroad. Some of the topics included a graphic depiction of the effects of U.S. bombing on Iraqi civilians by pro-PLO journalists Andrew and Leslie Cockburn, an allegation by a British documentary team that Oliver North used Anglican Church official and hostage negotiator Terry Waite as a dupe, and a Hodding Carter late-hour hatchet job on former CIA Director Robert Gates, just before the Senate was to vote on his confirmation. The redoubtable Moyers contributed *High Crimes and Misdemeanors*, his 90-minute indictment of Presidents Reagan and Bush for their roles in the Iran Contra Affair. (Perhaps Moyers should share his secrets with independent prosecutor Walsh, who was unable to establish criminal culpability). Not once during the program were conservative points of view, such as the questionable legality of the Boland Amendment, given an airing.

Yet *Frontline* went on to weave even more Republican-skewering fantasies, the most notable being its two lengthy investigations of the "October Surprise" conspiracy theory. Robert Parry produced two programs outlining the paranoid claims of disgruntled Carter official Gary Sick (in yet another just-published book) that the 1980 Reagan presidential campaign conspired to keep Americans hostage in order to steal victory on election day. Parry's first program aired in April 1991. But even after *The New Republic*, *Newsweek*, and even *The Village Voice* proved the story fraudulent, *Frontline* devoted another full hour to the charge the following year. In it, Parry took back some of his initial claims but introduced another set of equally silly accusations. These included the charge that the CIA sent him his original sources and had them lie in order to discredit him. A bipartisan congressional committee headed by Democrat Lee Hamilton has dismissed the October Surprise theory, but *Frontline* and PBS have yet to air an apology or retraction.

Only two programs out of the 25, *Cuba and Cocaine* and *The Last Dictator*, veered from the standard left-wing perspective. *The Last Dictator* might be called a revisionist left-wing perspective, downplaying the brutal acts of the tyrant in favor of his policy fiascos, such as his failures at growing giant strawberries. Even mistakes like that couldn't break his fatherly connection to Cubans: "Many...will never forget how once he restored their national pride."

Besides topical issues, *Frontline* producers have a rather interesting perspective on history and often play fast and loose with the facts. A look at the American Indian Movement was entirely sympathetic to the domestic terrorist group responsible for murders, an armed siege, and the storming and vandalizing of the Bureau of Indian Affairs in the '70s. The BIA sacking was only apparently a PR problem: "But when the occupation ended, television reports focused on major damage to the property. AIM had gone to Washington as a civil rights organization...and they returned to South Dakota with the reputation as a radical political group." Their violent occupation of Wounded Knee was not the result of terrorism but a noble protest, according to "correspondent" Milo Yellow Hair, himself a former member of the organization in question. "Although they were surrounded by government forces during a harsh winter, a sense of dignity emerged within the embattled camp. Inside Wounded Knee, the dream of a free Indian society was reborn." Giving a nod to one of the left's favorite causes, the documentary called into question the murder conviction of Leonard Peltier.

Last season, *Frontline* spent an hour rehearsing author Anthony Summers' unproven charges that FBI Director J. Edgar Hoover was a homosexual transvestite. And what self-respecting PBS series could resist waving the bloody shirt of the Vietnam War? A British documentary rebroadcast in 1991 contained a minute-by-minute description of the My Lai massacre, complete with interviews of guilt-ridden, sobbing vets.

Reviewing the endless stream of one-sided programs leads to the question: How inevitable is this? Does *Frontline* have an agenda, or is conservative exclusion simply an oversight? For the answer, consider *Frontline*'s story selection process, which outlines the essential elements for documentaries requesting funding or airtime. Nowhere in the three-page document do the words *balance* or *objectivity* appear. In 1987, *Frontline* executive producer David Fanning explained: "We feel it is part of *Frontline*'s mandate to raise consciousness."

Apparently Fanning's goal of consciousness-raising didn't extend to the brutality of communism. In 1990, Jorge Ulla and Nestor Almendros were looking for a PBS venue to air their aptly-named documentary *Nobody Listened*, the story of Castro's sadistic prison system. After it was rejected twice by PBS's other documentary series, *POV*, *Frontline* also balked on airing the film. Don Kowet of the *Washington Times* reported that one producer told the Academy Award-winning cinematographer Almendros: "*Frontline* does not produce anticommunist programs." In 1986, producer Ofra Bikel commented on her documentary *The Russians Are Here*, which described problems Russian immigrants have adjusting to the United States. Her film's purpose? "To show that when you take people from a country like Russia and put them in a country like America, you're not necessarily doing them a favor." Bikel was also the producer-narrator of *Frontline*'s treatment of the Anita Hill-Clarence Thomas debacle.

An uninformed viewer, however fair-minded, couldn't help concluding after watching the last three seasons of *Frontline* that the United States is wrecking the planet, that Republicans regularly shred the U.S. Constitution at home and abroad, and that dissenters from the liberal consensus on welfare and civil rights are racists. Shutting out conservatives does not serve the public interest nor does it fulfill the mandate of the Public Broadcasting Act. Since there are no conservative series to balance *Frontline*, *Frontline*'s own lack of balance is all the more disturbing.

—*David D. Muska*

FRONTLINE *AND* CIR: *A* PARTISAN MATCH

When *Frontline* began its 1992-1993 season, its producers did not lead with a documentary of their own but introduced a 90-minute attack on General Motors made by the Center for Investigative Reporting, a San Francisco-based collective of radical journalists. *Frontline* is so fond of CIR that it not only has given the organization its season opener more than once, but it saved the group from folding in 1989 with CPB-provided funds, now a hefty share of the CIR budget.

Who is CIR, and what is its journalistic philosophy? "We don't consider investigative reporting to be something that includes investigating welfare mothers," CIR co-founder David Weir explained to a *Newsweek* reporter in 1982. Much closer to its heart is the bashing of a symbol of corporate America like GM. While CIR did raise eyebrows with one of its first stories, a magazine article on the criminality of the Black Panther Party (for which COMINT editor David Horowitz was a primary source), CIR has traditionally limited its subjects to comfortable left-wing conceptions of corporate and military malfeasance.

Although CIR has always placed most of its journalistic output in print, often in socialist journals like *Mother Jones* and *The Nation*, they also struck investigative deals with the networks from the late '70s to the late '80s. But when network news budgets shrank as the '90s approached, CIR was left high and dry. By the summer of 1989, the entire CIR staff was forced to take an unpaid vacation. It was during this crisis that *Frontline* (and CPB) came to the rescue. In the January/February 1991 *Washington Journalism Review*, reporter Mike Hudson explained: "A year later things had changed. Except for Weir, everyone was back, the center was at full strength and CIR was scrambling to finish a documentary for PBS's *Frontline* on the world trade in toxic waste." The name of that documentary was *Global Dumping Ground*, first aired on October 2, 1990, and narrated by Bill Moyers, complete with a spin-off book.

Hudson's 1991 story also explained: "CIR recently received $75,000—its largest grant ever—from the Florence and John Schumann Foundation in Montclair, New Jersey....In the spring of 1989, Moyers had helped raise money for the toxic waste documentary and volunteered to serve as executive editor. [In 1991], Moyers became president of the Schumann Foundation and helped CIR win the large grant." Moyers also serves on a board of advisers to CIR with another member of the public broadcasting community, NPR's Susan Stamberg.

CIR grant proposals go out with a Moyers plug: "As the major media organizations around the country scale back their investigative reporting efforts in fear of criticism and the bottom line, the Center for Investigative Reporting serves an increasingly vital function. To remain viable as an active investigative center and resource, CIR needs your support. The work they produce speaks for itself, and so does the need for it."

PBS also helped CIR in 1990 by contracting them to assist in the launching of *Health Quarterly*, a new show hosted by Peter Jennings. Orchestrated by CIR executive director Sharon Tiller, CIR staffers Sarah Henry and Constance Matthiesen served as associate producers on the first show. As part of the "research and reporting" for the PBS segment, Matthiesen later published a warm and fuzzy *Washington Post* profile of David Himmelstein and Steffie Woolhandler (Nov. 27, 1990), the Harvard health-care socialists who organized Physicians for a National Health Program. Matthiesen's *Post* profile was short on investigation and long on adulation: "When [Woolhandler] begins to speak, the aspiring doctors are suddenly quiet—struck not just by her powerful voice, which is softened by a rich Louisiana accent, but by her devastating critique of the health care system they are about to enter." Matthiesen ended the story: "[One] medical student is insistent: 'Do you really think someone on welfare should have the same health care as someone who has money?' Before Woolhandler can answer, other soon-to-be doctors in the auditorium answer with an emphatic 'Yes!'"

After *Global Dumping Ground* (heralded as its "first independently-produced documentary"), CIR contracted with *Frontline* for a series of documentaries leading up to the 1992 election, for which CIR reported that Fanning's crew "generously agreed to provide half the funding for each production." This is especially important since *Frontline* is funded directly by the Corporation for Public Broadcasting and has no underwriters.

The Spring 1991 edition of CIR's newsletter at the time, *In House* (now expanded and titled *Muckraker*), touted their PBS link: "The documentary series represents a major shift by CIR into independent production....By setting up an independent production unit within CIR, our reporters and producers can now shape stories for broadcast much as we have done for years in print."

Those "shaped stories" included *The Great American Bailout*, an investigation into the savings and loan scandal, which contains a reasonable summary by CBS reporter Robert Krulwich but also insinuates that the S&L bailout was delayed until after George Bush won the 1988 election. Neither CIR nor *Frontline* has announced a revisitation of the S&L story in the wake of President Clinton's involvement in the failure of Madison Guaranty Savings & Loan and its ties to the Clintons' partnership in the Whitewater Development Company.

Other "shaped stories" included the first two documentaries of the 1992-93 season, which both aired days before the 1992 election. On October 20, *Frontline* weighed in with a show decrying the lack of a "national energy strategy" (in other words, government intervention in the form of price controls, gas taxes, import fees, etc.). The theme of the program was summarized by freelancer Nick Kotz and CIR's Rick Young in an editorial for *The Washington Post*:

> The United States has 5 percent of the world's population, yet we consume 25 percent of its energy. Our infatuation with fossil fuels is poisoning the planet....Energy Secretary Watkins' early attempts to forge a national energy agenda met stiff resistance from a White House unwilling to accept a larger government role in energy policy and opposed any actions that required taxes and interfered with the "free market."

On October 27, Krulwich hosted a show on campaign finance practices, predictably skewering both parties (but with twice as much attention to the Republicans) for being in the grip of corporate money. The show included no defenders of current campaign finance laws or critics of liberal "reform" groups like Common Cause.

CIR's relationship with public broadcasting continues to prosper. As if CPB's indirect funding of CIR through *Frontline* wasn't enough, it now directly funds CIR to produce a three-hour series, *School Colors*, that will follow a group of students through their senior year at Berkeley High School. Their direct mail now boasts of a new *Frontline* investigation with another left-wing agenda—the 1872 Mining Law (which provides for private use of federal lands) and the "wise use" movement that opposes the major environmental groups.

Frontline's contracts with CIR—a group never devoted, and in fact opposed, to the idea of balance within a program—raise questions about the show's selection of topics, experts, and reporters. But CIR is not the only radical group of filmmakers *Frontline* has pledged to help out. When Globalvision, a production company run by radicals Danny Schecter and Rory O'Connor, had their left-wing PBS series *South Africa Now* canceled, they joined the *Frontline* stable.

Their work for *Frontline* included *The Resurrection of Reverend Moon*, a documentary on how the Reverend Sun Myung Moon had "reemerged as a major media, financial, and political power in the new conservative establishment" and *The Bank of Crooks and Criminals*, an investigation of the BCCI banking scandal. Globalvision now produces a new show for PBS stations, *Rights and Wrongs*, anchored by *MacNeil/Lehrer*'s Charlayne Hunter-Gault.

Almost every outside producer or reporter selected by *Frontline*—from producers like Globalvision and Andrew and Leslie Cockburn to reporters like Bill Moyers, Roger Wilkins, and William Greider—shares CIR's mission of using public television to promote the ideas of the left.

The mere form of *Frontline*, 60 minutes of uninterrupted, single-issue investigative journalism, gains them plaudits from a journalistic establishment that often fails to distinguish between the show's form and its often-biased content. *Frontline*'s own publicity boasts: "Among TV critics and print editorialists, *Frontline* has established itself as what the *Cleveland Plain Dealer* called 'the most consistently important weekly hour on television, the crown jewel and standard-bearer for the mission of public television." In a perverse way, that's true: *Frontline* does set the standard for public television's mission: not to serve the public, but to serve itself.

—*Tim Graham*

POV: "OP-ED PAGE OF THE AIRWAVES"

As though public broadcasting's programming lacked a left-wing component for balance, PBS and the National Endowment for the Arts created the summer documentary series *POV* (*Point of View*). Last year, with a newly appointed Clinton staff at the helm, the NEA upped its support for the show from $250,000 to $375,000.

A *POV* news release proclaims:

Co-executive producers Ellen Schneider and Marc N. Weiss firmly believe that many viewers appreciate opinionated and passionate television. "*POV* functions like an op-ed page of the airways. The point is to get people talking to each other and debating issues long after the closing credits. That's a terrific role, that television, particularly public television, can play."

In talking to the TV press, Weiss and Schneider insist their op-ed page is like the one in many newspapers, a collage of diverse viewpoints, not just opinionated and passionate television from the left. Weiss told the *Seattle Post-Intelligencer*: "There is no political litmus test, no ideological agenda." Ellen Schneider parroted to the Associated Press: "There is no political litmus test...*POV* has no ideological agenda."

That may satisfy Sheila Tate that *POV* is run in the spirit of the Public Broadcasting Act, but a look at any season of *POV* shows that its real mix is a sprinkling of apolitical films amidst a sea of far-left propaganda. In each of the last two seasons, the only fig leaf of political balance came from the most acceptable anti-communism in liberal circles, criticizing China: Iris Kung's *Escape from China* in 1994 and Mickey Lemle's *Compassion in Exile* about Tibet in 1993.

Even left-leaning *Los Angeles Times* TV critic Howard Rosenberg calls *POV* "the nonfiction film series that conservatives often cite to bolster their fallacious argument that PBS is somewhat to the left of Fidel Castro." But *POV*'s record of strident leftism even involved Castro: Weiss twice turned down the late Nestor Almendros' searing documentary on Cuban human rights abuses, *Nobody Listened*, for "presenting point of view as fact." The rest of *POV*'s schedule suggests that point of view often triumphs over fact.

This year's list of programs follows the regular pattern: two art-house releases, Ross McElwee's *Time Indefinite* and *Hearts of Darkness*, which is about the filming of *Apocalypse Now*; Kung's anti-China film; two films on women, *Dialogues with Madwomen* and *Memories of Tata*, which focus on mentally ill women and physically abused women, respectively; two shows on gays and AIDS, *One Nation Under God* and *The Heart of the Matter*; two films on blacks, *End of the Nightstick* and *Passin' It On*, one promoting the Black Panthers, the other promoting the Black Panthers' law collective; and one on a lone left-wing anti-government protester, *The Times of a Sign*.

Where many markets led with McElwee's likable film, some markets (including Washington, D.C.) began the season with *One Nation Under God*, a film denouncing a therapeutic "cure" program for homosexuality. Films on "homophobia" and AIDS are a *POV* staple. In 1991, *POV* gained its greatest notoriety by airing the late Marlon Riggs' *Tongues Untied*, which many PBS stations refused to air because of its full frontal nudity, images of black men rollicking in bed, and repeated profanity.

Marc Weiss now defends the film: "We knew it was a risky film, but we also thought if we didn't put it on, there would really be no reason for the series to continue. It was important not to pull back and say 'this might be too hot to handle.'" But *POV* did drop *Stop the Church*, a 29-minute film celebrating the ACT-UP raid on St. Patrick's cathedral in New York City, in which activists invaded the church sanctuary—which not even the Communist government of Poland had dared to do—to throw condoms at bewildered Catholic worshippers during mass.

In 1992, *POV* began with Riggs' *Color Adjustment*, in which he decried TV's "profoundly conservative bias" and complained about the absence of gays from television families: "Have we exchanged the myths of pre-television America for new fictions just as confining, for impossibly rigid, homogenized fictions of the family, and the American dream, and that this is the price of the ticket to acceptance?" In 1993, the show led off with *Silverlake Life: The View from Here*, Tom Joslin and Mark Massi's chronicle of their dying from AIDS.

In *One Nation Under God*, Teo Maniaci and Francine Rzeznik attack the ex-gay support group Exodus International and therapists seeking to cure people of homosexuality, relying largely on ex-ex-gay Exodus founders Michael Bussee and Gary Cooper, as well as gay author Martin Duberman and Joan Nestle of the Lesbian Herstory Archives. The two-hour film reaches its low point in moving from the testimony of therapists to footage of Nazi concentration camps. *Los Angeles Times* critic Robert Koehler noted: "*One

Nation displays as much hate of that group [ex-gays] as some fundamentalist Christians display toward gays and lesbians." It also rehashes gay activist rhetoric, claiming at one point: "In March of 1987, the AIDS Coalition to Unleash Power, better known as ACT-UP, came into existence. In October of that same year, Ronald Reagan was finally to utter the word AIDS. By that time, 25,000 were already dead." But President Reagan appointed a commission on AIDS in July 1987, making the show's claim false. Maniaci and Rzeznik also don't mention the fact that federal AIDS spending already totaled $771 million by the end of fiscal year 1986, six months before ACT-UP was founded. Gay activists like Virginia Apuzzo boasted of their regular contacts with the Department of Human Services, the Public Health Service, and the Social Security Administration after a 1984 meeting with HHS Secretary and Reagan appointee Margaret Heckler.

The filmmakers' approach is highlighted by *POV*'s on-line discussions after the program. Maniaci expressed hope his film would combat homophobia: "I think that people on the far right will probably never change their opinions, but that there are a lot of moderate people who may be swayed to change their homophobic opinions after having seen this. I think a lot of homophobia is based on invisibility. The more people see and recognize gay people, the more those walls will be broken down." Maniaci praised his promoters: "I think PBS tries to present a broad spectrum of programming, but that it also receives a lot of flack from conservative constituencies."

Asked about the film's content, Maniaci said: "I spoke about how I felt that people have a right to be ex-gay if they want to be, and they took that as an affirmation of their stance. I think the film is fair, though, in that it allows them to say everything they want to say."

But Dr. Elizabeth Moberly, a therapist who is often featured in the film, took issue with Maniaci's journalistic methods: "When filmmaker Teo Maniaci interviewed me at the ex-gay Exodus conference in Texas, [in] 1990, he concealed the fact that he is himself gay. I asked him if he had any personal stake in this and he claimed that he hadn't. He pretended to be heterosexual."

In an on-line discussion after *End of the Nightstick* about anti-police brutality activism, a questioner asked:

"Wouldn't you say that young poor black males in this country are already living in a police state, by most definitions of a police state?" Producer Cyndi Moran replied: "I think a lot of people that we talked to would agree with you. That was a point made, not in so many words, in the documentary." Another producer, Peter Kuttner, agreed: "One interviewee uses the word genocide. A strong word, but one which does graphically describe what many young people see as the destruction of a community." To which a viewer responded: "*End of the Nightstick* confirms my belief that we live in an increasing [sic] oppressive society, even for poor white males like myself. Good film!"

Passin' It On marked the rare airing of an Independent Television Service project, this one the story of Dhoruba Bin Wahad, the Black Panther who was convicted of fatally shooting two police officers sitting in their squad car but was released on a technicality (see "Panther Outrage," page xx). *Los Angeles Times* TV writer Robert Koehler wrote: "*Passin' It On* appears to be the left's latest media effort to rile up the right." The film not only relentlessly pleads Wahad's innocence, it spreads the pathetic propaganda line that the Panthers were really community service activists dedicated to feeding kids breakfast. The film glorifies Wahad and includes a soundbite from a student proclaiming, "Since he was freed, so to speak, he's basically traveled around this country and this world and kicked the United States Government's ass!"

The same tendency continued in an on-line discussion of the season-ending film *Times of a Sign*, which addressed Bill Breeden's decision to steal a John Poindexter street sign from Poindexter's hometown of Odon, Indiana. Breeden explained the film's audience: "It was a showing attended by approximately 100 people. And all of them peace activists and radicals so it was a rather biased audience. But they loved it. It brought the house down, many times."

When asked if he had been to Nicaragua, Breeden replied: "I went to Nicaragua the following year. I drove a bus of medical supplies from Bloomington, Indiana, to Nicaragua, a large school bus. I found the people to be unbelievably strong, the country to be very free. This was prior to the election of Chamorro." When asked what his film would mean in the inner city, Breeden replied: "I think it means that people, regardless of where they live, have the responsibility and ample opportunities to resist fascism."

In the film, Breeden explained his conversion to anti-Americanism:

When a person has had their eyes wrapped or has been blind for a long time, the first rays of light are real painful. I know in my case the realization that everything I'd believed about the American system, about the great American Dream, was a farce, was extremely painful. It was like standing on a rug and someone pulls it out from under me when I begin to see poverty for the first time in the cities, when I recognize my own racism, which has coincided hand in hand with my religion for so long—all those things. All of a sudden, I didn't have any place to stand.

But Breeden, driving his old car with "Impeach Bush" painted on the back, came around. His wife spent weeks in Nicaragua with Witness for Peace, the pro-Sandinista group that tried to put itself in between Sandinista and Contra fighters. Near the film's end, Breeden's defense lawyer decries the injustice of John Poindexter and Oliver North going free, those responsible for "the first-degree murder of millions of people," when Breeden had to spend four days in the county jail for his prank.

POV would be the perfect starting point for establishing that PBS exists to serve the left. By its very nature, the show aims to defy standards of balance and objectivity. It serves as a dumping ground for films too obviously slanted for regular PBS airing, such as the revised version of Mark Mori's *Building Bombs. POV* serves the left, and the left touts its one-sided point of view. Take it from neo-Marxist Jeff Cohen of Fairness and Accuracy in Reporting, who said: "Corporations are responsible for public TV having a spectrum that extends from bland to conservative. The few exceptions are Moyers, some *Frontline* documentaries, and *POV.*"

—*Tim Graham*

PART V
FAIR: REVOLUTION BY OTHER MEANS

Fairness and Accuracy in Reporting, which received nearly $800,000 in grants last year and the support of Hollywood stars like Ed Asner, Jackson Browne, and Tim Robbins, is the left's leading media watchdog group. Last fall, FAIR executive director Jeff Cohen appeared on the *Donahue* show and said: "I'll quote Seymour Hersh, one of the great investigative reporters. He said 'Don't count on the *New York Times* to lead a social revolution. They won't even know about it for six months.'"

Cohen has made it his mission to change that. If he has his way, the media will not only report the revolution, they will be part of it.

Cohen founded FAIR in 1986 out of his opposition to the 1986 ABC miniseries *Amerika*, a futuristic imagining of a Soviet invasion of the United States that he thought was unfair to the Soviet Union. To FAIR, the media is guilty of conservative bias almost by definition, because major media outlets are owned by large corporations and influenced by advertisers, which are also often large corporations.

FAIR's bible, *Unreliable Sources*, written by FAIR staffers Martin A. Lee and Norman Solomon, identifies the corporate market economy as what's wrong with TV: "Financial interests play a major role in determining what we see and don't see on television. Most of the top network sponsors are powerful multinational corporations. These global mammoths dominate our broadcast and print media far more extensively than most people realize."

With this rehash of a Marxist world view, it's no surprise that "PBS is one of FAIR's main targets," as Cohen explains. In FAIR's eyes, public television ought to reflect the socialist principles of its public financing. But since public TV in America is compelled to function in a capitalist environment, it is subject to the same malevolent corporate influences that dominate the commercial media. FAIR refers to

PBS as the "Pro-Business Service" and has lamented that National Public Radio is no longer an alternative news source, having lost its "independent tone" and "moved to the mainstream."

To the Orwellians at FAIR, the American mainstream is hopelessly conservative and pro-capitalist, while "independent" is a synonym for politically left and economically socialist. FAIR's vocabulary is contagious. Although its political agenda is to push public broadcasting to the left side of the revolutionary barricade, and its economic outlook derives from 19th-century ideology, FAIR is invariably referred to by public broadcasting journalists as "liberal" and "progressive."

FAIR's COMPLAINTS ABOUT THE PBS SCHEDULE

FAIR's litany of complaint begins with the PBS lineup of talk shows, which it claims are dominated by "conservatives." (The quotation marks are necessary, because FAIR considers anyone to the right of Noam Chomsky and Ramsey Clark conservative.) "PBS does not offer one weekly show hosted by an advocate of the left," FAIR argues.

By contrast, PBS airs *The McLaughlin Group* and *One on One*, hosted by John McLaughlin; *Firing Line*, hosted by William F. Buckley; and *Tony Brown's Journal*, which is "hosted by a Republican." FAIR discounts the fact that each show often has liberal panelists or liberal guests. On *The McLaughlin Group*, Morton Kondracke, a Democrat, is a "foreign policy conservative," the liberal Jack Germond is a "centrist," and the very liberal Eleanor Clift is "no stranger to insider journalism," damned because she "covered the Bush inauguration in worshipful prose." Of *Firing Line*, FAIR complains: "While Buckley makes a point of choosing panelists to balance his conservatism, they are often establishment liberals."

Tony Brown of course began his show 25 years ago as a man of the left. In fact, the Buckley show was brought on-line to balance Brown's *Journal*. Having moved slowly to the right during the past quarter century, Brown declared himself a Republican in the fall of 1991. Ignoring this history, FAIR whines: "Isn't it about time PBS aired a weekly program reflecting more mainstream opinion in the black community?" FAIR's own written record belies the complaint. As recently as 1987, FAIR approvingly cited Brown as an "exception" to white male domination of PBS's airtime.

Yet even this eccentric accounting by FAIR of PBS talk shows is disingenuous at best. Consider what FAIR has omitted: *To The Contrary*, the new women's talk show from Maryland Public Television, is hosted by Bonnie Erbe, no conservative, and features two liberals and leftist Julianne Malveaux along with conservatives Kate O'Beirne and Linda Chavez, giving the show a 3-to-2 tilt to the left, counting the moderator; *Inside Washington* is hosted by liberal local Washington anchorman Gordon Peterson and airs on a dozen PBS stations, routinely featuring four (and sometimes all five) liberal panelists (Charles Krauthammer is its only conservative); *Washington Week in Review* is hosted by Paul Duke (no conservative) moderating a panel of routinely establishment liberal insider journalists. The recent national distribution of nightly talk shows hosted by liberal Dennis Wholey and former Bill Moyers producer Charlie Rose adds two more left-leaning talk show hosts to the PBS lineup.

In the 1992 season, Bill Moyers' weekly prime-time series, *Listening to America*, was, for the most part, a talk show hosted by a man of the left. Even FAIR, which has trouble finding liberals who are liberal enough, counts Moyers as one of its own. In 1990, Jeff Cohen told a C-SPAN audience: "Bill Moyers, of course, was an aide to a very conservative Democratic administration, [but] now is very much I would say a liberal or progressive." In 1991, FAIR activist Dennis Perrin concurred in another C-SPAN interview: "The only example that you can point out to me is Bill Moyers, who I will grant to you is definitely left-of-center." But FAIR never concedes the omnipresence of Moyers in its critiques of PBS.

Because of its Marxist approach to the world, FAIR's critiques often blame everyone but the reporters themselves for alleged bias in the news, focusing instead on the owners and executives. In an interview in *Unreliable Sources*, Jeff Cohen is asked: "For a group set up to criticize the media, doesn't FAIR have a lot of friends in the media?" Cohen answers: "That was a conscious strategy of ours, in keeping with our view that the media are not monolithic and that many in the working press are FAIR's potential allies. Our common foe is media conglomeration and callous media owners."

In fact, the paperback edition of *Unreliable Sources* includes a laudatory quote from a media friend in the *Washington Journalism Review*: "You gotta love these guys. Not only have Lee and Solomon written a timely consumer primer on conservative bias in reporting, they've done it with humor." The writer, Susan Farkas, is a producer at *Dateline: NBC*.

FAIR vs. MacNeil/Lehrer

As already noted, FAIR's critiques of PBS rarely focus on reporters and rely very little on a content analysis of its programming. FAIR's ideologically motivated approach to criticism is much in evidence in its 1990 assault on *The MacNeil/Lehrer NewsHour*. FAIR's evidence that *MacNeil/Lehrer* leans to the right consists of a poll at the Conservative Political Action Conference that declared it the fairest news show. (Conservatives do generally regard *MacNeil/Lehrer* as the most balanced of the prime-time news shows. But they also regard it as a liberal show. It's just the most balanced among a very liberal sampling.) If a conservative media group used a parallel argument, they'd be laughed out of court. But FAIR's study elicited major media attention. The study, conducted by Boston College graduate students William Hoynes and David Croteau, focused far more on the race, gender, and occupation of the guests than on what they actually said. Hoynes and Croteau theorized that the show's pro-establishment tilt was obvious in its guests' racial and gender makeup: "By itself the demographic makeup of these programs' guest lists does not guarantee a diversity of perspectives. However, demographic variety is one important sign of substantive diversity." FAIR's Martin Lee was more blunt about what the show's white male tilt allegedly proved: "Ted Koppel's, Jim Lehrer and Robert MacNeil's TV news shows, along with other shows, by discriminating against women and people of color—in a subtle yet insidious manner—promote racist attitudes in society as a whole."

The FAIR study "revealed" that *MacNeil/Lehrer*'s guests were 90 percent white and 87 percent male. Ironically, FAIR boasts that its report caused PBS to give air time to Noam Chomsky and the late *Progressive* editor Erwin Knoll, both white males. Of course, Chomsky and Knoll, despite their ethnic and gender handicaps, did manage to have the politically correct positions on the issues dear to FAIR.

On the other hand, *MacNeil/Lehrer*'s inclusion of Knoll on their regular panel of daily newspaper editors made no journalistic sense except as a payoff to FAIR. Unlike the others, Knoll was not an editorial-page editor of a daily newspaper with his finger on the pulse of a mass audience. He was an ideological warrior catering to a narrow and small ideological readership. The February issue of *The Progressive*, for example, featured as its cover story the case for "A New American Socialism" by Manning Marable. This "case" turns out to be the turgid argument of a modern-day King Canute trying to turn back the tide of history and resurrect a bankrupt and discredited ideology—hardly the stuff of contemporary journalism. (If Knoll's presence on the newspaper panel was more than just a payoff, surely there is at least as strong a case for the balancing presence of conservative opinion journal editors like John O'Sullivan and Bob Tyrell, whose magazines have four times the circulation of Knoll's. The editorial-page editors are generally bland and centrist as a whole, and there was no conservative balance to Knoll on the panel.)

FAIR's demand for fewer white males (based on the vulgar Marxist assumption that what you are is what you think) is also disingenuous when FAIR itself is put under the same ideological microscope. The majority of FAIR's staff and advisory board are white males, and at least seven of the white males are millionaires: Ed Asner, Jackson Browne, Adam Hochschild, Casey Kasem, Tim Robbins, Dr. Benjamin Spock, and Studs Terkel. The group is headed by Jeff Cohen, a white male; the publisher of *Extra!*, Martin Lee, is a white male; and the newsletter's editor, Jim Naureckas, is a white male. Cohen, Lee, and Naureckas are the principal spokesmen for the group and make the lion's share of its media appearances, leaving the support roles to women.

In other words, FAIR is making its own significant contribution to the lack of female and minority voices on the airwaves—in Lee's words, subtly "promoting racist attitudes in society as a whole."

FAIR's vulgar Marxists, Hoynes and Croteau, also found that 46 percent of *MacNeil/Lehrer*'s American guests were current or former government officials, 38 percent were professionals ("academics, doctors, and lawyers") and 5 percent were corporate representatives. "A total of 89 percent of *MacNeil/Lehrer's* U.S. guests represent elite opinion, while only 6 percent represent public interest, labor, or racial/ethnic organizations." Since *MacNeil/Lehrer* is a news program, however, it is hardly surprising that its guests feature newsmakers and newsshapers, which almost by definition make up an elite group.

FAIR's ideology-driven approach attempts to obscure its partisan bias by hiding its own side of the political debate under generic classifications: "under-represented" categories like "public interest, labor, consumer, peace, environmental, racial/ethnic and gay/lesbian" groups. If FAIR were honest, it would demand what it really wants: more radicals, socialists, and politically correct activists.

On the other hand, when counting elite heads to establish its negative view of programs like *MacNeil/Lehrer*, FAIR invariably overlooks the actual opinions the guests express. Someone like Robert White, a former ambassador to El Salvador, will be counted as a white male elitist ex-government official, yet White is a fierce critic of U.S. policy in Central America and political sympathizer of groups favored by FAIR heroes Chomsky and Knoll. Cohen, a lawyer, would himself be counted as a white male elitist.

Not surprisingly, given this Alice-in-Wonderland methodology, the FAIR study found *MacNeil/Lehrer* to be dominated by the political right: "Two conservative think tanks dominate the guest list: the American Enterprise Institute and the Center for Strategic and International Studies. AEI fellows appeared six times and CSIS appeared eight times in this six-month period." One doesn't need a calculator to figure that in a six-month period, 130 programs were aired with roughly 650 guests (at five guests per show). Of these, 14 came from the aforementioned think tanks. And of the 14, some scholars, such as AEI's Norman Ornstein and Middle East specialist Robert Hunter of CSIS, are hardly conservative Republicans. Some domination.

FAIR's study says nothing at all about the *MacNeil/ Lehrer* team of anchors, reporters, and commentators. It ignores not only the content and quality of their reporting but the racial and gender makeup of the staff. MacNeil and Lehrer—white males—are joined by co-anchors Judy Woodruff and Charlayne Hunter-Gault—both female and one African American. The show's reporters include Kwame Holman, a black former press secretary to Democratic Washington, D.C., Mayor Marion Barry; Elizabeth Brackett, a former Democratic committeewoman and candidate; and economics reporter Paul Solman, who helped found *The Real Paper*, a left-wing underground tabloid, in the '60s. (In 1990, Solman blamed conservative "tax rebels"—rather than liberal spenders—for Massachusetts' declining bond ratings under Michael Dukakis.) The show's regular commentators—former *U.S. News & World Report* editor Roger Rosenblatt, black columnist Clarence Page, and Anne Taylor Flemming—are all liberals.

FAIR vs. NPR

FAIR used a similar methodology in its recent attack on National Public Radio for being too "mainstream." FAIR again focused on racial, gender, and economic classifications of news and opinion sources: "NPR tilted toward government officials and representatives of establishment and conservative think tanks. Only 21 percent of NPR's news sources were women." Lifting a phrase from radical scholar Laurence Soley, FAIR refers to sources as "newsshapers," implying that the definition of what is newsworthy lies in the hands of interviewees and sources rather than editors and reporters. This is an absurdity, as anyone who has tried to get NPR editors (or any other editors) to cover a story they do not consider newsworthy will attest. Sources only become sources and interviewees only get interviewed *because* reporters and editors seek them out.

Needless to say, FAIR completely ignored the political affiliations of NPR's top brass, which would indicate a pronounced tilt toward the other end of the spectrum. NPR's president, Douglas Bennet, accepted a job in the Clinton State Department. Under Jimmy Carter, he served in several State Department jobs after working as a top aide to Democratic Sens. Abraham Ribicoff and Thomas Eagleton. Lois Schiffer, NPR's general counsel, a board member of the Women's Legal Defense Fund, was mentioned for a post in the Clinton Justice Department. Anne Edwards, an NPR senior editor, joined the Clinton-Gore campaign and now works on the White House staff. Bob Ferrante revolved into

NPR after serving as Democratic National Committee communications director for two years. He joined NPR in 1989 as executive producer for morning news.

FAIR also ignores current NPR vice president for news and information Bill Buzenberg, who publicly opposed Reagan's Nicaraguan policy and proclaimed "the administration has been slow in recognizing the more immediate threat from the right in countries such as El Salvador and Guatemala," and managing editor John Dinges, a former teacher at the Institute for Policy Studies. In fact, in 1987 FAIR credited Dinges with exposing the "lie" that the Sandinistas were arming Salvadoran guerrillas. Subsequent evidence, of course, shows that they were.

Past top NPR officials also have strong liberal and Democratic ties. Former Robert Kennedy staffer and McGovern campaign bigwig Frank Mankiewicz was NPR president from 1977 to 1983; Adam Clayton Powell III, son of Democratic Congressman Adam Clayton Powell and vice president of news programming from 1987 to 1990, left NPR to join Jesse Jackson's short-lived syndicated talk show; Paul Allen, an NPR producer from 1979 to 1985, left to join the staff of liberal Sen. Chris Dodd and, later, the Natural Resources Defense Council. On the other hand, there is not a single identifiable conservative or Republican in a top staff or executive position at NPR.

FAIR vs. CPB

In early 1993, Jeff Cohen wrote a long letter to CPB chairman Richard Carlson listing his objections to "right-leaning" public broadcasting. His complaints were treated as front page news in *Current*. In his letter, Cohen singled out an *unaired* new program, *Reverse Angle*, the pilot for a documentary series hosted by Fred Barnes and Morton Kondracke. Cohen wrote: "FAIR recommends that this [show] be abandoned." The reason? "Barnes and Kondracke are longtime panelists on *The McLaughlin Group*. Both are regulars on other TV networks....A new PBS show featuring these two would make a mockery of the mandate to 'provide a voice for the unheard.'" By the same argument, however, Bill Moyers' 100-plus hours on public TV in a wide range of formats makes an even greater mockery of the same mandate.

But that would be to take this March Hare logic far too seriously. Why does the presence of Barnes and Kondracke as familiar *hosts* preclude the presence on *Reverse Angle* of the voices of the unheard, appearing as sources and subjects? By this reasoning, every show, to avoid making a mockery, would have to change hosts every week (or, in the case of *MacNeil/Lehrer*, perhaps every day).

Cohen, who often calls FAIR an "anti-censorship group," followed his pre-emptive attack on a show that no one has seen by insisting, *pro forma*, that a cancellation of the show wouldn't be censorship: "FAIR would never question the right of these two men to be heard on TV; they already are heard—loudly." But this argument, too, runs directly counter to the argument that FAIR and other left-wing groups have made to the effect that any denial of airtime or government grants to controversial shows, performances, and artistic productions amounts to censorship. Religious groups were called censors for opposing the airing of Marlon Riggs' *Tongues Untied* on PBS, even though Riggs has had several shows on public television.

This isn't the first time that FAIR has exposed the flimsiness of its claim to be an "anti-censorship" group. The November/December 1988 edition of *Extra!* included two articles decrying the media's opposition to the United Nations' proposed New World Information Order, which would have allowed Third World governments to inhibit the flow of information from "imperialist" news outlets and reporters.

One of the articles complained that American media groups "organized widely-publicized international conferences to endorse 'free press' ideology and attack the NWIO. In short, the media not only reported on the debate, but were active participants in it." Note the quotation marks around "free press."

Finally, there is the irony of Cohen's use of the new CPB "Open to the Public" policy to call the CPB to account for its alleged bias against FAIR's agendas. After all, FAIR wasn't prominent in the campaign for balance that led to the "Open to the Pubic" policy. On the contrary. FAIR portrayed the balance campaign as a right-wing attack on public television intended to censor left-wing views. Perhaps a FAIR apology is in order.

Although FAIR is often obsessed with the secrecy of

"the national security state," it opposed the campaign to apply the Freedom of Information Act to CPB and criticized the call for public scrutiny of public television as an attempt to expand "undue government influence." FAIR opposes "undemocratic" corporate media ownership, but the group also opposes democratic reforms of public broadcasting (since, in FAIR's Marxist universe, only private corporations are a threat to democracy).

Most ironically, FAIR advocates additional taxpayer-funded radio and TV networks as the hope for a "democratized" media, while one of its own favorite political slogans is, "Separate the press and state."

In his letter to Carlson, Cohen singled out programs on business and the stock market as inherently biased because...they're about business. Again, content doesn't figure in the FAIR complaint. The fact that the *Nightly Business Report* is about business conditions and performance—basically how to make money—and features regular commentary, in any case, from liberals like Robert Reich and Lester Thurow, doesn't register on FAIR's scales. Cohen's letter to Carlson describes *Wall Street Week* as controversial, not only because of "the pronounced ideological biases of the host (Louis Rukeyser), but also because of the extremely narrow selection of guests. The core audience of such a show—active investors—represents only about 2 percent of the American public." Once again FAIR's penchant for the *non sequitur* rears its familiar head. If gays and lesbians measure only 2 to 3 percent of the population, as they do in most opinion surveys, would that be an argument against their representation on public television? In reality, FAIR's estimate of the number of stockholders among the American public is off by a factor of 10. There are 47 million stockholders in America, or 20 percent of the population.

For a "controversial" show, the only real controversy Rukeyser has caused is his effort to publish a for-profit newsletter of stock tips. To publicly attack Rukeyser (and to be taken seriously by publications like *Current)*, one would think FAIR would have many examples of Rukeyser's conservative bias on *Wall Street Week*. One would be wrong, however. FAIR has not provided a single one so far. Rukeyser is guilty by association with business and the stock market.

FAIR's Credibility Meltdown

Before the 1993 Super Bowl, FAIR held a news conference in Pasadena declaring that studies showed domestic violence increased during and after NFL football games. At the briefing, Sheila Kuehl of the California Women's Law Center cited an Old Dominion University study claiming that violence against women increased 40 percent after Washington Redskins games.

But on Super Bowl Sunday, *Washington Post* reporter Ken Ringle exposed what other media are now calling FAIR's Super Bowl Hoax. When Ringle called the author of the Old Dominion study, he said "that's not what we found at all." Ringle also pointed out that FAIR representative Linda Mitchell claimed she knew Kuehl was misrepresenting the Old Dominion study, but declared: "I wouldn't [challenge] that in front of the media...She has a right to report it as she wants."

Why would a group devoted to "accuracy in reporting" defend the right of a political ally to mislead reporters at their own news conference? FAIR's Super Bowl scandal should hang like a millstone around the group's neck for a story as phony as *Dateline: NBC's* exploding GM trucks. In both cases, making a politically correct point was more important than getting the story right.

Misunderstanding FAIR

The failure to pierce the veil of FAIR's Orwellian vocabulary and take into account its political agendas creates a misleading impression that FAIR's criticisms are parallel to those offered by other media critics and groups. FAIR is not really interested in establishing balance or diversity within the current framework of public radio and television. Its agenda is indeed revolutionary. It wants to redefine the political spectrum and rearrange the economic environment.

Confusion about FAIR's agenda strengthens the false impression that PBS and NPR programming falls between the two extremes of left and right. FAIR's vision of public broadcasting's future—more money, less public scrutiny—can even seem at times to be a carbon copy of the liberal consensus. In Cohen's interview in *Unreliable Sources* he predicts: "As a nationwide movement of media activists reaches a certain critical mass, FAIR will consider long-term campaigns aimed at a democratic restructuring of the media." Cohen even sees eye to eye with congressional left wingers on new taxes to pay for this restructuring: "Plentiful funding for truly public broadcasting could come from a variety of sources: a tax on imports and factory sales of radios, TVs, and VCRs; a tax on TV and radio commercials; a fee charged to private broadcasters when they acquire or renew their licenses from the federal government."

For a group of anti-corporate activists suspicious of the profit motive, it is interesting that FAIR never suggests that PBS's rampant merchandising of home-video tapes and children's television spinoff products should be used to finance expanded programming. For a group advocating revolutionary change, it's noteworthy that all that FAIR really proposes is to extend the present structure of public broadcasting while eliminating corporate funding. In fact, FAIR's fierce attacks on PBS and NPR reflect a view that public broadcasting is territorially theirs, a socialist base that ought to provide an uninterrupted platform for radicalism. FAIR's rhetoric about a "democratic restructuring" of media has little to do with democracy and everything to do with creating a nationalized, politically correct media. From FAIR's revolutionary perspective, almost nothing that the media— commercial and public—currently offer is really palatable: As long as the media fail to promote "revolution," they are hopelessly "establishment" (and therefore, by definition, "undemocratic"). The public broadcasting targets of FAIR's criticism should realize that there is little they can do to win FAIR's approval short of turning over their microphones and raising the white flag.

—*Tim Graham*

PART VI

NATIONAL PUBLIC RADIO

THREE LETTERS ABOUT CENSORSHIP AT NPR

In the May 27, 1991, issue of *Current*, the quasi-official publication of PBS, Bill Moyers launched into a malicious attack on COMINT and its editor. Moyers was responding to the lead article in COMINT'S first issue, "Missing Balance in PBS History." Moyers rejected COMINT's conclusion that there was an identifiable political bias in public television documentaries (a conclusion *New York Times* critic Walter Goodman found perfectly credible: see "Public TV Documentaries That Lean to the Left," *New York Times* May 6, 1991). Ignoring the entire public record of COMINT's appeals for balance, and without any evidence to substantiate the charge, Moyers wrote that "Horowitz...and his ilk do not want 'fairness and balance'— they want unanimity. They don't want 'media integrity'— they want media subservience to their ideology." The following letter about the controversy was written to Moyers by an NPR producer who is not allowed to write to *Current* and who must remain anonymous, under threat of being fired by his NPR station. Relevant excerpts from Moyers' reply follow the letter, along with COMINT's closing words for Moyers.

LETTER FROM AN ANONYMOUS NPR PRODUCER

July 23, 1991

Dear Mr. Moyers,
     After pondering your column in the May 27, 1991, *Current* I'd like to suggest another way to approach David Horowitz's criticisms of public TV.
     Let me preface this with two observations: So far as I

know, I am the only conservative form of life in the entire public-radio universe (I produce feature news stories and a classical music program on Station W---); and I'd have preferred to respond to you in the pages of *Current*, but I'd lose my job if I did so, since my own politically incorrect beliefs ride at the back of the public broadcasting bus. Those two facts in themselves say something about your thesis.

You'd probably agree that, in terms of general ideological orientation, public radio is not a lot different from public TV. Many of my friends move back and forth from one to the other with ease....I think both you and Horowitz had some good points. The real problem is the monolithic ideological conformity that prevails in both branches. In nearly a decade in this business, the most frequent comment I've gotten from public-broadcasting colleagues—by far—is something like, "Gee, you're the first conservative I've ever heard of in public radio."

This by itself is evidence of a serious problem, Mr. Moyers. I think it was Walter Lippmann who said, "Where all think alike, no one thinks very much." When there's nobody in the newsroom to challenge the conventional wisdom—or when those who can are afraid to speak up—opinions pass for facts, catchwords and slogans pass for reasoning. When a newsroom reaches a certain critical mass of people with identical world views, they find it inordinately difficult even to imagine seeing existence from a different angle. They can't even perceive their own uniformity. One of the ironies of my job is to work daily with people who cherish a self-image as iconoclasts, nonconformists, and heretics when in fact they are drearily orthodox on any question you care to name. The very fact that a conservative public-radio producer is regarded by his colleagues as a kind of walking oxymoron is a dead giveaway.

Back before I realized that in public broadcasting some free speech is freer than other free speech, I made the mistake of sending a letter to *Current* criticizing NPR's leftist tilt. I was told that if I ever did it again, I would be fired (on a pretext, my boss was candid enough to admit). Five years ago the editor of *Current* asked me to submit an editorial on the same topic. This time I checked with management ahead of time and was told that if I dared to submit the piece, I should "beware my job." The only two other conservatives I've ever known in the business—both of whom wised up and left—related similar treatment.

I get the impression you believe public broadcasting is actually a pretty non-ideological place, Mr. Moyers. Assuming you've actually spent some time at public stations, I wonder how you can sustain this belief. I had to run over to our local public TV station on an errand last year and was brought up short by the amazing number of politically correct bumper stickers in the parking lot. Then it hit me: It was fund-drive time, and the station's volunteers had turned out in force. Same story here at W---. During our spring and fall fund drives, the station blooms with T-shirt slogans like, "U.S. Out of Central America," "Keep Your Laws Off My Ovaries," "ACT-UP Gay Rights," etc.

It's not so much that I object to such sentiments. It's just that when you notice these are public broadcasting's most ardent supporters (and conversely that nearly all political and social conservatives view us as antagonists), you begin to suspect that perhaps David Horowitz is onto something. The leftists who support us are not stupid—they know we're on their side. And the conservatives who fault us are not, in your words, "partisan, self-righteous and authoritarian"; they can hear with their own ears that our coverage is slanted toward their opponents. Do you seriously suggest that neither liberals nor conservatives have the mother wit to see who's for them and who's against them?

After years in this business, my own impression is that public-broadcasting people not only are, at some level, aware of our industry's ideological imbalance but are touchy and thin-skinned about it. How else to explain the fact that a lone conservative like myself is not permitted to air our dirty little family secret—our liberal slant—in the pages of an industry tabloid? How else to explain the bitterly intolerant responses our conservative critics evoke from us? (Your own piece, Mr. Moyers, struck me as unnecessarily waspish and vindictive.)

Most of us in public broadcasting are so different from our conservative critics that it's almost as if we live in separate universes. Our easy belief in human progress and perfectibility, our free-floating agnosticism, our good-natured relativism; all these necessitate a major effort of the imagination to comprehend where our critics are coming from. We can make that effort and suppose that maybe, just maybe, they are honest people with legitimate grievances. Or we can dismiss them all as authoritarians who want not fairness but "subservience." As long as we continue to respond as you did in *Current*, we'll continue to be not public broadcasting, but a private communications system for the alienated New Class elite who are our main constituency.

Sincerely, [Name Withheld by Request]

BILL MOYERS' REPLY

August 7, 1991

Dear Mr. —,

I appreciate the care you gave to your letter to me of July 23 and the tone with which you wrote. My reply to David Horowitz may have been a little impassioned here and there, but he had unfairly attacked two of my documentaries and I was, shall we say, aroused....

I am not familiar with the "entire public-radio universe" or, believe it or not, with the public-television universe either. I rarely hear any public-radio stations except here in New York and seldom see any other public-television stations. So I cannot respond authoritatively to your characterization of either universe...

...l am saddened by your account of what happened to you when you wanted to exercise your own free speech. I have long thought that the best critics of any institution, public television included, should be the people who serve them, derive our benefits from them, care about them but nonetheless believe we are obliged not to serve them blindly but to prod, goad, and challenge them precisely because we care about them more than a free-swinging outsider can. I would like to have seen your letter in *Current*. Public broadcasting would be the better for it.

Actually, I wish there were more like you in our "universe" and more like me, too, and of others as well. I don't know if the result would be more liberal or conservative, but I do know it would be more—well, public.

With best regards,
Bill Moyers

Dear Bill,

Pardon us if we regard your reply as so much sancti-
monious eyewash. You are one of the most powerful figures
in public broadcasting. When it comes to abuses in other institutions of American life, your nose can be seen poking into
every nook and cranny to find out what's going on, and your
voice can be heard in millions of households exhorting
America to make it right. Do you expect anyone to buy your
alibi that you really don't know what's going on in public
broadcasting? You produced a PBS program about censored
stories. Here's one: *the totalitarian atmosphere in national public
radio.* Now how about taking care of the beam in your own
eye before you go pointing any more fingers at the motes in
everyone else's.

Sincerely,

The Editors of COMINT

NPR AND THE TOTENBERG AFFAIR

In September 1992, the nation was treated to a spectacle
that is regrettably becoming all too common a feature of
our troubled democracy: trial by television. In this case, the
trial was that of Clarence Thomas, the Supreme Court nominee accused of sexual harassment. His accuser was Anita
Hill, a law professor who had worked for him when he was
the nation's chief enforcer of civil rights. It is the nature of
television trials that the accused has none of the protection
of due process that our legal system provides. With his nomination in the balance, Thomas was forced to defend himself
against charges about incidents that were alleged to have
happened 10 years in the past, between two people, in private, with no witnesses.

The charges, of course, had already been heard by

the members of the Senate Judiciary Committee. These men, most of them lawyers, had decided that, as presented, the charges were not substantial enough to weigh in the balance against Thomas' nomination.

The reason for their decision was so simple and so basic to American principles of equity and justice that it is hard to fathom that anyone should call their judgment into question, although that is precisely what happened. In the American justice system there is probably no principle so sanctified as a defendant's right not to be convicted on the basis of charges made by a faceless accuser, the presumption of innocence until proven guilty. The right to cross-examine one's accuser and challenge his or her credibility is one of the cornerstones of a free society.

The Senate Judiciary Committee members dismissed the claims of Anita Hill because she insisted on making her accusations anonymously; her affidavit was an attempt to destroy Clarence Thomas' career from the shadows. It was not because they were men that the committee members refused to admit Hill's unsubstantiated allegations as evidence, but because they were Americans, mindful of the rights that provide the foundations of the nation's democratic order.

And it is there that these matters would have rested, except for the fact that someone with access to the committee's confidential files leaked Hill's accusatory affidavit to NPR reporter Nina Totenberg. This individual did so in violation of Senatorial rules, common ethics, and possibly federal law.

At the moment of the leak, reporter Totenberg had been presented with not one, but two stories. Both were sensational. Both had the potential to threaten the careers of national figures. But each had dramatically different political ramifications.

CHOOSING A STORY

The story not chosen was the leak itself. This breach of confidentiality was possibly not an isolated act but the culmination of a coordinated campaign to "Bork" the Thomas nomination—a verb coined to commemorate the divisive politics that have come to dominate the nomination process. The leaker had violated a cardinal rule of the Senate, and possibly federal law as well, in order to destroy a distinguished American's career. Was this a group effort? Was a Senator involved? Nina Totenberg now had the key which, if she had chosen to turn it, would have broken a national scandal. Perhaps the repercussions of such a scandal would have led to the reform of a nominating process, which all parties seem to agree is needed. But in exposing this scandal, she would also have ensured the confirmation of Clarence Thomas.

Perhaps that is why she chose the second reportorial path, which made her, willy-nilly, an accomplice to the unethical machinations of the anonymous party that sought to bring Clarence Thomas down.

After receiving the confidential information contained in the affidavit, Totenberg made a hasty effort to substantiate the accusations. She failed in this, just as the committee would fail in the supplemental hearing her revelations would make necessary. But she did succeed in acquiring the elements that would make it impossible for the committee to stick to its original position—a position that had protected both the accused and the accuser from the public circus about to ensue. Totenberg managed to locate a "corroborating witness," Judge Susan Hoerchner, in whom Hill had confided about her alleged sexual abuse without being specific as to detail or to the name of the party she claimed had abused her.

How did Totenberg locate Judge Hoerchner? Perhaps through James Brudney, the Metzenbaum staffer who directed Anita Hill's performance and whose law school roommate was Hoerchner's brother. In other words, perhaps by making herself even more complicit in the network that was conspiring to "Bork" the nomination. We don't know the answer, because Totenberg has chosen to maintain the confidentiality of *her* sources, while violating everyone else's.

In any case, Hoerchner's testimony was inconclusive. In order to "make" the second story, therefore, Totenberg had to flush Hill from her hiding place, where she had remained throughout the three months of the hearings now concluded, and thus to force her and Clarence Thomas to enter a debasing spectacle of accusation and counter- accusation about intimate manners without any possibility of resolution. And all before a nationwide television audience.

FORCING HILL TO TALK

Totenberg was able to accomplish this, where the male members of the Judiciary Committee had failed, because she did not feel bound by those ethical scruples that had prevented them from compelling Anita Hill to go public against her wishes. (It is one of the ironies of this whole affair that these much-abused males had more respect for the sensibilities and expressed concerns of Anita Hill than the female NPR reporter who eventually threw her to the lions.) All Totenberg had to do to accomplish this end was to threaten to divulge the contents of the confidential affidavit that Anita Hill had made and that some unscrupulous Senator or Senate staffer had placed in unauthorized hands. Which is precisely what she did.

Once Hill was confronted by Totenberg's threat to reveal the affidavit to the public, she consented to an interview. This allowed Totenberg to go public with the interview rather than the document itself, an act which might expose her to legal prosecution. With the interview in hand, Totenberg went on National Public Radio with her report:

> [Hill] told the Senate Judiciary Committee and later the FBI that she'd been sexually harassed by Clarence Thomas when she worked as his personal assistant in the early 1980s....According to Hill's sworn affidavit, a copy of which was obtained by NPR, Thomas, "spoke about acts that he'd seen in pornographic films involving group sex or rape scenes. He talked about pornographic materials depicting individuals with large penises and breasts."...She said she told only one person about what was happening to her, a friend from law school. The friend, now a state judge in the west, corroborated Hill's story, in part, both in an interview with the FBI and with NPR. She said that Hill had told her at the time of the alleged harassment in general, though not in detail.

Totenberg's report was carried nationally. The revelation embarrassed the members of the Judiciary Committee, who were instantly accused of not taking Hill's accusations seriously because they were insensitive males. In fact, their only real crime was in being sensitive to the demands of a system of justice that insists on accusers coming forward and facing those whom their accusations would destroy. By blackmailing Hill into coming forward, Totenberg had put the Judiciary Committee members in an impossible position. To get themselves off the hook, they decided to hold a hearing on the charges.

A TEST OF PRINCIPLE

At this point, NPR faced its own test of principle as the following questions presented themselves: Was Nina Totenberg's action in leaking what amounted to a confidential personnel file ethical? Was Totenberg herself part of the "special interest" network opposed to the Thomas nomination? Should an inquiry be held? Should she be censured? And, finally, should Totenberg be replaced as NPR's reporter for the hearings on Anita Hill's charges?

This last question presented itself irrespective of the answers to the others. Totenberg had become an integral part of the Anita Hill story. It is a basic principle of journalism that when a reporter becomes a part of the story, her objectivity has been compromised, and therefore she should be removed from the responsibility of reporting it. NPR, which is apparently immune to considerations of its own partisanship, as well as to the professional standards that govern other members of the media, chose to keep Nina Totenberg on the job, assigning her to anchor the Hill-Thomas hearing. These issues were raised with CPB, PBS, and NPR officials in a letter from COMINT when the hearings were concluded:

☛ We are concerned about the role NPR reporter Totenberg apparently played in this process and at the fact that her superiors have remained silent about her breach of professional ethics in publicizing [the] confidential material [contained in Anita Hill's affidavit] to the American public. We are appalled that even after the disclosure, NPR officials continued to assign Ms. Totenberg the responsibility of being the principal reporter and commentator for both NPR and the Public Broadcasting

Ser-vice in respect to the Senate hearings made necessary by this leak.

☛ On Saturday, Sept. 12, 1992, Ms. Totenberg conducted a television and radio interview with Sen. John Danforth, in which the Senator decried the unprecedented leaking of Anita Hill's accusations to the public as "despicable and disgraceful" and "probably illegal." As soon as the interview was over and the Senator was safely off camera and unable to reply, Ms. Totenberg told millions of public radio and television listeners across the country that "the history books are full of important things that have happened as the result of news leaks," thus justifying her unconscionable act. She went on to cite this leaking of a file on the character of Clarence Thomas to "the leaking of the Pentagon Papers" during the Vietnam War, as an example of a public service made possible by such methods. Thus is character assassination by the press made into a virtue by the perpetrator.

☛ This abuse of the publicly funded broadcasting system for partisan purposes is neither unique nor new. Ms. Totenberg, you will recall, was instrumental in leaking rumors about the personal life of conservative Judge Douglas Ginsburg that caused him to withdraw his own name from nomination to the United States Supreme Court. Totenberg, as was later revealed, had purveyed the re-criminations of an embittered ex-girlfriend who told her that Ginsburg had smoked marijuana during his college days, 15 years earlier. Public broadcasting officials apparently regarded this dishonorable performance as reason to put Ms. Totenberg in charge of the Thomas hearings for their networks.

We ask you to conduct an inquiry into the behavior of Ms. Totenberg during the hearings process. We ask you, further, to conduct an inquiry into the conduct of the NPR, PBS and WETA executives who put Ms. Totenberg in charge of reporting the supplemental Senate Judiciary hearings to attempt to undo the damage that her leak caused. We ask you to withhold CPB funds from NPR, WETA, and PBS until this inquiry is completed and steps are taken to ensure that NPR, WETA, and PBS reporting will conform to the requirements of the Public Broadcasting Act of 1967.

NPR STONEWALL

NPR's response came from NPR president Douglas J. Bennet. There was not going to be an investigation of possible partisan politics in NPR reporting, nor was there going to be an apology for any breach of journalistic ethics in having a story reported by a person involved in the story in question:

> November 4, 1991
> NPR News and PBS agreed to co-anchor the confirmation hearings jointly as a public broadcasting experiment. PBS chose Paul Duke for its co-anchor. NPR chose Nina Totenberg as its co-anchor, because she is one of the most knowledgeable reporters in Washington in matters involving the Supreme Court. When the Senate made the decision to reopen the hearings, NPR and PBS agreed that this was a continuation of the previous hearings, and therefore we decided to continue with the same anchors.

This evasive non-sequitur was followed by the customary self-pat-on-the-back that has become the signature of public-broadcasting officials:

> NPR's editorial process has been thorough, responsible, and in accordance with the highest standards of journalism. Correspondent Nina Totenberg has provided excellent work as both a reporter and live-events anchor on this story, as on many others. We are proud of her work and the overall coverage of this matter by NPR news.
> Sincerely,
> Douglas J. Bennet

In other words, NPR's president—a former bureaucrat in the Carter administration (and now a potential appointee in the Clinton administration)—regards his reporters as possibly above the law and certainly beyond the reach of the standards governing other professional journalists.

—David Horowitz

NINA TOTENBERG, PARTISAN JOURNALIST

For all of their prodding and preening, most national media reporters never escape obscurity except for a handful of star anchors and an even smaller group that's broken a Big Story that rocks the nation. National Public Radio veteran legal reporter Nina Totenberg first tasted stardom in destroying the Supreme Court nomination of Judge Douglas Ginsburg. But that demolition paled in comparison to Totenberg's outing of Anita Hill, who was forced to come forward with a 10-year-old story about alleged sexual harassment at the hands of yet another Supreme Court nominee, Clarence Thomas.

Few question Totenberg's ability to report the nuances of a court decision or her knack for ingratiating herself with important potential sources. But many have questioned her professionalism and adherence to journalistic ethics in the Ginsburg and Thomas nominations. Terry Eastland, a legal journalist and currently editor of the *Forbes Media Critic*, explained: "My sense is obviously, she has done some good reporting on legal issues, but Totenberg has become the person for those on the left to approach to post their complaints or gossip or negative ideas about Republican or conservative nominees. NPR's news division has become a hotline for the political left."

As detailed in Larry Sabato's book, *Feeding Frenzy*, Totenberg picked up the Ginsburg marijuana story from a liberal interest group that had been provided with the information by a disgruntled ex-girlfriend of the nominee. Totenberg then culled confirmation of the story from two of Ginsburg's Harvard colleagues and attributed the scoop to them instead of the liberals. This kind of covering of her ideological tracks is a Totenberg trademark.

In the January 1992 *Vanity Fair*, Ann Louise Bardach reported that Totenberg had also played fast and loose with journalistic rules with a reporter from the *Legal*

Times. Aaron Freiwald told Bardach that he had a juicy story on nominee Douglas Ginsburg's "resume enhancement" for Monday's editions and struck a deal with Totenberg that she could use it in exchange for an attribution to promote sales of *Legal Times.* An hour later, she was on the air presenting the story with no attribution for Freiwald. Totenberg said she already had the story before that, but she admitted to "one or two language overlaps."

The Anita Hill leak investigation conducted by special counsel Peter Fleming together with the additional investigative reporting of David Brock's recent best seller, *The Real Anita Hill,* reveal how Totenberg's coverage of the Hill-Thomas hearings also raises ethical questions and how that coverage depended heavily on liberal interest groups. Hill said she would not talk to Totenberg until she had received a copy of her affidavit to the Senate Judiciary Committee. Brock reports on how Totenberg complained to Ricki Seidman, a Ted Kennedy aide, that she could not secure Hill's affidavit. Seidman called James Brudney, an aide to Sen. Howard Metzenbaum, and Totenberg received a copy by fax. After interviewing Hill, Totenberg called Seidman, again, and Judith Lichtman of the Women's Legal Defense Fund, who had been dying to go to Totenberg with Hill's identity for weeks.

Once Totenberg broke the story, she had a special interest in maintaining that Hill's story was credible. After all, if Hill was found to be lying, then Totenberg's scoop would look more like blatant character assassination than a blow against sexual harassers on the Supreme Court. But PBS and NPR put her back on the air to analyze the second set of Thomas hearings, which were to address precisely the issue of Hill's veracity, just as Totenberg had covered the first set of hearing and as if she was not herself involved in the story and as though she were a beacon of impartiality. She was not.

Totenberg repeatedly used breaks in the hearings to defend herself and her liberal sources. On four different occasions, she praised the positive role of leaks. "The history books are full of important and historic events that were the result of newsleaks...[Watergate] would have just been a third-rate robbery if there hadn't been a lot of leaks disclosing what it had all been about. I don't mean to be defensive about this, but news leaks aren't always bad."

On eight occasions, Totenberg emphasized the credibility of Hill's "corroborating" witnesses who, except for Judge Susan Hoerchner, barely knew Hill at all (a point that Totenberg failed to make) and could not name Thomas as the harasser. When the pro-Hill panel was done and before panels of Thomas' defenders appeared, Totenberg declared: "I think this was a tough day for the Clarence Thomas side."

To help tilt the scales further, she and NPR reporter Mara Liasson continuously giggled while describing the testimony of Thomas supporter John Doggett. (No such giggles had been heard when Anita Hill produced a "boyfriend" with whom she had a telephone relationship as a character witness.) At the end of the Sunday hearings, after 11 character witnesses were called for Thomas, many of whom were female and worked with him and Hill on a daily basis, Totenberg declared: "By and large, I'd say the big news of the day was the very first panel of the day, those who were corroborative witnesses for Anita Hill."

As the hearings ended and the Senate voted, Totenberg wondered three times if Justice Thomas could be fair to the liberal interest groups that opposed him (and helped her to get the Hill scoop).

Totenberg also drew attention to herself by claiming to *Washington Post* reporter Howard Kurtz that she quit the now-defunct *National Observer* in the '70s because she had been subjected to sexual harassment. *Wall Street Journal* Washington bureau chief Al Hunt, an *Observer* colleague, cried foul, writing that Totenberg was fired from the newspaper for plagiarizing a *Washington Post* article in 1972. In a very Clintonian dodge, Totenberg responded by declaring "What I did or didn't do almost 20 years ago isn't the issue."

After the hearings, Totenberg continued to promote Hill's credibility. Totenberg told *Vanity Fair* that she "checked Anita Hill's credentials up the wazoo and everybody said she was a saint, that her integrity was the highest, that she was a Bork supporter, a conservative, and an Evangelical." But Brock, whose book documents Hill's long-standing liberal commitments, noted that in a question-and-answer period after a speech at Stanford University a few weeks later, Totenberg answered a question as to whether Hill would be nominated to the Supreme Court: "If you want someone even remotely of her political/judicial persuasion, you're going to have to elect a Democratic President."

When special counsel Peter Fleming began to investigate the question of who leaked the Hill affidavit in violation of Senate rules, Totenberg defended herself à la Oliver North and shredded all the incriminating documents. Totenberg also refused to take note of Anita Hill's post-hearings declarations to *Essence* magazine that she opposed Robert Bork and Ronald Reagan. When David Brock's first *American Spectator* exposé of Hill appeared, Totenberg told interviewer David Tosatti: "I had heard a good deal of that and did not consider it proven...My standards for what goes on the air are high, and I have not found anything to date sufficient to put on." If Totenberg had to have an allegation "proven" before she put it on the air, she would never have broken the Hill story. Totenberg has continued to ignore Brock's massive case against her own version of Anita Hill to this day.

Totenberg's partisan pattern of reporting has continued. During the 1992 House Bank scandal, Totenberg reported that Special Counsel Malcolm Wilkey's investigation invaded the privacy of House members. (The right to privacy isn't exactly Totenberg's strong suit, at least not where conservatives are concerned.) At Lani Guinier's nomination for associate attorney general for civil rights, the *Washington Post* reported that Totenberg hugged Guinier. On NPR's *All Things Considered* on June 4, 1993, Totenberg openly complained that the White House would not let her help Guinier explain her views, which would have aided her confirmation: "I personally offered an on-the-record interview with her so that she could explain her views in these articles, because I have known her for some time, and I think she would have trusted me not to do a hatchet job on this. They were not interested in doing this. They were interested in burying her."

Nina Totenberg is a partisan journalist, good at what she does, but in dire need of balance.

—*Tim Graham*

CAMERA vs. NPR

L ast year public television was criticized for anti-Israel bias by the Boston-based Committee for Accuracy in Middle East Reporting in America (CAMERA). This year CAMERA issued a report extending its critique to National Public Radio. The report, based on a content analysis of NPR broadcasts for a six-month period in 1991, was authored by CAMERA president Andrea Levin. It has been answered by NPR's managing editor John Dinges.

COMINT decided to look into the dispute between CAMERA and NPR. We began with a review of Levin's report and the correspondence between Levin and Dinges and other public-broadcasting officials. We also interviewed the principals in the dispute at length and include their commentary on the written record as an afterword. We conclude our report with some reflections on its significance for the new "Open to the Public" policy of CPB and the larger question of establishing standards of balance and fairness throughout the public-broadcasting system.

CAMERA's COMPLAINT

On Oct. 30, 1992, CAMERA president Andrea Levin complained in a letter to Corporation for Public Broadcasting Chairman Sheila Tate that National Public Radio is "relentlessly hostile to Israel and highly distorted in its Middle East coverage generally."

In her letter, Levin says CAMERA had written to NPR president Douglas Bennet a year earlier, in August 1991, but Bennet failed to respond. Another complaint was filed with NPR vice president for news and public affairs Bill Buzenberg in October, 1991. According to Levin, Buzenberg also did not answer. Levin says she only received a reply in mid-December, 1991, and not from Bennet or Buzenberg but from a subordinate, NPR managing editor John Dinges. Dinges made NPR files available to CAMERA researchers. According to Levin, Dinges said NPR would conduct its own study of Middle East coverage. Levin said CAMERA then designed its new study to overlap the same time period as the proposed NPR study. Levin complains that the promised NPR study was never conducted.

CAMERA representatives met with NPR officials to present their complaints on June 1, 1992, but Levin says that she was disappointed in the meeting. When CAMERA "presented detailed evidence drawn from NPR's own archives, officials at the meeting dismissed the data. Further, and most importantly, we regret to say, the meeting yielded no sign whatever of more balanced and accurate reporting in subsequent months." Levin concluded her letter to Tate by calling on CPB to take her data seriously and protect the American public "against such abuses of power under the laws that require balance and objectivity in programming" alleged against NPR.

CPB responded a little over a month later. Levin received a letter signed by Richard Carlson soliciting comments on the new "Open to the Public" campaign. Although the letter did not go into the particulars of her complaint, Levin told COMINT she was encouraged by Carlson's reply and was preparing a list of suggestions to improve the fairness of NPR coverage. She was hopeful that CPB would take action to correct past mistakes.

NPR'S RESPONSE

NPR managing editor John Dinges has a different view of these exchanges. He thinks Levin's charges are unfounded He feels that NPR's coverage of the Middle East has been fair and balanced. He believes NPR has been cooperative with CAMERA and responded fairly to Levin's complaints.

In his letter of November 19, 1991, Dinges wrote to Levin that "partisans on all sides of the controversy criticize us. Many of the letters are the mirror image of your complaints, except they come from people espousing the various Arab and Israeli points of view that you consider are overrepresented on our programs." He said those charges, like CAMERA's complaints, "do not stand up when NPR's programming is measured according to the highest standards of professional journalism." He said that NPR could not possibly be biased against Israel because their own guidelines "specifically rule out advocating a particular point of view."

Dinges said he would look into Levin's charges himself. "I have begun to compile a coverage review of NPR stories and interviews concerning Israel for the period Aug. 8 to Nov. 8, 1991. I believe that study will back up the fairness and balance we have consciously ensured in our day to day coverage." Dinges concluded, "I hope I will be able to explore with you the balance that is indeed present in our overall treatment of an issue. If there are deficiencies, we will discuss that, too, and we will correct them."

As a result of Dinge's intervention, CAMERA researchers were permitted to go through the NPR transcripts. The first publication of a critical article in the Spring 1992 *CAMERA Media Report* brought an immediate reply. Dinges complained that Levin was being unfair to NPR. In a letter dated May 16, 1992, Dinges wrote: "In the interest of fair play, I hope you will consider supplying your readers, many of whom are listeners to NPR, with our response to your charges."

Dinges argued that CAMERA's criticisms were "based not on journalistic criteria for fairness, but on the organization's desire to ensure favorable coverage for its issue." Dinges complained he had not been informed of the CAMERA analysis before publication and charged "there has been no word of any analysis to back up your charges against NPR with something approaching objective evidence." He objected to the CAMERA newsletter's charge that "NPR presents an overwhelming array of left-wing, sometimes even lunatic-left speakers and virtually excludes other views." Dinges also rejected the charge that "we at NPR 'suppress' Israeli centrist opinion." He said "it is inconceivable to me that any objective observer looking at our coverage would find the presence of leftist voices on Israel to be 'overwhelming' [as Levin had charged]."

Dinges objected to the characterization of NPR's choice of interview subjects as "leftist and anti-Israel." He strongly defended Seymour Hersh, author of a book claiming the Mossad betrayed vital American military secrets to the Arabs. "How Hersh could be described as a leftist is beyond me. He is one of the most highly regarded investigative reporters in American journalism." Dinges found complaints about other NPR interviewees, whom CAMERA complained were biased, equally misguided. "Leslie and Andrew Cockburn were interviewed a year ago in connection with their book on U.S.-Israeli relations on *Fresh Air*, a program that interviews scores of authors. Christopher Hitchens has not been interviewed at all on NPR about Israel, according to a check of all programs of the past two years."

Dinges said that NPR had not suppressed the Israeli center. He replied to Levin, "If there is any part of the political spectrum that receives full attention on our air, it is the center...CAMERA, however, seems to exclude from the category 'center' anyone with anything critical to say about Israel."

Dinges remarked that CAMERA was wrong to claim that pro-Arab and anti-Israeli experts dominate NPR programming. "During the period in question, we interviewed Palestinians about the peace talks on some days, and we interviewed Israeli spokespersons on other days." He challenged Levin, "If you or anyone else can demonstrate, on the basis of concrete examples, that we have not achieved this kind of balance over a period of coverage...then we will take steps to remedy it."

Dinges concluded by attributing damaging agendas to Levin and her organization:

> CAMERA seems intent on using unsubstantiated charges to create a campaign among NPR's Jewish listeners to cut off funding to NPR's member stations if NPR does not conform to CAMERA's concept of how Israel should be portrayed. I should note that since CAMERA began this campaign to cut off NPR funding, one of your own board members, Rev. Robert Drinan, a former congressman and staunch defender of Israel, has resigned from the CAMERA board. We will respond to CAMERA's activities by setting the record straight and appealing to our listeners to judge us by what we actually put on the air, not by CAMERA's inaccurate and often vicious portrayal of us.

CAMERA'S CONTENT ANALYSIS

The Fall 1992 CAMERA Media Report was put together in response to Dinges' challenge. The issue was headlined "Focus on NPR" and featured the results of a six-month study of NPR's Middle East coverage from July 1, 1991, through Dec.

31, 1991. Levin says these dates were chosen to bracket the period August 8 to Nov. 8 selected by Dinges in his November 19, 1991, letter. Researchers used the NPR index to find 278 references to the Arab-Israeli conflict and then selected a subset of stories indexed by the keyword "peace." These were indexed by topic. A sample of 39 stories from *Morning Edition* and *Weekend Edition* was examined in greater detail, including full identification of speakers and interview subjects.

CAMERA says that its 39-story study shows "evidence of the tilt in NPR coverage." Forty-three Arab speakers were interviewed and, of those, 36 were Palestinian. By contrast, only 22 Israelis appeared in the sample. CAMERA suggested that by focusing on Palestinian moderates and excluding Israeli centrists, a slanted picture of the conflict was created. No representatives of rejectionist PLO "hardline" factions or the Muslim fundamentalist Hamas organization were interviewed among the Arab subjects. By contrast, 10 of the 22 Israelis were non-government speakers. Seven of these were from the far-right and three from the far-left. No centrist Israeli Labor Party spokesmen were interviewed. No speaker articulated centrist "concepts of territorial compromise or security concerns." The study found that five out of seven of the extended interviews were with Arab spokesmen, three of these with Hanan Ashrawi, the leader of the Palestinian delegation at the peace talks. The study contrasts the soft questions provided to Ashrawi with the challenging remarks presented to the two Israelis.

The major finding of the study is that NPR did not cover issues vital to a balanced understanding of the conflict: the military threat to Israel by the Arab states, the nature of Israel's security concerns, the Arab refusal to recognize Israel's legitimacy and right to exist, and the stated aims of Palestinian groups such as Hamas "to destroy Israel." The study also accused NPR of ignoring major stories of Arab anti-Semitism, Arab treatment of minorities, the Syrian occupation of Lebanon, and the killing of Palestinians by other Palestinians.

CAMERA devoted an entire section of its report to analysis of the reporting of NPR correspondent Linda Gradstein, who was accused of pushing a "political agenda" by failing to report Israeli security concerns, falsely claiming that "Israeli soldiers are killing Palestinian men in increasing numbers," when the number of deaths had declined from 270 in 1989 to 74 in 1992, and general misrepresentation of the facts. For example, Gradstein was accused of mistranslating the Palestinian war chant "With fire we will liberate Palestine" as "We will never forget you" in order to present a more innocuous picture of the Palestinian agenda. From citations such as these, CAMERA concluded NPR "ignores Israeli concerns and purveys Arab agendas."

NPR REJECTS CAMERA's CONCLUSIONS

On Nov. 24, 1992, Dinges wrote to Levin to complain that "your charges are unfounded and based on an incomplete and one-sided analysis of our coverage. Your study appears to have been designed not for objectivity, but to confirm your already strongly held opinions." According to Dinges, the entire premise of CAMERA's study was erroneous:

> [Your reports] say almost nothing about what we actually reported, focusing instead on a list of stories you contend we should have covered but did not...It has nothing to do with an objective or fair analysis of the stories we in fact reported. Inexplicably you almost totally ignore the scores of stories we aired about Israel and other Middle Eastern countries...These constituted the heart of NPR's coverage.

Dinges said that Levin's study omitted *All Things Considered*, and "it defies reason to formulate such sweeping charges about NPR's coverage of any issue when you have omitted half our daily news product." Dinges also claimed that by omitting NPR's regularly scheduled newscasts, CAMERA ignored "a major part of NPR's total news product."

Conceding that he was "troubled by your assertion that NPR interviewed almost twice as many Arabs as Israelis in its coverage," Dinges said he had examined every broadcast of NPR's *All Things Considered, Morning Edition*, and *Weekend Edition* from Oct. 16 to Nov. 18, 1991, "which was one month of the period you studied."

He said his study found that NPR had interviewed 31 Israeli officials and experts, 32 Arabs, and 30 third-party analysts. Of the Israelis, Dinges claimed half were government officials and half were "clearly in the spectrum of mainstream, centrist opinion in Israel." Dinges observed that CAMERA had claimed that NPR had "aired not a single report" during the study period about Hamas but said that he had found four reports in the same period.

Dinges made one concession to CAMERA. "It is true," he wrote, "that with notable exceptions such as the conflict with Iraq, NPR gives relatively more coverage to Israel and the Arab-Israeli conflict than to non-Israel related events in Arab countries." But Dinges felt this was a valid journalistic judgment, reflecting "the news interest in the region for US listeners, an assessment shared by virtually all major news organizations in the United States."

Dinges also objected to the criticism of Gradstein, calling it an *ad hominem* attack. "We categorically reject your charge that she has in any of her reporting injected a political agenda....It is the duty of a journalist to prevent any personal views from coloring his or her reporting. Gradstein has been scrupulous in that regard, as evidenced by an objective reading of her reports." He charged that CAMERA'S claims were "intended to intimidate her and NPR into skewing our coverage of the Middle East to reflect CAMERA's own political agenda. That we will not do."

Dinges reiterated his conviction that "any reasonably objective scrutiny of NPR's coverage of the Middle East will conclude that our treatment of Israel has been fair, balanced, and devoid of any of the malicious or political intent CAMERA ascribes to it." He again pointed out Father Drinan's resignation from the CAMERA board, "after learning of the unfounded attacks on NPR."

CAMERA RESPONDS TO NPR

Levin characterized Dinges' defense of NPR coverage as a "total evasion of CAMERA's principal criticisms" and viewed it as part of "the network's continuing attempt to stonewall substantive criticism of its coverage of Israel and the Middle East."

Levin rejected Dinges' claim that her charges were "unfounded," "one-sided," or "a collection of characterizations and positions that [CAMERA] would have liked our reporting to support." She chastised Dinges for claiming that a demand for full and balanced coverage was "the advocacy of what it terms a position." She noted that CAMERA advocates "the free flow of complete information to the American public, not 'support' for a position." Levin added that Dinges, in effect, concedes her charge in his reply: "Most telling is NPR's inability to refute CAMERA's damning discovery that in six months of intensive coverage of Israel, for which 278 Middle East stories are indexed in NPR's own archives, not one addressed the military threat to Israel....NPR has never denied these gaping omissions in coverage."

Levin also responded to Dinges' claim that NPR coverage had equal numbers of Israeli and Arab representatives. She noted that Dinges had never undertaken the study of programming from August 8 to November 8 promised in his letter of November 19, 1991. Levin pointed out that Dinges had selected one month of coverage only after an outcry from CAMERA. Meanwhile, CAMERA had taken a look at broadcasts during the selected period from October 16 though November 18 and had come to different conclusions.

CAMERA counted not 93 speakers, as NPR maintained, but 114. Of those, 67 were Arabs and 47 were Israelis. She argued that this greater statistical imbalance "showed an unmistakable skewing in the direction of *ad hominem* representation of Arab views." Levin noted the sample "also replicates the original CAMERA study in that no representative of the mainstream Labor party is among the non-government speakers." She also pointed out that there was not a single speaker from Hamas or any of the radical PLO groups. This gave a false impression of Palestinian views as being more moderate than they were in reality.

Levin also rejected Dinges claim that there were four stories on Hamas. She noted that CAMERA's criticism centered on NPR's failure to report Hamas' goal of destroying Israel. CAMERA found five, not four, references to Hamas. Of those, CAMERA found all but one to be passing allusions. The one story that did talk about Hamas at all, CAMERA argued, did not describe the goals of the organization: namely, the destruction of Israel and annihilation of the Jews.

Regarding NPR's editorial decision to downplay coverage of Arab countries, Levin called Dinges' defense of the policy a "dereliction of responsibility to listeners...Whole nations, conflicts and calamities go unreported, creating a dangerously misshapen version of Middle East reality." In her answer to Dinges' charge that her attack on Linda Gradstein was *ad hominem*, Levin said that the criticism was justified. "Her reports are quoted verbatim and analyzed, and her publicly stated political views are shown to permeate her reporting." Levin contrasts Gradstein's lengthy coverage of a Popular Front for the Liberation of Palestine funeral—with Gradstein's mistranslation of "With fire and blood we will redeem Anton" to the less threatening "Anton, Anton, you were murdered. We promise to continue your struggle"—to Gradstein's four-sentence account of the stabbing murder of Israeli teenager Helen Rapp with "three of them critical of Israelis angered by the killing."

Dinges reply to these charges is: "I don't speak Arabic, so I can't really judge, but I don't believe you can construe from that evidence of a campaign. Certainly, if it was a mistranslation, it was a mistake."

Regarding the resignation of Father Drinan, Levin asserts he was pressured to resign by Dinges himself in an attempt to discredit CAMERA instead of responding to its criticism. Since Dinges raised the issue of board resignations, Levin refers to the case of former CBS News president Richard Salant's, who quit the NPR board because the radio network accepted targeted foundation and corporate grants for news coverage. She quotes Salant as saying: "It's a bad idea because news judgments should be made...strictly on the basis of news value, and not whether you get money to cover some things but not others."

Finally, in response to Dinges' request that Levin publish his replies in CAMERA's newsletter, Levin said she would be willing to publish Dinges when CAMERA obtained

a similar opportunity to address its concerns to NPR's constituents, the 14.5 million weekly listeners to whom the network's reporters have regularly broadcast a seriously skewed version of the Middle East. NPR has yet to respond to this proposal. As it has from the outset, the net-work admits to no flaw whatever in its coverage, is indignant at public criticism, and thinks it is entitled to argue its case to CAMERA members while

refusing to grant CAMERA an equal chance
to make its case to NPR listeners.

COMMENTS ON THE DEBATE

To date, the Corporation for Public Broadcasting has not
made any decisions in the case of *CAMERA vs. NPR*. CPB's
vice president for corporate information, Phil Smith, told
COMINT: "I believe we have responded to CAMERA." Andrea Levin said she thinks the CPB response—which is a description of the "Open to the Public" campaign and request
for input—"is a tremendous step forward." Levin hopes to
pursue her claim against NPR through the balance process
CPB establishes.

Pending the official investigation by CPB's new balance department, COMINT conducted independent interviews with Andrea Levin, John Dinges, Georgetown University professor Father Drinan, and Harvard Law School professor Alan Dershowitz.

Dinges told COMINT that Levin "has accused us of
terrible things, propaganda campaigns, systematically excluding points of view." He said, contrary to CAMERA's
charges, NPR is very sensitive to complaints: "We even put
corrections on the air. It's one thing to point out mistakes.
It's another thing to claim we have some kind of axe to
grind. We reject that 100 percent."

Dinges said that CAMERA's charges were totally
spurious and without foundation and that "any objective
observer, who has any credentials in journalism and some
credibility within the profession," would agree with NPR. He
argued that criticism of NPR was criticism of the entire
American journalistic community.

"We are very highly respected within the American
journalistic community," Dinges said. "The system of American journalism is self-policing within the profession. We
are not subject to the dictates of government or special interest groups."

"The criticisms of our coverage have come from one
interest group," he said, adding, "we have received some
criticism from Arab groups, but not as strong." Dinges asked
that NPR should be judged by the same standards by
which one judges the *New York Times* or the *Washington
Post*. "I don't think they have made a case that has any le-

gitimacy according to the standards of American journalism," he said. "NPR's system is no different from any other news organization."

When asked about Andrea Levin's charge that Richard Salant had resigned from the NPR board because he thought that NPR's system of underwriting for content was unethical—and unlike that of any newspaper or commercial news service, where it might be considered "payola" or "plugola"—Dinges replied: "I don't believe that anything Richard Salant said had anything to do with the Middle East. We have never received a grant that has anything to do with Middle East coverage."

However, Andrea Levin told COMINT that one could not be certain that money from the Ford Foundation and the German Marshall Fund for NPR's international coverage was not paying for coverage from the Middle East. "How do we know where the money comes from?" she said. "We know Germany played a role in arming Iraq and elsewhere. The Germans built poison gas factories in Libya. How can we be sure?" The Ford Foundation has international programs active in the Middle East. Levin noted that other NPR funders, such as the MacArthur Foundation, have exhibited partisan tendencies on this issue.

Dinges defended NPR's use of earmarked funds against Levin's criticism. "The big grants for foreign coverage are less tied to specific topics than grants for other coverage," he told COMINT. "We don't have a grant that even mentions the Middle East." However, he said, NPR does have "a 100-page International Coverage Report provided to some of the funders, which gives coverage plans and projections for the foreign desk for the whole year." When asked for a copy of the annual plan, Dinges demurred. "I don't know whether the development office makes that available except to funders," he said. Dinges conceded that criticism of targeted funding "should be part of the entire public broadcasting debate" but that it was not relevant to NPR's Middle East coverage. "She [Levin] just answered the Drinan resignation by bringing up Salant," he said.

Regarding the controversy over NPR's coverage of Hamas, Dinges faxed COMINT a transcript of an October 29, 1991, segment of *All Things Considered* hosted by Robert Siegel. Dinges said of CAMERA, "For them [CAMERA] to say NPR didn't do any stories on Hamas, and we sent them this story, which is dedicated entirely to a split in the Palestinian camp, it's wrong. A reporter would never get away with that."

Levin told COMINT that she stands by the charge made in CAMERA's publication, that NPR has never done a report on "Hamas, its goals, and its potential impact on the achievement of peace."

Indeed, the episode faxed to COMINT by Dinges did discuss Hamas but only in the context of its fight with Yasir Arafat's Al Fatah (described in the report as peace-seekers) over the Madrid peace talks. Just as CAMERA claims, the NPR report did not mention that Hamas called for the destruction of Israel or that Hamas distributes the notorious anti-Semitic tract, *The Protocols of the Elders of Zion*. NPR did not note, for example, the claims in Hamas' charter that "the Zionist invasion" is behind "the Freemasons, the Rotary and Lion's Clubs, and other sabotage groups."

Instead of being about Hamas' plans for Israel and the Jews, the NPR report Dinges supplied was about an internal fight among Palestinian groups over whether to negotiate at all. It contained only Palestinian criticism of Hamas for challenging PLO leadership in Gaza and threatening PLO supporters. It concluded with Siegel editorializing about the PLO in what seemed a testimony to their moderation and benevolence: "They've already accepted a two-state solution that some Palestinians find insufficient, and now they've accepted an invitation that many find demeaning. If they fail to deliver anything from Madrid to the denizens of Gaza's sordid refugee camps, there is another Palestinian movement that's prepared to seize the day." Siegel did not quote a single Israeli in his account.

Dinges supplied COMINT with an additional breakdown of NPR interview data from Oct. 16 to Nov. 18, 1991, to refute CAMERA's analysis. It had a new total of 111 Israel-related interviews. Of these Dinges found 31 Israeli officials and experts, 35 Arab officials and experts, 53 third-party analysts, 10 Israeli citizens, 8 Arabs or Palestinians, and 5 others. He said CAMERA had "no basis for dividing up the 'third parties' among Israelis and Arabs." Levin stands by her numbers but told COMINT she would be happy if an impartial third party were to investigate these matters. Dinges said NPR files were open for anyone to come in and check his numbers.

COMINT called Father Drinan, former liberal Massachusetts congressman and author of the pro-Israeli *Honor the Promise*, about his resignation from the CAMERA board. His account of his resignation differed from both Dinges' and Levin's. Dinges read COMINT a letter to NPR in which Drinan reportedly said: "I am afraid this organization [CAMERA] has an agenda which is one-sided and unrelenting. Please feel free to use my resignation in any way you see fit."

Although Drinan supports NPR, he told COMINT the dispute was not the only cause of his departure from CAMERA. He said he had resigned after receiving a letter from a rabbi in South Carolina saying the group was one he should not be associated with. Drinan says of his letter of resignation from the CAMERA board: "I don't think I gave reasons." He notes there were some other board members whom he found "odd" and says he found Levin "a broken record." Drinan says he had joined CAMERA because "who could be opposed to the objective?" However, he felt CAMERA "made some reckless charges...they harassed the *Boston Globe* a lot, and they just didn't communicate with me."

Drinan defends NPR against CAMERA's charges. "I'm a regular listener," he says, "and I don't honestly detect any bias. It's as objective as you can be about this tormenting question." He added that he would rather CAMERA had chosen other subjects to study. "You could say the Quakers are more biased against Israel than NPR. Or 'Peace Now.' Have they attacked those people?"

Levin maintains Drinan was pressured to leave her board. In her opinion he found it personally uncomfortable, as a prominent liberal spokesman, to be on the same masthead as well-known conservatives like M. Stanton Evans and associated with an organization engaged in criticism of cherished liberal institutions like NPR and the *Boston Globe*. Dinges still maintains it was the NPR issue that led to Drinan's departure.

Another well-known liberal, Harvard's Alan Dershowitz, differs from Drinan in his assessment of CAMERA. "An attempt to smear Levin just won't work. I think what she's doing is absolutely great," he says. "I'm allergic to anything that even smacks of censorship of any kind," he says, "and I'm a supporter of CAMERA, both morally and financially." Dershowitz thinks Levin "has had a real, positive impact."

He says: "The truth is that NPR has a bias against Israel. I listen to NPR and I hear it. There is a strong bias towards presenting the points of view of Palestinians and Israeli doves. The only time non-doves are interviewed is to mock them."

When asked what objective evidence he has, Dershowitz replies that his own personal experience is relevant to the issue. "NPR has never interviewed me about Israel. Why? Because I don't fit their model." (COMINT has received similar complaints from *New Republic* editor-in-chief Martin Peretz.) Dershowitz feels that if NPR were interested in presenting a balanced view of Israel, he would be a logical commentator. "Anyone who's read *Chutzpah!* would know it's not only a personal but a professional interest," he says. His professional career at Harvard and his own work on human rights have made him an expert on issues of civil liberties, but, he says, "I have not been called once on the story of these deportations [of 400 suspected Hamas supporters to Lebanon]. My perspective has never been presented to the listeners of NPR. I challenge NPR to give me an opportunity to present a non-ideological human rights perspective on Israel. I've been approached by other news organizations, but not by NPR."

When COMINT relayed Dershowitz's comments to Dinges, he said that NPR would consider putting Dershowitz on but that there were a great many experts on human rights, including many Harvard professors, who were clamoring to get on NPR.

LESSONS

The conflict between Levin and Dinges, CAMERA and NPR, with each side finding allies for their claims, has expanded into a public campaign with possibly damaging consequences for NPR funding, because there still is no institutional mechanism—a Standards and Practices department—at NPR or anywhere else in the system that can address these charges in a reasonable and timely fashion. At present CPB is the only part of the system that has announced any practical steps towards creating such a mechanism.

The case of CAMERA is instructive because it is so inevitable. A group interested in a particular area of news reporting conducts a study that finds NPR's reporting biased. NPR rejects the study on the grounds that it is the product of a special interest group. (Yet, what other kind of group would have the concern or the resources to bring such a claim?) Because unanswered criticism can nonetheless damage NPR's public image and access to funds, NPR conducts its own study. The complaining group, in this case CAMERA, rejects the NPR study because it is conducted by John Dinges, the very NPR official whose judgment has been called into question. It is a prescription for endless conflict and trouble.

Back and forth go the charges, but there is no third party to step in and take even a semi-dispassionate look, no referee to commission an independent study or to negotiate a compromise solution.

The CAMERA vs. NPR dispute underscores the importance of establishing Standards and Practices departments at every major entity in the public-broadcasting system, including stations. For the present, CPB has taken the lead in expressing a willingness to be an honest broker in determining the validity of balance charges. COMINT suggests that the case of CAMERA v. NPR be one of the first to receive the attention of CPB's new review process.

—Laurence Jarvik

NPR's TROOPERGATE

Veteran listeners of National Public Radio, who may have been curious as to whether its liberal news team would treat the new Clinton administration with the same journalistic aggressiveness as its Republican predecessors, received their answer with the first scandal to reach into the White House. When *The American Spectator* (soon followed by the *Los Angeles Times*) broke the story charging that Bill Clinton had used Arkansas state troopers to secure sexual liaisons with women, NPR treated the story differently than it had similar stories in the past. While NPR reporters exhibited a zeal worthy of the tabloid press in pursuing sleazy personal charges against Supreme Court nominees Douglas Ginsburg and Clarence Thomas, the standard suddenly became much higher when the accused turned out to be a Democrat.

On Dec. 21, 1993 NPR White House reporter Mara Liasson forwarded the allegations and then announced: "Now, all of these allegations are being flatly denied by the White House. Today, Mrs. Clinton was asked about them in a wire service interview. She called them 'trash for cash.' She said they were outrageous, terrible stories and attacks on her family." But the First Lady had not said the stories were untrue. Nor, two days later, in an interview with Liasson, did the president flatly deny the allegations as Liasson had claimed: "The president confined himself to lawyerly answers, refusing to specifically deny the troopers' allegations."

On Dec. 22, Liasson and NPR anchor Linda Wertheimer (wife of liberal lobbyist Fred Wertheimer) interviewed Clinton at the White House. Wertheimer practically prompted Clinton as to how to reply to the allegations: "Mr. President, we know these men have been aided and advised by people who are political enemies of yours, but we also know that these men worked very closely with you for a long period of time. Why do you think they're doing this?" Clinton answered that this was bringing pain to the family at Christmas, that he had not abused his office, and that "I just don't think I should say any more about it."

Wertheimer then asked: "You called some members of your old detail, not the people, I understand, who are involved in these stories, but other people, which of course opens up those kinds of questions. I wonder why you did that?" Clinton replied almost whiningly: "Well, we answered that too. I just don't want to—don't want to do anything to prolong this. I have answered those questions and I don't have anything else to say."

If the cover-up had been attempted by George Bush instead of Clinton, one can imagine Wertheimer smelling the discomfort and pushing further. Instead, Wertheimer moved quickly to unburden Clinton from his distress: "On this day, you're answering these kinds of questions and you're 58 percent in the polls, and there's been this kind of push-pull, up-down aspect to your first year, it seems to me, Mr. President. Is this just the nature of trying to govern in the '90s or do you think there's something about you that causes it to happen?" How many loopholes can you find in that question?

The interview continued with Wertheimer and Liasson asking a number of questions about defense and foreign policy, and then Wertheimer finished with a moment of baby-boomer fellow-feeling:

> You talked about your age, and your election, of course, was a personal milestone for many people of my age. A young president, after many years. I was up late last night, you know, working on this interview, three o'clock in the morning. And I—and the thought just popped into my head—"I wonder if President Clinton wakes up at three o'clock in the morning sometimes and thinks, 'I am the president?'"

During the congressional authorization debate when the issue of bias in public broadcasting was in the air, NPR officials were quick to assure the public that they would be just as tough on a Democratic administration as they had been on Republican ones. But there was no evidence of that in NPR's coverage of Troopergate. NPR journalists have been known to pursue a story doggedly to find out whether charges like these are true or not. But in the case of the trooper story, the news outlets of NPR were slaves to the normal news cycle: Once the First Lady and the president had addressed the story, its news value was over. Prolonging the story would be misbehavior.

Having never really been picked up by NPR reporters, the story moved on to the analysis phase. On December 26, NPR senior news analyst Daniel Schorr disdained the reports as well as the White House's reaction to them. He related his longtime aversion to sex stories:

> When the Senate Intelligence Committee, in a report in 1975, made a veiled reference to President Kennedy's affair with a mistress of Mafia boss Sam Giancana, I did not pursue

the lead. I guess that was a mistake. I generally stayed away from the Gary Hart womanizing story and when I once referred to it in a commentary on NPR, he called me to say that I was buying the conventional wisdom about that episode and that the conventional wisdom was wrong. And I didn't argue with him.

Schorr continued:

> Now, here are the Clintons appearing in Christmas-tide magazine photos as a model, happy family on top of the world. But against the background drumbeat of unseasonable and unpalatable allegations about their private lives. What do you have here? A couple of Arkansas state troopers out for a book and a buck? And Arkansas lawyers who have been gunning for the Clintons? Eleven thousand words in an ultraconservative magazine by David Brock, who did a job on Anita Hill. Surely I don't have to deal with that.

An interesting comment, considering the "ultra conservative" *Spectator* has featured articles by House Whip Newt Gingrich, ABC reporter Brit Hume, and CPB president Richard Carlson and criticized Pat Buchanan as a "fascist" during the '92 campaign. When was the last time an NPR commentator referred to *The Nation* as an "ultra-left" magazine?

But Schorr felt he did have to deal with the story in any case—because the Clintons had. The president had called the troopers in question in an attempt to quash their testimony, and the First Lady had condemned the story when it broke, thereby giving it "legs." "So you think the Clintons have problems? Just think about my problem trying to practice respectable journalism when nothing out there looks very respectable." Poor Daniel Schorr. Unnoticed by the sole "national correspondent" for NPR were the actual reasons the story had significance—the possibility that the president had abused public officials to service a pattern of compulsive sexual behavior and the tarnish that such behavior would put on his role as the nation's moral leader.

Like the rest of NPR, Schorr never agonized over the newsworthiness of Anita Hill's uncorroborated charges or the malicious gossip of the ex-girlfriend of a Supreme Court nominee who claimed he once smoked a marijuana joint at a private party. They never gazed at their navels and despaired at trying to look respectable when the reputations of conservative public figures were being thrown into the gutter.

Not only was NPR not going to be part of the investigating team this time, as the Liasson-Wertheimer nterview showed, it was determined to form a palace guard for the embattled Clintons. On December 27, when NPR guest commentator Kevin Phillips suggested the trooper story might have an impact on the voters' trust in their presidential leader, reporter Cokie Roberts quickly neutralized the suggestion, saying health care was more important. Paul Duke, the long-time moderator of the PBS show *Washington Week in Review*, declared on December 31: "One of my losers of the year is David Brock, who wrote that slimy magazine article that revived all those old charges about Bill Clinton's personal behavior, and I regarded that as journalism which is truly out of bounds." But when Duke's colleague Nina Totenberg broke Hill's sexual allegations with help from liberal interest groups out to hang Thomas, Duke defended them:

> There's criticism being directed at these groups, but it seems to me, this is in the American spirit. This is in the oldest American tradition of lobbying, where people organize for their causes and they band together...and then they go out and they work for legislation...and so I think some of the critics are off base when they condemn this so strenuously, because these groups are representing significant segments of the populations.

Duke, who co-anchored the Hill-Thomas hearing with Totenberg and Liasson, has made his program a forum for the liberal-media point of view. On December 24, *Los Angeles Times* Washington bureau chief Jack Nelson complained:

> *The American Spectator* broke this story, as Gwen mentioned, because they're a very right-wing ideological publication....What really happened was there was a conspiracy in my opinion, by right wingers, including some right-wing journalists, to press this newspaper into running this story before it was ready to, trying to get it out, and so they spread the rumor all around town that I threatened to resign if it didn't run.

But when liberal journalists and interest groups broke the Hill allegations, as part of a concerted effort to destroy Thomas, the *Washington Week* panelists didn't see a nasty personal attack from the left. In fact, they managed to interpret this as an attack from the right. Nelson:

> I've been in this town for 21 years, and they play a vicious brand of politics in Washington. This was as vicious a fight as I've ever seen, except it was totally one-sided...When you had Alan Simpson standing up there like Joe McCarthy, reaching in his pockets and saying "I'm getting stuff through faxes, and all over the country," he sounded just like Joe McCarthy. And you had Arlen Specter, who was a prosecutor at one time, saying that [Hill] committed perjury, when probably you couldn't find another prosecutor in the country that would tell you she had committed perjury.

Time's Julie Johnson agreed, calling Specter "the Great Inquisitor" and disdaining his "low-blow hit on perjury."

Yet no one was a match for Totenberg herself. After scuttling Republican nominees with tales of personal foibles, she actually decried the trooper story on the talk show *Inside Washington* on December 31. "You get allegations that are printed in a fringe magazine, or at least a magazine with a very definite political agenda, and then you see...how long it takes the rest of the press to come and bite." But remember that during NPR's coverage of the Hill-Thomas hearings, Totenberg defended her leak as a heroic act, comparing it to the leak of the Pentagon Papers and the Watergate story: "That would have just been a third-rate robbery if there hadn't been a lot of leaks."

On the New Year's Eve edition of *Inside Washington*, she also pooh-poohed the growing Whitewater scandal:

> When the American people hired Bill Clinton for this job, they knew he was no saint. He virtually told them he was a sinner. It's not at all clear to me that the Clintons did anything illegal or even improper at Whitewater. But because of the records that haven't been turned over, there remain questions and there may remain questions forever. This is the kind of thing that's never resolved 100 percent.

Earlier Totenberg had made the same proposal to abandon a story before it had really gotten off the ground in respect to the House Bank scandal: "I think that this has become a metaphor for the distemper of the country. It has no merit as a really good scandal. There's no public money involved...It was a lousily run bank and that's stupid and probably someone should pay, but it's not major." Of course, the House Bank was controlled by the Democratic majority. Former House Sergeant-at-Arms Jack Russ, a major figure and fixer in the Democratic leadership, was convicted of embezzlement. Being a zealous investigator of Republicans and an ardent defender of Democrats apparently qualifies Totenberg to be a star "reporter" for NPR.

So far in the Clinton era, NPR has shown no inclination to investigate Democrats with the same passion as they prodded and poked the Republicans during the Reagan-Bush years. It makes one wonder how seriously CPB is taking its responsibilities to live up to congressional demands for balance.

—*Tim Graham*

NPR AND HILL
AND JONES

The baby-boom generation at NPR that sang Fleetwood Mac songs along with the Clinton campaign in 1992 continues to struggle with the political baggage of Bill Clinton's sexuality. In December 1993, NPR reporters struggled with the revelations of Arkansas state troopers as briefly as they could. Then in February, Paula Jones announced at a Washington press conference that she had been sexually harassed by Clinton and was considering a lawsuit.

For three months, NPR ignored the story, a striking contrast to its treatment of similar charges by Anita Hill that she had been sexually harassed by Supreme Court nominee Clarence Thomas. It was NPR's Nina Totenberg who pressured and then forced Anita Hill to go public with the story, even though her claims lacked the corroboratory witnesses available to Mrs. Jones. A July 28, 1994, *All Things Considered* satire by the "Reduced Shakespeare Company" clearly defined the differences between the Jones and Hill charges within the NPR culture. In a routine that savaged all sides, one satirist declared: "We should be talking about the most important issue of President Clinton's administration." Another replied: "The inevitable Paula Jones issue of *Playboy*?" Then Mrs. Jones filed suit.

On the day the Jones suit was filed, May 6, 1994, Totenberg finally arrived on the story for *All Things Considered*. After presenting the claims of the suit and statements from lawyers on both sides, Totenberg wrapped up the story: "The Jones allegation has, of course, raised parallels between her case and that of Anita Hill's. Some women's rights groups normally supportive of the Clinton administration have privately squirmed at the parallels but publicly offered tentative support." Totenberg quoted Marcia Greenberger of the National Women's Law Center suggesting Jones would get fairer treatment in court than Hill did before the Senate Judiciary Committee. (No one asked whether Clarence Thomas—the accused—received fair treatment in being tried out-side a court of law.) Totenberg ended by quoting a statement from the National Organization for Women: "We continue to monitor this case, but we will not take the right wing's bait by heralding or attacking either person."

On *Weekend Edition* the next day, Totenberg said that, "after talking to some lawyers," the chances of the suit's survival was not good. When host Susan Stamberg asked if comparisons to Anita Hill were "fair," Totenberg continued to press her long-held notion that Professor Hill had corroboration: "They both have corroboration, though in fact, Paula Jones has more specific corroboration. But in nei-ther case is there any eyewitness to what happened." It's big of Totenberg to admit that, but three of Hill's four "corrobo-rators" were not precise or contemporary, most being told of Hill's alleged harassment years after it would have occurred.

Totenberg also suggested that Jones's motives might be impure:

> Paula Jones, according to her lawyer and one sister, was interested in money. Her lawyer acknowledges that he approached the White House, or tried to approach the White House, seeking money in exchange for her si-lence, and one sister says she was interested in money. Anita Hill never asked for money. Paula Jones made her charges at a press con-ference that was arranged for by Bill Clinton's sworn political enemies. Anita Hill went directly to the Senate Judiciary Com-mittee privately, and when the committee didn't pay any serious attention to her charges, her story was leaked.

Of course Hill did not go directly to Congress. She was pushed and pulled into that role, and it would be sur-prising if none of these people egging her on failed to men-tion the rewards that might come to someone who played heroine to the feminist mass. As it turned out, she did make millions in the aftermath of the hearings and has made it clear in the aftermath that—although she disingenuously de-nied it under oath—she had an ideological interest in stopping Thomas' nomination.

The contrast between Hill and Jones on this particular issue of partisan interest is striking. While Jones' lawsuit is definitely supported by conservative groups, she is politically unsophisticated. If Jones were a shrewd ideologue, she would have held a press conference at the same time she filed suit and chosen a nonpartisan location; instead she let her lawyer persuade her to appear before a conservative PAC. Hill, on the other hand, was an active feminist at the University of Oklahoma long before she made the accusations and told interviewers she was opposed to the direction Reagan and Thomas were moving on affirmative action. The fact that she lied about these views to Congress shows just how politically knowledgeable she was. Like Jones, Hill's testimony was solicited by liberal politicians (Ted Kennedy, Howard Metzenbaum) and interest groups (Alliance for Justice, People for the American Way). The testimony was supervised by a team of liberal lawyers, including Georgetown's Susan Deller Ross and Harvard's Charles Ogletree. Totenberg herself was an integral part of the liberal strategy to bring Hill forward.

The Jones story went uncovered by NPR until the May 13 *Morning Edition*, when a comment by ABC reporter Judy Muller was aired: "On the radio came the news that Paula Jones had filed a sexual harassment suit against President Clinton. 'Oh no,' said the cab driver, 'Not again,' and I knew just how he felt. As the two of us listened to the sordid details of the lawsuit, I realized my compassion fatigue had been replaced by scandal fatigue."

Muller cited polls that most Americans didn't care about Clinton's personal life, then added: "We may question Paula Jones's motive and her timing, but we cannot determine the truth of her accusations, and so we are captives to the legal process that will determine the truth, more or less, even as our tolerance for another scandal goes into overload."

Muller complained Americans will hear about Clinton's private parts more than his public policy and concluded:

> For many Americans, it is much more than
> they want to know. For many Americans,

scandal fatigue set in long ago, beginning with Gennifer Flowers and escalating in the torrents of Whitewater, a story few seem to care about, and even fewer comprehend. The Paula Jones story is much easier to comprehend, of course, but the question remains: How much do we care? I have a feeling that in places like Chicago's Robert Taylor Homes, where just walking to school is a life-threatening proposition, the answer to that question is "not very much."

This is a clever ending, but you could say the same for any political scandal: Did threatened inner city residents care about Iran Contra? Note how Muller's "scandal fatigue" began with Gennifer Flowers and escalated with Whitewater and wasn't bothered by media allegations of the "Secret Team" running the Western hemisphere from CIA headquarters or the "October Surprise" or Clarence Thomas' alleged conversations behind closed doors—all public-broadcasting staples.

The tone of coverage did improve as the Jones story aged. On May 20, 1994, reporter Lynn Neary did a very balanced job on a story angle the rest of the national networks tried to ignore: hypocrisy, or the switching of positions since the Hill-Thomas hearings. Neary interviewed four women in her story: conservatives Bay Buchanan and Free Congress Foundation legal analyst Marianne Lombardi and liberals Deborah Ellis of the NOW Legal Defense and Education Fund and attorney Deborah Katz. Neary even gave the conservative women the last word: "Lombardi says she is convinced that no feminist organization would ever come to her defense in a sexual harassment case simply because she is conservative."

On June 11, NPR news analyst Daniel Schorr took on the issue:

Well, here we are doing a little light wallowing in scandal on this Saturday morning, and so the latest on Paula Jones. A court document filed by state trooper Danny Ferguson...the good news for President

Clinton is that Ferguson says he never told Paula Jones that Clinton wanted to meet her. She said she wanted to be his girlfriend. Bad news, however, for the president is that Ferguson says she did go to his room. That seems to contradict the White House assertion that she was never in a room alone with him, so win some lose some.

But host Scott Simon editorialized in his transition to discussing Rwanda: "Let me take you from the ridiculous to the horrifying, if we could."

On NPR, Jones is a troublesome bimbo, a tabloid nightmare like Lorena Bobbitt or Tonya Harding. Anita Hill, meanwhile, remains the heroine of the liberal myth that NPR reporter Nina Totenberg did so much to create.

—Tim Graham

PART VII

PACIFICA RADIO
PROMOTES HATE

On Feb. 1 and 2, 1992, public radio station KPFK-Los Angeles, turned over its transmitters from 9 a.m. to midnight to Louis Farrakhan, Leonard Jeffries, and a general parade of anti-Semitic racists, for what was billed as *Afrikan Mental Liberation Weekend*. Minister Farrakhan warned listeners that whites and Jews were "the pale horse with death as its rider and hell close behind" that for centuries had wreaked destruction on red, yellow, brown, and black peoples in Africa, Asia, and the Americas and on Palestinians in the Middle East. Not to fear, however, a "reckoning" was about to come, Farrakhan assured the audience.

The organizer of the weekend event was Dr. Kwaku Person-Lynn, who had his own special message, which was as follows: Real Jews are black. White Jews are "hypocrites" for claiming to be Jews. White Jews add injury to this insult by forcing the real Jews, the Falashas of Ethiopia, to give up their "original" Judaism "in order to stay alive." As might be expected, this message elicited phone-ins by callers convinced that Jews were "devils."

Afrikan Mental Liberation Weekend is an annual production of KPFK. Its message is wholly in tune with the station's programming, which features fringe radicalism and general hatred of whites, America, and all things capitalist. Other programs, for example, have been devoted to hour-long diatribes by Farrakhan lieutenant Steve Cokeley informing listeners that a recent measles epidemic was a "genocidal plot" by whites against the black community and that the problem with blacks was that they "didn't deliver retribution." During a recent fund drive, a KPFK station announcer decried the manipulativeness of commercial networks, which, by featuring stories on Olympic gold medal winner Chris Yamaguchi, "tried to make us think America was a decent country." Another pledge-week announcer stressed that no other station had reported to its listeners the "fact" that orphans were being "disappeared" in Latin America by the U.S. government and "murdered for their body parts," which were then shipped to U.S. hospitals. Needless to say, there is not the slightest hint of the balance required by law in KPFK programming.

KPFK-Los Angeles is a Pacifica station and receives a Community Service Grant from the Corporation for Public Broadcasting of $134,126 a year. Why?

—David Horowitz

MY LIFE AND TIMES AT PACIFICA RADIO

KPFK is one of a chain of stations owned by the far-left-of-center Pacifica Foundation, a chain that includes stations WBAI in New York City, KPFA in Berkeley, KPFT in Houston, and WPFW in Washington, D.C. The foundation's name hints at pacifism and its role since the '50s in seeking nuclear disarmament by the West, but its stations have always been willing to give ample airtime to those ready to take up arms against American interests inside or outside of the United States.

Coming to KPFK, I soon discovered, was like entering a zoo or joining a circus. In addition to the predictable Marxists and extremists from one or another ideological, racial, sexual, or ethnic minority, one found a fascinating variety of eccentrics. At odd hours the station aired enthusiasts for folk music or literary criticism or science fiction, and in the early years after my arrival such programs were not necessarily colored by any omnipresent political filter. In many ways, KPFK was then genuine Free Speech Radio, at least for those given airtime.

My hour of airtime each week was bequeathed by dapper William F. Buckley-like conservative Randy Darden, a sometime Hollywood actor, who had enjoyed my morning talk show on University of Southern California station KUSC. I would become the token right-winger on KPFK, the figleaf that station bosses could point to when accused of broadcasting only leftist political views.

But then as now, my views were not conventionally conservative. I was a Libertarian ready to replace government bureaucracy with free-market institutions.

To reach the Pacifica audience accustomed to leftist rhetoric, I declared myself the station's "resident right-wing anarchist." An odd label on any other station, on KPFK it struck a resonant chord because the title "anarchist" is respected on the left. From this podium I could simultaneously go to the rhetorical right *and* left of any caller on any topic. My first appearance started at 11:00 p.m. on a Friday night and flooded the station's telephone lines with enchanted listeners who had never before encountered the radical individualist view of the world that stretches from Thomas Jefferson to Milton Friedman. And as my first quarter hour of intellectual ferment ended, the host who followed me baptized my program with outre theme music "River of S—" by the latter day beatnik group The Fugs.

For several years, I felt at home in the Pacifica bestiary. Like so many others there I was unconventional, an outspoken critic of the government and military conscription if not of the Vietnam War itself, a defender of civil libertarianism and the right of minorities to be free from persecution. On my show I supported gay rights and relentlessly promoted animal rights long before the cause became popular. I participated actively and gave much free time to help pitch for money during fund-raising drives, and I recommended what would become the bumper sticker slogan of the station—much to the consternation of the Nuclear Regulatory Commission: the words "Radio Active" and, aptly, the official symbol used as a warning for hazardous radioactivity. When listeners were polled by the station, I was usually found to be among its three most popular personalities.

But I had one failing that would be my undoing: As an individualist, I was of course anti-socialist and anti-Communist. By the mid-'70s, with the fading of the flowering of ideas the '60s engendered, the leftism at KPFK, as elsewhere in the counterculture, settled back into the hands of the remaining lefties, the hard-core Stalinists. Purges began at the station, with some refugees fleeing across town to National Public Radio station KCRW in Santa Monica.

My own live talk show was ended, but I was allowed to continue giving pre-recorded 15-minute commentaries on a news program. One day the new news director at the station told me he once had been an anarchist but that time in Italy talking with members of the Red Guard had converted him to the higher truth of Marxism.

Then, in late January 1980, my commentaries were suddenly removed from the air, even though I remained popular with listeners. I was denounced repeatedly on air in a tone reminiscent of Stalin's show trials of the '30s, allegedly for making unspecified "racist" and "sexist" remarks in a commentary.

Oddly, no tape from my commentaries was aired as evidence of these heresies—even though the station had tapes of everything I had said. I was given no chance to discuss or rebut these vague, false, and bizarre accusations on air. (I was later told that one of my sins was to ask why Jane Fonda, amid her demands that the U.S. nuclear industry be shut down, had hypocritically never made similar criticism of unsafe reactors in the Soviet Union—the Chernobyl meltdown was to happen years later. I was also told that my sin was even simpler: that in 15 minutes a week I could undo the propaganda effect of days of leftist programs, so I had to be removed.)

Days later, in early February 1980, I forced my way into a meeting of program hosts at the station. The Marxist news director, flanked by the station manager and program director, was giving orders to the two dozen people present. "From now on," he said, "all programs will be expected to carry messages of Class Consciousness, including the music programs!"

Until that moment, Stalinism had been an abstraction to me, but now I looked around at the faces of longtime friends, many of them stiff with terror. I continued to appear on more powerful local radio stations such as KABC and would soon be invited to join the family at KCRW for the next five years (although with my expression restricted to scientific, not political, topics by order of the dogmatically leftist station manager, formerly manager of KPFK, who wanted no Libertarian ideas on her airwaves). But for these frightened programmers, their tiny shows on KPFK were all they had or would ever have. As I watched, their human dignity, self-esteem, and sense of freedom evaporated, leaving the cold blank stares of submission I had seen years earlier in the eyes of people in Havana when I was there doing a piece for the *Los Angeles Times*. A totalitarian chill filled the room.

And, as in Stalin's Russia, no one said a word in opposition. All those who opposed Communism on the air had been swiftly purged. The surviving air personality whose voice came closest to anti-Communism, ironically, was the old Communist party organizer Dorothy Healey, who had taken to wearing black armbands in the wake of the 1968 Soviet invasion of Czechoslovakia. I had once, in the name of free speech, brought her to lecture a class I taught at the University of Southern California, much to the distress of school officials, and I considered her a friend—but she said nothing in opposition to the purges at KPFK. Her show continued, critical of the Soviet Union but advocating a utopian Marxism. And within days of this terrifying dictation to station programmers, KPFK's management was back on the air asking listeners to contribute money to Pacifica to "preserve Free Speech Radio in southern California."

Should a station such as KPFK exist? Despite my bad experiences there, I believe it should. It also brought me wonderful experiences, new ideas, delightful friends, and an encounter with a listener who became my wife 17 years ago. And although I no longer desire to live at the circus or in the zoo, it is nice to be able to visit these odd and different creatures occasionally by tuning my radio down to the non-commercial bottom end of the FM dial. Moreover, with the ebb and flow of time, new management running KPFK at this moment has invited me back to deliver occasional commentaries on tape—although the invitation may disappear when they read this article, the left being notoriously thin-skinned and unable to tolerate dissent or honest criticism. The bulk of KPFK's airtime remains filled with predictable "politically correct" viewpoints, including some from the same people who led the Marxist purge of opposing opinion in 1980.

Among those I interviewed 20 years ago on KPFK

were visiting representatives of the violent leftist Kabouter movement in the Netherlands. In Holland, they told me, if enough citizens signed a petition the government would provide a radio station managed by the petitioners. By this method the Kabouters had gotten their own radio station, VPRO. Its typical programming, they told my audience, might feature a half-hour do-it-yourself show on how to build a bomb followed by a half-hour program telling listeners where to find NATO military installations and offices near their neighborhoods.

In the United States, Pacifica Radio has at times been remarkably similar to this Kabouter station in the Netherlands. It has turned over the bulk of its airtime to those most hatefully opposed to American society and values. In some cases it has acted as a megaphone for black anti-Semitism, for class and race hatred and warfare, and for open advocacy of violence.

But at least in Holland scarce claims of territory on the electromagnetic spectrum are granted by democratic petitions; Pacifica gained its monopolies on scarce broadcast frequencies in some of America's largest cities by the royal favor of bureaucrats or the ideological favor of leftist politicians. You and I will never be allowed to have a radio station, so we must beg or buy airtime from those already holding government monopoly licenses; the obverse of the old saying is also true, "license is not freedom." For those desiring to be heard in the free-speech radio dialogue on Pacifica's fiefdoms of the public airwaves, the signs make clear that "No Politically Incorrect People Need Apply."

But even more troubling to me than the implicit censorship and denial of free speech in these privileged monopolies is that KPFK has carried out such broadcasts with taxpayer money, $134,000 each year of funding from the Corporation for Public Broadcasting, which gets *its* funds from taxpayers who voted in significant majorities for Ronald Reagan and George Bush.

Two centuries ago, Thomas Jefferson confronted a world where the King taxed Quakers, Baptists, and non-believers to fund the state church, the Church of England. In his 1779 statute to abolish such taxation, Jefferson wrote that "to compel a man to furnish contributions of money for the propagation of opinions which he disbelieves and abhors is sinful and tyrannical."

By such reasoning, should you or I be taxed to broadcast the eccentric—but in most instances far leftist—views of the elite selected to voice their opinions on Pacifica Radio?

The Voice of America is by law not permitted to broadcast into the United States, because its programs are officially deemed to be "propaganda" aimed at promoting the government's point of view. This official point of view, the assumption goes, could tailor taxpayer-supported Voice of America newscasts to favor the reelection of incumbent politicians. But how different is Pacifica Radio?

My own bias is this: Let KPFK and the other Pacifica stations remain on the air so long as listeners support them voluntarily. But in the name of free-speech radio, we should eliminate the tax subsidy you and I have been forced to pay to keep KPFK's left-polarized signal on the air.

—*Lowell Ponte*

WAITING FOR THE SECOND ROUND AT KPFK

Pacifica Station KPFK-Los Angeles, is a 110,000-watt public-radio station whose signal can be heard all the way from Los Angeles to San Diego, an area of more than 20 million people. During the cold war, its public-affairs programming was devoted to the promotion of Marxist guerrilla movements and Communist police states. It even gave over its air time to a pro-Khaddafi group during the air raid on Libya. It has from time to time aired hour long harangues by Louis Farrakhan, Farrakhan lieutenant Steve Cokely, and other purveyors of racial hatred.

On May 6, 1992, a week after the riots began, a

KPFK host introduced Farrakhan lieutenant Steve Cokeley, who was on a phone line from Chicago. Cokeley, who made a name for himself by accusing Jewish doctors of injecting blacks with AIDS, used his air time to insinuate that the Federal Emergency Administration might have played a sinister role in either setting or conspiring to prevent the control of the fires set during the riots (a week later, attorney William Kunstler was claiming on KPFK that the FBI had set some of the fires). Then Cokeley concluded:

> Let me just say one last thing. Many people from around the country are making a surprise visit to Los Angeles, myself and others included will be showing up there shortly. We are bringing...some names of those people, who—if there ever was a second round—and we should thank Los Angeles for Westwood, Beverly Hills, and other portions, where the whites called this an unusual phenomenon, that the blacks went into the white neighborhoods, and that happened all over the country. And that is a unique and different response...[than] we've seen in the past.
>
> —*David Horowitz*

BROADCASTING HATE

A storm of controversy has surrounded Pacifica-owned KPFK of Los Angeles since its annual *Afrikan Mental Liberation Weekend* aired at the beginning of February 1993. The *Weekend's* organizer and host, Dr. Kwaku Person-Lynn, welcomed to "progressive" Pacifica a swarm of anti-Jewish and anti-white racists, led by Professor Leonard Jeffries and Minister Louis Farrakhan.

Professor Jeffries' contribution to the *Weekend* was his usual mix of Afrocentric pseudo-history and racism. He was, in fact, slated to appear at a Los Angeles conference on "The

Holocaust and the First Amendment," the organizing theme of which would be to question the existence and uniqueness of the destruction of European Jewry by Hitler's Reich. In the end, Dr. Jeffries did not show up for this memorable event because of the adverse publicity that greeted its announcement and his feeling that he already had "more problems than he could deal with." Thus, he missed meeting with such notable hate-mongers as Willis Carto, treasurer and founder of the neo-Nazi Liberty Lobby, Mark Weber of the Institute for Historical Review (the nation's leading Holocaust deniers and also a Liberty Lobby front-group), and Hans Schmidt, a former member of the Hitler Youth. The only thing the participants seemed to have in common was a shared hatred for Jews.

Jeffries has a warm admirer in KPFK's radio host, Dr. Person-Lynn, who teaches at Cal. State-Dominguez Hills and who regards Jeffries as an African American "hero." According to Dr. Person-Lynn, Jews who are white are not really Jews. They call themselves Jews, they may think they are Jewish, but they are usurpers and exploiters of the real Jews. The real Jews are black, naturally. This explains why, in attacking the associate director of the Anti-Defamation League in Los Angeles on the KPFK show, Person-Lynn called him a "psychotic, idiotic European Jew." In Person-Lynn's perverse vocabulary, "European" is a negation rather than a modifier.

In a letter to the same director, dated Feb. 11, 1992, Person-Lynn went even further:

> ...the Anti-Defamation League is really a closet white supremacist organization...you are going to have to face the reality that people are not afraid of you, your organization, or that tired out term anti-Semitic. We can see through that. We are aware of your efforts to condemn and wrongly label universal Afrikan leadership and scholarship, just because they do not spout your "party line"....The station and I both knew of your predictable attacks, because of your efforts to lie and hide the fact that European Jews were heavily involved in the financing of the

slave trade, the slave trade itself, and as slave owners. Maybe you should enroll in my class so you can learn something about your own heritage, and who you and Judaism evolved from, which started among Afrikans in Ethiopia and Egypt, who were black, in case you did not know.

Dr. Person-Lynn's listening audience was even more outspoken. One caller stated: "The Jews haven't seen anything yet. The Jews stole our birthright. What is going to happen to them is going to make what Hitler did seem like a party."

Publicly funded KPFK is the most powerful FM station in Southern California, reaching audiences from San Diego to Santa Barbara and from the California Coast to the California Desert, an area and population larger than most states in the Union. Its news and programming can be heard on 53 affiliated and subscriber stations nationwide. Its regular fare of radical extremism and racial divisiveness was only highlighted by Person-Lynn's 26-hour *Weekend*. Listeners hungry for more could tune in every Wednesday, for example, to *The Family Tree* (where a host recently asked the listening audience "Haven't you noticed how all the people getting blacks in this city—[D.A.] Ira Reiner, [Judge] Joyce Karlin—are Jews?") Or they could treat themselves to the paranoid ravings of Farrakhanite Steve Cokely, a welcome guest on KPFK, or to the conspiracy theories of KPFK regular Ambrose Lane.

But *Afrikan Mental Liberation* was such an overdose of venom, that it set off a reaction, first in the local Jewish press and then at CPB. Board member Vic Gold led the attack, calling for disciplinary action against the Pacifica network. Pacifica president David Salniker responded to the CPB board's complaints by promising to take remedial measures and, in particular, prevent Kwaku Person-Lynn from hosting shows on his own in the future. Kenneth Karr, a KPFK advisory board member, was also suspended for allegedly referring to UCLA as "Jew-CLA."

That was in 1992. In 1993, *Afrikan Mental Liberation Weekend* was aired again on February 13 and 14. In the weeks before airtime, KPFK general manager Bill Thomas made assurances that all tapes to be played on the *Weekend* would be checked before being aired and that "Person-Lynn would be accompanied by two co-hosts who would rebut the most controversial speakers." Both co-hosts, however, were prominent members of the Jeffries-Lynn subculture of Afrocentric conspiracy theorists. One co-host, Ambrose Lane, "reportedly changed his mind after a confrontation with Person-Lynn in the studio" before airtime, while the other, UC-Santa Barbara Professor Gerald Horne, "phoned in for only two brief commentaries," perhaps because Person-Lynn introduced him as "KPFK's designated Negro."

That Dr. Person-Lynn gets what he wants at KPFK is apparently nothing new. There are two reasons for this. One is his popularity with the KPFK audience, as reflected by his ability to raise funds—he brought in $15,000 during the *Weekend's* pledge breaks, an unusually large amount. The other is fear. When he thinks he's been "dissed," Dr. Person-Lynn has been known to resort to intimidation, threats, or actual violence. Suzy Weissman, a program host at the station, told a journalist that in 1984 Person-Lynn phoned her at three in the morning, called her a "Jew," and accused her of sabotaging his fundraising efforts. Ian Masters, a host at the station, reported Person-Lynn had threatened another staffer with a shotgun. Person-Lynn admits there was such an incident, but says he was armed with a crowbar rather than a gun. Clare Spark, former program director at the station, said that Person-Lynn once became outraged at switchboard operator Andrea Enthal, accusing her of turning down microphone levels during one of his programs. He then threw Enthal against a wall, fracturing her thumb. Ironically, the dispute arose over a Martin Luther King Day broadcast.

Even though Dr. Person-Lynn's promised "co-hosts" turned out not to be co-hosts at all, the 1993 *Afrikan Mental Liberation Weekend* went on as scheduled. The only apparent change from the previous year's 26-hour marathon was that the Louis Farrakhan speech was replaced by a racist sermon from Elijah Muhammad. Otherwise, the featured guests were pretty much identical. And so was the message: the ongoing "war" of blacks against whites.

Once again, Professor Leonard Jeffries was a prominent guest. Perhaps because of the still-simmering controversy over the program of the previous year, Dr. Jeffries resorted to damage control and a more oblique and cryptic mode of address in peddling the same noxious doctrines.

Thus, referring to a *New York Post* editorial accusing him of promoting a race-based conspiracy theory of AIDS, Jeffries explained: "And so I've said we need to look at all the possibilities. Given the knowledge of the Tuskegee experiment in syphilis, in a black institution among a black population, organized by the U.S. government and leading health officials, an experiment that went on for 40 years even after penicillin was developed, we have to look at all the possibilities that might be real for us in terms of where these devastations like AIDS come from. So, certainly, I made my analysis on that."

In explaining that he was not singling out the Jews in previous public attacks, Jeffries made the following clarification: "[It is] the rich bankers and merchants [who] have a fraternity of interests that they operate with. Doesn't make any difference whether they're Jewish, whether they're Christian, or whether they're Muslims." He then made the not so subtle transition to the same line of attack anyway:

> We do not need to be blinded by a civil rights coalition movement so that we cannot see that while there was a civil rights movement and certain people saw a common interest in that, there were economic interests across these groups that were working against us. And are continuing to work against us. Continuing to establish imperialism and neo-colonialism. Continuing to establish the impoverishment of Black people and people of color around the world. Continuing to work in South Africa against the interest of Black folk. Because they want the gold and the diamonds. Continuing to work in this economic realm which is so important to them so they are willing to compromise the historical integrity of Israel having risen up out of the ashes of European Jewry devastated by the Nazi holocaust. The State of Israel's in-

tegrity is compromised by leaders who have
an economic interest to wed themselves to
the fascists of South Africa.

Professor Jeffries rambled on in this segment of his
interview until he arrived at a point where he could report
on his meeting with the former Mayor of New York,
Edward Koch. According to Jeffries, Koch asked him to
document his claims of extensive Jewish involvement in
the slave trade:

> Where do you want to start? Do you want to
> go back into the Spanish Sephardic Jewish
> community? Then we get Stephen Bir-
> mingham's book, *The Grandees*, which deals
> with the Jewish Sephardic community in
> Spain and Portugal....Do you want to go to
> Amsterdam? Then get a book by Jonathan
> Israel on European Jewry in the age of mer-
> cantilism, 1550-1750. And here's a picture of
> the Amsterdam synagogue, which was the
> center for slave trading for the Dutch. And it
> was round this synagogue that the slaving
> system was established...as a system. Before
> that time, the Dutch and the English had
> been slaving as some [kind] of pirate opera-
> tion. They would send out fleets to rob the
> Spanish galleons....Well the Jewish mer-
> chants said, Let's make this thing into a
> business!...[F]ill these same ships with these
> Africans, take them across the ocean, make a
> profit on not only the trading of the cheap
> goods for Africans...take the products of the
> New World, put them in the same hold of
> these same ships, and bring them back to
> Europe, and establish a system.

If it is even worth observing, the work by Jonathan
Israel, *European Jewry in the Age of Mercantilism 1550-1750*,
deals with slavery on only two pages, offering absolutely no
support for Jeffries' claim of Jewish primacy in the slave
trade. Further, there are no photographs of the Amster-

dam synagogue in the book—and, indeed, no photographs at all.

The kind of racist Know-Nothingism featured on *Afrikan Mental Liberation Weekend* is not unusual programming for KPFK or the Pacifica stations nor are the paranoid conspiracy theories it favors confined to the left. In this one instance, at least, there is balance at Pacifica.

Thus Pacifica's flagship station, KPFA-Berkeley, has been home to right-wing conspiracy theories focusing on the Council on Foreign Relations and the Federal Reserve system—staple demons of the John Birch Society. During the prelude to the Gulf War, with much of the left, including its Berkeley contingents in a fevered state, KPFA discovered Craig Hulet, conspiracy theorist extraordinaire, whose paranoid fantasies were put on tape and offered as a KPFA premium:

> George Bush is a threat....[He] has perpetrated the most heinous race war against [the] black [and] Hispanic community... since slavery. This drug war has nothing to do with drugs. It's been directed primarily at the black and hispanic communities. That's who's been assaulted, that's who's been arrested. That's who's going to the prison camps....Blacks...They're not afraid of the Klan...they're not afraid of the David Dukes. What makes them afraid...is a man like President Bush who can somehow woo the entire nation while he bombs a Third World brown people into the stone age....We've got a man in the White House that is more fascist, more racist, more dangerous than any man on the planet.

Hulet's appearances on KPFK led directly to the formation of "study groups" in the San Francisco Bay area, where intrigued Pacifica listeners could further pursue his conspiracy fantasies—and buy his tapes. Following Hulet's lead, the groups studied the Federal Reserve System with the aid of books and videos by Eustace Mullins, a favorite right-wing expert on the Federal Reserve System. Eustace Mullins is author of *The Biological Jew* and is one of the nation's leading anti-Semites.

◆ ◆ ◆

According to its 1991 Annual Report, Pacifica Radio exists:

☛ to promote cultural diversity and pluralistic community expression,

☛ and to contribute to a lasting understanding between individuals of all nations, races, creeds, and colors.

Pacifica has not lived up to its stated ideals. Idiotic conspiracy theories leavened with racist hate-speech neither promote cultural diversity, nor contribute to any understanding, lasting or otherwise, between individuals of different nations, races, creeds, and colors. According to the latest available figures, Pacifica receives roughly $1 million a year from the Corporation for Public Broadcasting. Pacifica-owned and operated KPFK receives around $173,000 of that total, while the Pacifica flagship station, KPFA, receives around $290,000. If Pacifica wants to indulge in the kind of programming detailed above, they should do it with their own funds, not at taxpayer expense.

—*Alex Safian*

STATEMENT
BY VICTOR GOLD

Member of the Board of the Corporation for Public Broadcasting

April 6, 1993

The Board of the Corporation for Public Broadcasting has rejected a proposal made by me to stop CPB funding of public-broadcasting stations that repeatedly sponsor and air anti-Semitic, racist, and other hate programs.

The board, acting behind closed doors and in my absence, instead supported the position taken by CPB president Richard Carlson and chairman Sheila Tate that, while CPB "decries" hate programming, it will continue to furnish federal funds to stations blatantly guilty of it.

The board's action, taken at its April 1-2, 1993, meeting in Lincoln, Nebraska, is not only hypocritical and disingenuous, it raises serious questions as to whether CPB is capable of fulfilling the mandate recently given it by Congress to assure "balance" as well as responsibility in public broadcasting.

My proposal, submitted to members of the CPB board at its Lincoln meeting, reads as follows:

> While reaffirming the First Amendment right of every public broadcasting station to broadcast diverse and alternative programs and opinions, the board of Corporation for Public Broadcasting condemns and deplores the dissemination of material that defames any race, religion or minority and directs the corporation staff to consider any station's repeated programming of such material as one criterion by which to determine the absence of "excellence" and "quality" in the future funding of such station.

I initiated this proposal after a persistent pattern of anti-Semitic programming by radio station KPFK-FM, Los Angeles, over a two-year period, 1992-93. During this time, the station received some $365,115 in so-called Community Service Grants from the Corporation for Public Broadcasting.

These federal funds went to support the operation of a station that annually sponsors a 26-hour talkathon billed as Afrikan Mental Liberation Weekend and termed a "hatefest" by members of the Los Angeles Jewish community. In 1992 and 1993, the program featured, at length, diatribes from such anti-Semitic, racist demagogues such as Louis Farrakhan, Professor Leonard Jeffries, and Steve Cokely, whose "community service" included the outrageous and inflammatory charge that a "Jewish doctors' conspiracy" exists to inoculate African-American infants with the AIDS virus.

Perhaps, as the only Jewish member of CPB's board, I am, as Mr. Carlson has stated, especially "emotional" in my concern about such programs. However, as noted in my previous appeals to the board for action, I am equally "emotional" over KPFK-FM's irresponsibly featuring speakers who defame Asians, Hispanics, and member of the gay community.

Given this background, how does CPB's leadership and board justify giving federal money to such a station? It is Mr. Carlson's contention that CPB's sanction against stations that program such material should, to quote him directly, "be rhetorical, not financial." In short, lip service.

CPB chairman Tate, offering her rationale for subsidizing hate broadcasting, cites the First Amendment. But the issue here is not freedom of speech in broadcasting. Rather, it is whether Congress has furnished millions of federal dollars to CPB in order to subsidize, in the name of "community service," the defamation of any race, religion, or minority.

This clearly cannot be the case. For this reason, given the CPB board's reluctance to act against anti-Semitic hate programming, I, as a CPB board member, call upon the appropriate committees of Congress to re-examine CPB operations to determine whether the corporation continues to serve a positive functional role in public broadcasting.

"PACIFICA IS FIRST A POLITICAL ORGANIZATION"

The above statement is not quoted from an editorial in the pages of COMINT. It is a sentence taken from the resignation statement of Andrew Phillips, a veteran broadcaster who was for the last four years program director at WBAI, Pacifica's New York station. In his farewell letter, Phillips pointed out that WBAI has only 13,000 subscribers in a city of 8 million:

> While Public Radio has continued to grow, Pacifica is in slow decline. Currently each of Pacifica's five stations is running a deficit

which collectively amounts to hundreds of thousands of dollars.

Part of the explanation for this decline, in Phillips' view, is Pacifica's character as a political organization:

> Pacifica is first a political organization. Broadcasting is of lesser importance. I don't believe it was always this way nor was it the vision of Lew Hill, Pacifica's founder, but it is what we have become. A glance at agendas of Pacifica board meetings tells the story....To succeed, these priorities must be reversed. We first need to "create" or "grow" our public—to encourage an audience to enter our tent before we begin to perform. I am not a propagandist though I believe there is a place for propaganda in a broadcasting system like Pacifica's. But more important is the creation of the apron and adequate publicity and moral and financial support before the polemics begin. There has to be intelligence and there has to be art. And there has to be the courage to change. It is not the fault of the volunteer producer staff that Pacifica has not succeeded. The fault lies at the top.

Pacifica's support base is small because the partisan politics it promotes is a fringe politics. We called Cheryl Thompson, the program director at WPFW, Pacifica's Washington station, and asked her whether she would agree with a description of her station's programming as "left and far left." She said "Yes." We asked whether she was running any conservative shows. She answered: "If you want to run Rush Limbaugh, no we don't do that kind of programming."

Is the use of taxpayer funds to subsidize a station whose programming is far left to left (or far right to right) a legitimate function of government? Can anyone at CPB provide us with an interpretation of the Public Broadcasting Act's balance provisions that would qualify for Community Service Grants a network that regards itself as a partisan political institution?

—*David Horowitz*

PART VIII

THE CORPORATION FOR PUBLIC BROADCASTING

EXPLANATORY NOTE

The Corporation for Public Broadcasting was established by Congress in 1967 to oversee noncommercial educational radio and television service in the United States. It both funds public radio and television stations and regulates their activities. By law, it is also responsible for ensuring that stations adhere to the requirements of the Public Broadcasting Act of 1967 for balance and objectivity. In 1992, a series of amendments were attached to the CPB authorization bill, requiring the corporation board to enforce the balance provisions of the Public Broadcasting Act.

AMENDMENTS TO THE PUBLIC TELECOMMUNI- CATIONS ACT OF 1992

I. BROADCASTING OF INDECENT PROGRAMMING: FCC REGULATIONS

The Federal Communications Commission shall promulgate regulations to prohibit the broadcasting of indecent programming (1) between 6 a.m. and 10 p.m. on any day by any public radio station or public television station that goes off the air at or before 12 midnight; and (2) between 6 a.m. and 12 midnight on any day for any radio or television broadcasting station not described in paragraph (1).

The regulations required under this subsection shall be promulgated in accordance with section 553 of title 5,

United States Code, and shall become final not later than 180 days after the enactment of this Act.

II. OBJECTIVITY AND BALANCE AMENDMENT

Purpose: To promote programming objectivity and balance. On page 11, immediately after line 4 of the Inouye amendment to the committee amendment, insert the following new section:

SEC. 16. Pursuant to the existing responsibility of the Corporation for Public Broadcasting under section 396(g)(1)(A) of the Communications Act of 1934 (47 U.S.C.396 (g)(1)(A)) "to facilitate the full development of public telecommunications in which programs of high quality, diversity, creativity, excellence, and innovation, which are obtained from diverse sources, will be made available to public telecommunications entities, with strict adherence to objectivity and balance in all programs or series of programs of a controversial nature," the Board of Directors of the Corporation shall:

(1) review the Corporation's existing efforts to meet its responsibility under section 396(g)(1)(A); (2) after soliciting the views of the public, establish a comprehensive policy and set of procedures to—

(A) provide reasonable opportunity for members of the public to present comments to the Board regarding the quality, diversity, creativity, excellence, innovation, objectivity, and balance of public broadcasting services, including all public broadcasting programming of a controversial nature, as well as any needs not met by those services;

(B) review, on a regular basis, national public broadcasting programming for quality, diversity, creativity, excellence, innovation, objectivity, and balance, as well as for any needs not met by such programming;

(C) On the basis of information received through such comment and review, take such steps in awarding programming grants pursuant to clauses (ii)(II), (iii)(II), and (iii)(III) of section 396(k)(3)(A) of the Communications Act of 1934 (47 U.S.C. 396(k) (3)(A)) that it finds necessary to meet the Corporation's responsibility under the section 396(g)(1)(A), including facilitating objectivity and balance in programming of a controversial nature; and

(D) disseminate among public broadcasting entities information about its efforts to address concerns about objectivity and balance relating to programming of a controversial nature so that such entities can utilize the Corporation's experience in addressing such concerns within their own operation; and

(E) starting in 1993, by January 31 of each year, prepare and submit to the President for transmittal to the Congress a report summarizing its efforts pursuant to paragraphs (1) and (2).

III. AVAILABILITY OF INFORMATION FOR PUBLIC INSPECTION

Purpose: To make certain changes concerning the Board of the Corporation for Public Broadcasting and to make certain information available for public inspection.

Sec. 14. (a) CPB INFORMATION.—Section 396 (l) of the Communications Act of 1934 (47 U.S.C. 396(l) is amended by striking paragraph (4) and inserting in lieu thereof the following:

(4)(A) The Corporation shall maintain the information described in sub-paragraphs (B),(C), and (D) at its offices for public inspection and copying for at least 3 years, according to such reasonable guidelines as the Corporation may issue. This public file shall be updated regularly. This paragraph shall be effective upon its enactment and shall apply to all grants after January 1, 1993.

(B) Subsequent to any award of funds by the Corporation for the production or acquisition of national broadcasting programming pursuant to subsection (k)(3)(A)(ii)(II) or (ii)(II), the Corporation shall make available for inspection the following:

(i) Grant and solicitation guidelines for proposals for such programming.

(ii) The reasons for selecting the proposal for which the award was made.

(iii) Information on each program for which the award was made, including the name of the awardee and producer (and if the awardee or producer is a corporation or partnership, the principals of such corporation or partnership), the monetary amount of the award, and the title and description of the program (and of each program in a series of programs).

(iv) A report based on the final audit findings resulting from any audit of the award by the Corporation or the

Comptroller General.

(v) Reports which the Corporation shall require to be provided by the awardee relating to national public broadcasting programming funded, produced, or acquired by the awardee with such funds. Such reports shall include, where applicable, the information described in clauses (i), (ii), and (iii) but shall exclude proprietary, confidential, or privileged information.

(C) The Corporation shall make available for public inspection the final report required by the Corporation on an annual basis for each recipient of funds under subsection (k)(3)(A)(iii)(III), excluding proprietary, confidential, or privileged information.

(D) The Corporation shall make available for public inspection an annual list of national programs distributed by public broadcasting entities that receive funds under subsection (k)(3)(A)(ii)(II) or(iii)(II) and are engaged primarily in the national distribution of public television or radio programs. Such list shall include the names of the programs (or program series), producers, and providers of funding.

IV. INDEPENDENT PRODUCTION SERVICE INFORMATION

Section 396(k)(3)(B)(iii) of the Communications Act of 1934 (47 U.S.C. 396(k)(3)(B)(iii) is amended by adding at the end the following new subclause:

(VI) The Corporation shall not contract to provide funds to any such independent production service, unless that service agrees to comply with public inspection requirements established by the Corporation within 3 months after the date of enactment of this subclause. Under such requirements the service shall maintain at its offices a public file, updated regularly, containing information relating to the service's award of funds for the production of programming. The information shall be available for public inspection and copying for at least 3 years and shall be of the same kind as the information required to maintained by the Corporation under subsection (l)(4)(B).

SIGNIFICANCE OF THE 1992 ACT

With the president's signing of the Public Telecommunications Act in 1992, a long legislative battle was concluded. The bill ensures federal funding of the public-broadcasting industry through 1996, which will be another presidential election year. It came on the 25th anniversary of the Public Broadcasting Act of 1967 and, in the words of the new CPB president Richard Carlson, affirms that the experiment launched by this legislation still has "strong, nationwide support." And that is a fact. The leader of the legislative critics of current public broadcasting policies, Republican Majority Leader Robert Dole, is himself a contributor to the public broadcasting system. Most of the other critics are as well.

It would be seriously, if not dangerously, misleading therefore, to remain content with the positive result of the reauthorization effort—i.e., that it was ultimately successful. The far more significant revelation of this year of conflict lies in the damage the nine-month-long battle inflicted on the industry's image and finances and the deep and abiding dissatisfactions with the direction of public broadcasting that the battlelines revealed.

Thus, one outcome of the congressional fight was an amendment to the authorization bill that would "prohibit the broadcasting of indecent programming" during hours when children may be watching. The amendment was provoked by a series of questionable programming decisions made by PBS staff and constitutes the most restrictive legislation in the 25-year history of the public-broadcasting system. The amendment was proposed neither by Jesse Helms nor any other Republican legislator, however, but by Democrat Robert Byrd of West Virginia, the president pro-tempore of the Senate. The amendment was passed by a vote of 93-3.

What this vote reveals is that the PBS leadership is seriously out of touch with the sensibilities and judgments not only of its core supporters in the U.S. Senate, but of the American people as a whole. This is no place for an institution that considers itself a public trust. Nor is it an appropriate position for an institution that is dependent on government support for its continued health and survival.

Congress' unanimous endorsement of an additional amendment on "objectivity and balance" makes the same point even more strongly, if that is possible.

The amendment, sponsored by Robert Dole, enjoins the Corporation for Public Broadcasting to implement the provisions of the Public Broadcasting Act of 1967, which require "objectivity and balance in all programs or series of programs of a controversial nature."

When Congress voted unanimously to approve this amendment, John Lawson, director of national affairs for America's Public Television Stations, sought to downplay its significance. In a statement to *Current*, he noted that its provisions "basically set up a procedure to implement authorities and responsibilities that the CPB Board already has."

This is true. But precisely because it is true, the significance of the congressional mandate is nearly the opposite of what Lawson claims. That significance is to underscore a long-standing dereliction of duty, and a failure of responsibility, on the part of the CPB board *and* staff in implementing the provisions of the 1967 act. It points in particular to the failure of CPB's general counsel Paul Symczak, whose job it is to alert the appointed CPB board to its responsibilities under the law. Instead of guiding the CPB board to implement the objectivity and balance requirements of the Public Broadcasting Act, counsel Symczak and CPB staff have normally sought to deflect CPB board members from these very obligations, invoking the doctrine of noninterference in matters of programming as a rationale for the omission.

Lawson's interpretation of the amendment misunderstands the significance of the congressional action. What Congress has done is to tell the CPB board that the policy of ignoring the objectivity and balance provisions of the 1967 act is unacceptable and must be changed. The reason change is necessary is not merely that the present policy violates existing law (though that in itself should be sufficient). It is that, from a practical standpoint, public broadcasting cannot survive if it functions as a partisan voice whose mission is to oppose the values, policy preferences, and interests of half the community that supports it.

The 1992 platform of the Republican Party contains the following statement: "We deplore the blatant political bias of the government-sponsored radio and television networks. It is especially outrageous that taxpayers are now forced to underwrite this biased broadcasting through the Corporation for Public Broadcasting. We call for sweeping reform of CPB, including greater accountability through application of the Freedom of Information Act, a one-year funding cycle, and enforcement of rigorous fairness standards for all CPB-supported programming."

The importance of this statement for public broadcasters lies in the grievance it articulates and in the political constituency it represents. Public broadcasting exists in the environment of a two-party system composed of Democrats and Republicans. That is the basic fact from which all constructive thinking about the future of public broadcasting must begin. Whatever the outcome of the next election, whatever the resulting political balance, at some point in the electoral future the Republican Party is going to secure the power that will enable it to de-fund the public broadcasting system if its grievances are not addressed. That is the reality that anyone concerned with the future of this system must now begin to face. Taking steps to address this problem is the task that any responsible leader of the public broadcasting system will want to assume.

CONSERVATIVES AND LIBERALS AGREE: PBS TILTS LEFT

On January 12, the Corporation for Public Broadcasting held a hearing on balance and objectivity in Washington, D.C., and invited members of watchdog groups to present testimony as to how well they felt CPB was living up to its legal obligations under the Public Telecommunications Act of 1992.

Testimony was presented to a panel consisting of Sheila Tate, chairman of the Corporation for Public Broadcasting, Richard Carlson, president of CPB, and Fred DeMarco, CPB vice president for station relations. Fourteen people gave testimony, representing a diverse collection of groups, including the Gay and Lesbian Alliance Against Defamation, the Center for the Study of Popular Culture, People for the American Way, the Media Research Center, the Family Research Council, the American-Arab Anti-Discrimination Committee, CAMERA, AIM, the Human Rights Campaign Fund, the National Rifle Association, the Association of Chinese Americans, Accuracy in Academia, FAIR, and the Anti-Defamation League of B'nai B'rith.

The event, which took place in a rented hotel room, presented a decisive refutation to public broadcasting's claim that it receives equivalent criticisms from liberals and conservatives. In fact, with the exception of the die-hard Marxists from FAIR, the criticism could not have been more one-sided.

On the liberal side, Jill Bond, testifying for People for the American Way's "Artsave" project, came to "affirm our support for the role public broadcasting plays in providing quality programming and a diversity of points of view." The only criticism Bond had was that the corporation was spending too much time and resources on "alleged problems of programming imbalance." Bond argued that public broadcasting should "move away from the politically driven debates over balance and objectivity" and instead concentrate on technological issues.

Cathy Renna, spokeswoman for GLAAD, a liberal homosexual advocacy group, congratulated public broadcasting for airing programming favorable to liberal approaches to gay and lesbian issues. So did Gregory King of the Human Rights Campaign Fund, who noted that "the Corporation for Public Broadcasting, through your support of National Public Radio and the Public Broadcasting Service, has had an important impact on the ability of lesbian and gay Americans to emerge from the shadows of society into the sunlight of American life." He urged CPB to "continue to provide leadership in using the airwaves...to break the bonds of bigotry."

Only the perennially unsatisfied leftists from FAIR broke this united front of support for the *status quo*. Don

Hazen, representing the group, even objected to the form of the corporation and its presidentially appointed board—a structure that Lyndon Johnson and the liberal Great Society had put in place 25 years earlier. Hazen then went on to say that FAIR hopes that Congress will *repeal* the balance and objectivity requirements of the Public Broadcasting Act—no mealy-mouthed liberals, these Marxists. For the thousandth time, Hazen reiterated FAIR's complaint about the overrepresentation of corporate spokesmen and white males everywhere and asked for a regular show about labor as well as a talk show hosted by someone "left of center." Apparently Charlie Rose, Bonnie Erbe, Paul Duke, Dennis Wholey, Gordon Peterson, the omnipresent Bill Moyers, and Robert MacNeil and Jim Lehrer are right wingers on FAIR's political spectrum. Responding to COMINT's argument that PBS documentaries are overwhelmingly weighted towards liberal and left-wing perspectives and concerns, FAIR claimed that documentaries constituted only 8 percent of the PBS schedule and that talking-head shows, including *MacNeil/Lehrer*, were tilted to the right. This charge could only be supported by FAIR's "study" of PBS programming, in which a left-wing government official is identified by FAIR's scholars as a white male from an elite group, hence conservative.

If the liberal interest groups at the CPB hearing found the *status quo* satisfactory, however, conservatives had much to complain about.

Jim Warner, legal counsel of the National Rifle Association, made the point that his group had been attacked by an NPR commentator as the "Negro Removal Association" and that NPR had not responded to a request for airtime in reply. He noted that the basis of the FCC "fairness doctrine" was a scarcity of frequency and that CPB had the legal basis to issue a "fairness doctrine" because of the scarcity of federal money at its disposal. Since CPB could not fund everything, it should fund programs on the basis of fairness.

Tim Graham of the Media Research Center testified that since passage of the Public Telecommunications Act of 1992, "the actual on-air content of government-funded news programming on PBS and NPR has shown few signs of improvement." He cited the failure of PBS's *Frontline* to report the findings of a bipartisan congressional panel exonerating Reagan campaign officials of "October Surprise" charges, despite two *Frontline* programs falsely accusing them of the same. Graham noted *Frontline* had failed to correct its "secret team" assertions regarding the assassination of Eden Pastora, despite the contrary findings and change of heart of journalists Martha Honey and Tony Avirgan, who originated the accusations. Graham pointed out that the *MacNeil/Lehrer NewsHour* never corrected KQED reporter Spencer Michaels' report on taxes, which blamed Proposition 13 for the failing infrastructure of a town, despite 15 years of tax increases to the inhabitants of the town. He quoted from Glenn Garvin's article "Why I Hate NPR," which pointed out that for three days NPR had aired Clinton administration positions on the stimulus package without a single Republican response. He concluded by noting that *Frontline* "has begun its 1993 season without any programs on the scandals surrounding President Clinton or Democratic leaders in Congress, despite executive producer David Fanning's claim that the PBS slant against the Republicans "simply meant they investigated those in power."

Reed Irvine of Accuracy In Media argued that public broadcasting was tied to the American system of higher education and that its programming priorities reflect the same problem of political correctness as faced in American universities. He said that constant rejection from PBS was discouraging to those with conservative viewpoints and told how his own programs about Vietnam faced opposition from PBS executives in the '80s.

Robert H. Knight of the Family Research Council and Joe Goulden of Accuracy In Media singled out the PBS series *Tales of the City* for criticism. Goulden did a frame-by-frame analysis of a San Francisco bathhouse sequence, which he called false and misleading because the character ends up with a woman, having heterosexual sex. He added it was a disservice to glamorize bathhouses because the promiscuous homosexual sex that occurs there spreads a fatal disease. "I shudder at the thought of young San Francisco homosexuals being lured back into what are tantamount to suicide clubs by your false depiction," Goulden told the panel.

Knight called *Tales of the City* "a slick piece of gay propaganda that presents '70s gay life in San Francisco as superior to marriage and family, with few apparent consequences from promiscuous sex or illicit drugs." Knight pointed out that there is a "terrible tragedy unfolding among homosexual men" and that "more than half the gay men in San Francisco are now HIV-positive, and thousands more suffer from gay bowel syndrome, hepatitis A, B, and C, syphilis, gonorrhea, and a host of other sexually transmitted diseases directly traceable to gay sex practices such as anal sex. Yet the one guy dying from an incurable disease in the mini-series is a heterosexual businessman who learns to let go of his silly traditional values, such as fidelity to his wife, and chases the bohemian dream." Knight asked that CPB balance its programming with shows on successful abstinence programs, what actually occurs in abortion clinics, the impact of pornography on individuals, condom research, Charles Murray's findings on illegitimacy, the beneficial effect of religion on social pathologies, and the risks of gay sex. He asked that CPB air the Family Research Council's documentary *The Children of Table 34*, which alleges criminal sexual abuse by Kinsey's sex researchers.

Ginny Gong of the Association of Chinese Americans called for more sensitive depictions of Asian Americans, Russell Mokhiber of the Arab American Anti-Discrimination Committee called on CPB to include more Arab American commentators and complained that the *MacNeil/ Lehrer NewsHour* interviews with Arabs "were cold and removed, without any warmth for the people or feeling for their concerns."

Andrea Levin, executive director of CAMERA, and Michael Lieberman of the Anti-Defamation League of B'nai B'rith presented evidence of anti-Israel bias on PBS and NPR.

COMINT editor David Horowitz noted that CPB had not put any enforcement mechanisms into place despite the passage of 18 months since the Senate debate raised the balance issue. He pointed out that his own complaint against station KBOO's admitted bias towards the "liberal-progressive" political agenda was dismissed by CPB executive Fred DeMarco without investigation. He noted that ITVS had failed to live up to its congressional mandate and yet was not disciplined by CPB. Horowitz also argued that the failure of CPB to act in the case of Pacifica's anti-Semitic broadcasts had encouraged a coup at Pacifica's Washington station, WPFW, and "puts into question the seriousness of CPB's commitment to balance." He noted that there was a systemic bias against conservatives and Republicans and that he did not know of a single full-time conservative on-air personality or programming executive, and he called on the system to permit cultural and political diversity as well as diversity in terms of race and sex.

Unfortunately, CPB panelists Tate, Carlson, and DeMarco chose not to comment on the testimony or ask questions of the witnesses, with the exception of one closing remark from Sheila Tate, who announced the CPB board "does not intend to pass judgment on individual programs. We do not intend anything that will chill programming." Tate did not explain how CPB could honor its commitments to Congress and observe the provisions of the Public Broadcasting Act while turning a blind eye to the way it actually spends its programming funds.

—Laurence Jarvik

CPB REPORT: A WASTE OF $500,000

On February 1, 1994, the Corporation for Public Broadcasting released a report on its efforts to meet a congressional mandate to see that the fairness and balance provisions of the Public Broadcasting Act were met by the Public Broadcasting System. These included: (1) to review its efforts, if any, to meet these provisions in the past; (2) to solicit the views of the public as to whether its programs were, in fact, fair and balanced; (3) to review its national programming to see if the programming was balanced; (4) to take any necessary steps to achieve balance where imbalance was detected; (5) to spread the word of its activities and share its experience towards achieving balance throughout the system; and (6) to report annually to Congress "summarizing its efforts pursuant to these directives."

The *Report to Congress on Steps Taken by the Corporation for Public Broadcasting in Response to Section 19 of the Public*

Telecommunications Act of 1992: The First Year is CPB's effort to meet the congressional mandate. Unfortunately, it does no such thing.

The report shows that the CPB board has completely ignored four of the six congressional directives, fulfilling only the last, which requires the report itself (and even this has come a year late), and the second, which requires soliciting input from the public. As we shall show, CPB has erroneously construed this latter effort as a public relations exercise, and a poorly conceived one at that.

CPB's failure to confront the problem of balance, which the congressional directives instruct it to deal with, flows from a decision by the CPB board not to look at its programming (a violation of directives 3 and 4). As CPB board chairman Sheila Tate said at the CPB's Washington hearing: "The board does not intend to pass judgment on individual programs." But if the board does not intend to pass judgment on individual programs, how can it meet the congressional mandate? The answer is, it cannot.

As a matter of fact, the CPB board does not even have an official principle of balance by which to judge its programs in the first place. For example, is the principle of balance to be applied to individual programs, to programs in comparable time slots, to programs within similar genres? Is it to be applied to the overall schedule? As we pointed out more than a year ago, there is no CPB policy that answers these questions. Hence, there can be no CPB assessment as to whether its programming is balanced or not. If the CPB board had even attempted to comply with the first congressional directive ("review its efforts to meet its responsibilities" under the Public Broadcasting Act) it would have realized this and proceeded in a very different manner than that summarized in its report.

What the CPB board did do, at a cost of $500,000, was launch an "Open to the Public" campaign, as though accessibility was the only problem that caused Congress to hold up its authorization for nine months and issue the six directives. This was one of the problems and is dealt with in one directive. All the other directives are about fairness, balance, and objectivity and about establishing and enforcing standards of journalistic integrity and responsibility. These are the directives CPB ignored.

Since the CPB board did not review its standards of balance, did not rectify their deficiencies, and did not apply them to its programming, it is extraordinary to read in the CPB Report that "[the CPB board] has not found any glaring pattern of bias, social slant or partisan predisposition." How, in the absence of any articulated standards of balance, can CPB conclude that its programming is balanced? In fact, even within the "Open to the Public" framework through which CPB has chosen, in effect, to evade its responsibilities, the CPB Report refutes this claim. Though absent from the executive summary of the report, compelling evidence of bias in public broadcasting is contained in the voluminous documents appended as "Tabs."

THE REPORT

After summarizing the components of the "Open to the Public" program, the report describes the establishment of an "Office of Public Access." It then describes "Preliminary Meetings With Interested Groups." Actually, it refers to two such meetings in December 1992 and January 1993. Although the Report does not mention any particulars of the December event, an article in COMINT did. At the meeting, Diane Kaplan of Alaska public radio asked CPB to promise never to commission any balancing programming, a sentiment echoed by PBS chairman Jerry Baliles and others in attendance, who preached defiance of the congressional mandate for balance. Perhaps this atmosphere explains the deficiencies of the CPB effort as revealed in its report. It does not, however, excuse them.

The report then refers to the January 12, 1994, public hearing hosted by CPB in Washington, D.C. (see "Conservatives and Liberals Agree: PBS Tilts Left," page 243). The report does not mention that this particular hearing was not part of the original CPB schedule for "Open to the Public." It was not a "town meeting" like the other sessions, but a forum for groups with an interest in public broadcasting, and was convened only after considerable pressure on CPB by COMINT and others. The hearing was eloquent testimony to the bias in public broadcasting. Liberal interest groups like People for the American Way and the Gay Lesbian Association Against Defamation praised public broadcasting for being in the progressive vanguard, while conservative groups like the Family Research Council and AIM complained that that was exactly what it was doing.

Next, the report refers to a post-office box set up by CPB. CPB says that it forwards letters to "the appropriate producer, station, or organization for response." But Congress did not intend CPB's balance efforts to be a mail-drop service. The obligation was that CPB should read its mail and respond by examining and—where it was deemed necessary—adjusting its programming decisions. This mail-drop admission alone calls into question CPB's good faith in respect to the congressional directives.

Reading on, one is struck by what appears to be a willful decision to deny the obvious. CPB admits it has received some 3,682 postcards protesting two documentaries, Rachel Carlson's *Silent Spring* and *In Our Children's Food*. This volume of mail is clear evidence of a perception of bias, even if it is part of an orchestrated campaign, as CPB alleges. Some significant part of the public has felt injured enough to complain. Did CPB review the complaints, assess the program, and make a decision? No. Incredibly, a flood of mail protesting two documentaries is interpreted by the report as "no evidence of bias." Four hundred letters protesting *Journey to the Occupied Lands* are similarly dismissed. The reason given is that letters of complaint are "not statistically valid." So why solicit them?

The CPB report then refers to its toll-free phone number and the 6,011 calls it received. Here we encounter a similar pattern of denial. CPB concedes that 59 percent of the callers expressed "unfavorable or strongly unfavorable opinions" but then dismisses the implication by suggesting that the callers were organized. This is an admission either that CPB is incapable of analyzing this data in a productive way or that the open phone line is a waste of time.

CPB admits it received 1,385 calls about *Journey to the Occupied Lands*, a program the watchdog group CAMERA has argued is biased. If there are 1,000 complaints about a program, isn't that evidence of bias? If not, why are people complaining? Again, the reader is referred to raw data, rather than receiving the review of programming mandated by the law. No effort is made to reply to the analysis provided by CAMERA of the bias in the program; no CPB guidelines exist for an independent observer to judge whether the program meets a CPB standard or not.

It is the Town Meetings—the centerpiece of the "Open to the Public" campaign—that are cited in the report as evidence of "overwhelming support of public broadcasting." COMINT has already described the South Carolina town meeting fiasco in its last issue—a closed meeting with an audience that had been pre-screened by a marketing company to produce a favorable response. The Seattle town meeting was attended by a reporter for the *Seattle Times*. The reporter quoted one participant to the effect that the meeting was "a well-orchestrated PR exercise." The reporter, Chuck Taylor, himself observed that the audience was selected by CPB. Even so, there were complaints about bias. The Texas meeting also included testimony criticizing bias in public broadcasting, witnessed at the time by a COMINT reporter via satellite hookup, and ignored in the report.

RESEARCH

Perhaps the most egregious section of the report is that dealing with CPB's so-called research. As the *Seattle Times* noted regarding the local CPB poll, which found only 7 percent of viewers reporting bias, "the source of last night's input was selective. That poll by Elway Research Inc. questioned in detail only those who felt they were familiar enough with public broadcasting stations to form an opinion. That means regular viewers and listeners. Would they be viewing or listening regularly if they didn't like the spin?"

The CPB "national poll" was equally flawed. In a presentation at the Washington press conference, the two pollsters admitted that respondents had overreported their viewing of PBS, and the poll permitted them to characterize public broadcasting without reference to specific programs save the *MacNeil/Lehrer NewsHour*. But *MacNeil/Lehrer* has been cited by COMINT and other critics of PBS bias as among the most balanced programs on public airwaves. If COMINT had been polled by these experts using this frame of reference, PBS would have received high marks as well. The failure to include *Frontline*, *POV*, and *Bill Moyers' Journal*, to name a few more appropriate examples, cannot be chalked up to a mere statistical problem, especially when the results of even this questionable poll show 45 percent of viewers think PBS should be more balanced and define "liberal" as children of different ethnic backgrounds playing together on *Sesame Street* (which pretty much equates conservative with un-American). Other examples of poor questions in the poll included one defining bias as "showing only one side or point of view"—which is less self-evidently bias than "favoring one side or point of view"—and skewing results by only using a subset of 471 respondents out of 1,000 polled to answer questions about *MacNeil/Lehrer*.

The poll survey referred to "documentaries" without distinguishing between *National Geographic* and *Frontline*. Even so, with 10 being balanced and 1 being very biased or slanted, PBS shows only rated a 7.65—which, by definition, is not balanced; 10 is balanced. Thus—if one were fair-minded, as the report is not—one could extract, even from the flawed survey data, enough evidence to indicate that there is bias in public-broadcasting programming. On the two specific questions about documentaries on environmental issues, 45 percent of the respondents say that PBS programs are slanted in favor of environmentalists (matching the thousands of "orchestrated" postcards complaining about *Return to Silent Spring*), and 45 percent also say documentaries about political movements in other countries are slanted (matching the thousands of "orchestrated" responses protesting *Journey to the Occupied Lands*.) Again, this is clear evidence of the bias disclaimed by the CPB report.

The flawed CPB poll also noted that six in 10 upper-income households and conservative Republicans thought public broadcasting was biased. This is all the more impressive and glaring evidence of bias in public broadcasting, when one considers that the pollsters *never even asked* if public broadcasting was biased towards Republicans, although they did ask if it was slanted towards Democrats. When asked why they omitted the second largest political party, the pollsters told a press conference that in talking about public broadcasting in focus groups, the word *Republican* never even came up! You don't have to be a rocket scientist to interpret that datum's implication as evidence for bias in the public-broadcasting system.

Referring to "Colloquia On Standards Of Integrity and Responsibility" sponsored by CPB (actually one colloquium at the University of South Carolina), the summary ignores statements made by panelists to the effect that public broadcasting was set up to foster "social change" and should continue in its mission. This was merely a reflection of the liberal (and unbalanced) composition of the panel. The idea that public broadcasting's mission is "social change" is not shared by conservatives and violates its legal mandate. But how could the panel not reflect the status quo bias of the system, since CPB makes no effort to correct this bias by balancing its panels?

Not surprisingly, the CPB report includes a provision for the establishment of (its normally unbalanced) panels to review programming. But the law itself specifically directs the CPB board to review programming because of its dissatisfaction with the existing panel process, which is open to stacking by career bureaucrats, to conflicts of interest, etc.

The CPB report's conclusion contains this pathetic complaint:

> Implicit in the issue of balance and objectivity, on the other hand, is the difficult if not painful question of what to do with the information which "Open to the Public" has laid at public broadcasting's doorstep. As tastes differ, so do interpretations of whether the system's principles or operating style are in need of repair.

This is just an admission by the CPB board that it is not up to the task that has been set for it by Congress and by the terms of the Public Broadcasting Act. The issue of balance and objectivity in public broadcasting is not a matter of personal taste any more than any other difficult public decision is a matter of taste. The whole point of the law is to get CPB and the public broadcasting community to establish some agreed on principles of balance and objectivity and to enforce them. Unfortunately, as we have many times pointed out, the system at present has no clearly established "principles" that it can put on the table for the rest of us to evaluate. Or that it can enforce on programmers who are abusing public monies by putting together program schedules that are not reasonably balanced. The law says quite clearly that CPB must "take any necessary steps in the awarding of programming grants to meet the Corporation's responsibility." If there is evidence of a pattern of bias in public broadcasting—and there is, clearly, even from the manipulated and unsatisfactory evidence gathered for the CPB report—then CPB is obligated to award programming grants to rectify the imbalance. If it does not do so, it is in violation of the law.

By attempting to deny the obvious, CPB is trying to avoid its responsibility under law and is close to being in contempt of Congress. CPB has forgotten the lesson of the authorization debate. If the public-broadcasting community ignores half its public constituency, it will pay a price. Representative Dick Armey—the author of a bill to defund public broadcasting entirely—has, in the intervening time, become the Republican Party Whip. Meanwhile, many Democrats have joined Republicans in expressing their dismay at the current public-broadcasting schedule and have voted to freeze or cut CPB funds. It should not be forgotten that the congressional mandate on balance was unanimously agreed to by both sides of the House. If conservatives on both sides of the aisle make significant gains in the midterm elections, public broadcasting will need every conservative friend it can get. If public broadcasters continue to proceed along the lines of the CPB report, however, they will discover such friends difficult to find.

—*Laurence Jarvik*

CONTEMPT OF CONGRESS

In 1992, a series of amendments were attached to the reauthorization bill for the Corporation for Public Broadcasting. These amendments spelled out in detail the obligations of the corporation's board under the terms of the Public Broadcasting Act and outlined specific tasks the board would be required to undertake in order to fulfill them. Congress took this extraordinary step because of the previous failure of the board to live up to the terms of the act. It had failed to ensure that programming was fair, objective, and strictly balanced as the law required. At the time of the reauthorization, a new CPB board with a new chairman, Sheila Tate, pledged to carry out the will of Congress as expressed in these amendments.

More than two years have elapsed, enough time to assess the sincerity of the CPB in its resolve to carry out this mandate. Unfortunately, the record is as negative as it is clear. Led by its retiring chairman, Sheila Tate, the CPB board has for two years ignored the provisions of the law and thumbed its collective nose at Congress.

If this seems a harsh judgment, consider the facts: Except for soliciting public comments and providing a summary report on these comments—which was submitted a year late—the CPB board has done nothing else to carry out its obligations under the law:

☛ It has not reviewed national programming for quality, diversity, objectivity or balance;

☛ it has not taken steps in awarding programming grants to provide balance;

☛ and it has not disseminated among public broadcasting entities information about its efforts to balance programming so that the entities can follow its example.

Led by Sheila Tate, the CPB board categorically refused to fulfill these obligations. The rationale for this contempt of Congress was that CPB is a government agency and therefore for CPB to review programming—as Congress has required—would be to violate the First Amendment rights of public broadcasters. Accordingly, Tate, with the CPB board following, has ignored all requests for program review. The board has failed to undertake initiatives to fulfill the congressional mandates to review its practices from the viewpoint of balance, to provide funds to balance the existing schedule, or to provide leadership to the stations and distributing entities in establishing guidelines and procedures to do the same.

The argument that a review of programs would violate the First Amendment rights of broadcasters is a spurious one. If it were not, the board would have made this argument to Congress in the first place, at the time the authorization was debated. Instead, Tate and the CPB board pretended to Congress that they were ready to comply with the legislators' wishes, even though they had no real intention of doing so. Tate and the board then used the First Amendment argument to bully critics of the existing schedule and to ignore any serious discussion of possible reform.

As a result, instead of leading the efforts to comply with the congressional mandate, Sheila Tate and the CPB board have set a negative example for the entire system. In the two years since Congress enacted the amendments not a single step has been taken to: 1) establish standard guidelines for ensuring fairness and balance; 2) establish procedures that would promote balance while guarding editorial freedoms; 3) provide funding to redress the imbalances that currently exist in the program schedule.

We will just note, for the record, that there is still no balance to the $11.5-million per annum *Frontline* series nor to the $9-million per annum ITVS operation. New series, such as *The Charlie Rose* show, which airs nightly on the PBS feed, and *Rights and Wrongs*, which airs weekly on more than 100 PBS stations, have appeared in the last year without any gesture of balance. National Public Radio has yet to hire a senior producer, national correspondent, national reporter, or news manager with conservative credentials.

As we have pointed out many times in the past, when the CPB board fails in its responsibilities to ensure the integrity of the system, it fails as well in its role as a "heat shield." It leaves Congress with no option but to write new legislation with provisions that will be impossible to ignore.

—*David Horowitz*

THREE MEMOS, 1994

Public Broadcasting: A Democratic Boondoggle

Year after year, Republican legislators appropriate hundreds of millions of dollars to public-radio and television broadcasters, who return the favor by promoting the agendas of their political opponents.

During the 1992 presidential elections, public television ran two hour-long shows charging that then-President George Bush and former President Reagan "stole" the 1980 election by cutting a deal with the Ayatollah Khomeini to delay the release of American hostages in Iran. There was no opportunity given to Republicans for a reply.

Nor were any apologies or corrections offered by PBS when the "October Surprise" theory was dismissed as unproven by a Democrat-controlled committee of Congress. A year earlier, PBS ran a one-and-a-half-hour "documentary" on Iran Contra by Democrat Bill Moyers that accused President Reagan of "High Crimes and Misdemeanors." There was no opportunity for a Republican version of this history or a rebuttal of Moyers' partisan message.

During the 1992 election campaign, PBS ran six hours of programs by Moyers, a former LBJ speechwriter, and by another liberal Democrat, William Greider, on how badly the country had fared under 12 years of Republican administrations. There was no opportunity given to Republicans for response. There were no shows about the unprecedented expansion of opportunities for Americans during the prosperity generated by the policies of the Reagan years. During the closing month of the 1992 election campaign, PBS also ran *LBJ*, which was a four-hour celebration of Lyndon Johnson's Great Society programs, and a four-hour tribute to the Kennedy family. And this is just a sampling of the taxpayer-funded programs on public radio and television that helped to put the Democrats back in the White House.

What did public broadcasters do for Republicans in election year '92? They ran a biography of Richard Nixon to remind the public that the only president ever forced to resign was a Republican.

Given this bias, it was hardly surprising that staffers at public station WGBH-TV, Boston, who were reporting the election results for the national PBS feed, cheered *on camera* when the announcement came that Clinton went over the top.

It is indicative of the overall political culture of public television that PBS has never aired a program celebrating the victory in the Cold War that was won under the leadership of the Republicans and Ronald Reagan, even though this was the most important event of the last half century. Perhaps that is because, during the last decade of the Cold War, PBS was running hour after hour of television programs praising the Marxist guerrillas in El Salvador and the Marxist dictatorships in Cuba and Nicaragua on the last Cold War frontier.

This political partisanship is a direct violation of the Public Broadcasting Act of 1967, which requires that tax-payer-funded public affairs shows be strictly balanced and fair. To rectify this, Congress took action in June 1992 to re-mind public broadcasters of their responsibilities under the law. Led by Sen. Bob Dole, the Congress enacted amend-ments to the reauthorization bill that required the Corpora-tion for Public Broadcasting to review its programming and take steps to balance its product.

In the two years that have elapsed since this man-date, the CPB board has steadfastly refused to examine programming and carry out this mandate. In that time, not a single program or programming schedule has been spe-cifically reviewed for balance. Nor has a single program been funded for balance. CPB board chairman Sheila Tate has said categorically that the CPB board "does not intend to pass judgment on individual programs." In case after case, she has refused to look at the programming schedule of public radio and television stations for evidence of bias and has prevented CPB president Richard Carlson and his staff from doing so.

When media critics complained about the anti-Re-publican bias in public broadcasts during the '92 campaign, PBS and NPR officials responded by saying that, as journal-ists, they were "adversarial to power" and would be just as critical of a Democratic administration as they had been of Republicans. This has proven to be an empty promise. We now have a Democratic administration. What has been pub-lic broadcasting's response?

Now that a Democratic president has come under press scrutiny, public broadcasting has become the White House's most friendly network. There has not been a single documentary television program devoted to Whitewater or any other Democratic Party scandal, such as the attack on the Branch Davidian compound at Waco that left 50 chil-dren dead.

While *The New York Times*, CNN, and the *Los Angeles Times* have vigorously pursued the Whitewater story, *All Things Considered* reporters Linda Wertheimer and Mara Liasson have applied their journalistic imaginations to suggesting excuses for the president and First Lady and commiserating with them over the prying sensationalism of the national press.

Nina Totenberg, who bent journalistic ethics and skirted the borders of the law to break the story of Anita Hill's accusations against Clarence Thomas, dragged her feet in covering Paula Jones's complaint and played no role in getting it a public hearing. Nor has she expended any effort to get the many other women who have been identified by Arkansas troopers to come forward.

While taxpayer-funded broadcasters circle the wagons around the Clinton White House, Republican legislators should be thinking about what this means for their own electoral chances this coming November.

They should consider that public broadcasters estimate their audience at 100 million Americans a week, that National Public Radio reaches the most politically active and educated segment of the population, and that a poll of public broadcasters revealed that more than 80 percent are liberal Democrats. Small wonder that Sen. Robert Dole has said that every time he turns on NPR he thinks he's listening to the Democratic National Committee.

The public-broadcasting network is a Democratic lobby in every congressional district in the nation. This state of affairs violates the law and distorts the electoral process. Republican legislators—and all those interested in the health of the two-party system—should hold up reauthorization for the Corporation for Public Broadcasting until its board agrees to take steps to balance its programming and to abide by the spirit and letter of the public broadcasting law.

—David Horowitz

How PBS Documentaries Serve the Clinton Agenda

On May 24, PBS's *Frontline* aired *Public Lands, Private Profit*, which promoted legislation to raise fees charged mining companies. This tie to legislation and larger agendas is not unusual for PBS documentaries, especially given the environmentalist bias of the network's nature specials—for example, PBS refused to air *The Greenhouse Conspiracy*, a British program exposing the prediction as a hoax. In addition to well-known anti-Christian and anti-Israel programming and pro-Castro, pro-Mandela, pro-gay documentaries, there are less familiar examples that show how PBS fits into liberal Democrats' political and legislative agenda. In many cases, the "outreach campaign" features promotion of activist organizations, distribution of printed materials, coordination with schools, and 800 numbers (case in point, Bill Moyers' special on campaign finance reform had an on-air "dial 1-800-VOTE-SMART." The number is now disconnected.)

Because one cannot legally buy time on PBS or NPR, and because there is no mechanism to insure a right to reply, the endorsement of political positions by public broadcasting helps groups organize support. Further, although audiences may be small, shows are usually written up in newspaper columns, creating a multiplication effect for the original broadcast. *The New York Times* might not cover a story, but it might review the PBS documentary, thereby recirculating the story through the *Times*.

Here are some cases:

Support for the Clinton Health Care Plan

1. HEALTH POLICY: In 1992 the Robert Wood Johnson Foundation gave two $10-million grants to WGBH for coverage of health issues. This supported *The Health Quarterly* with Roger Mudd, a series cancelled after a year—and Clinton's election. Health coverage was a major campaign issue for Clinton, and the Johnson Foundation is closely associated with the Clinton plan. This year Bill Moyers hosted a PBS special on the crisis in health care, and PBS has announced a special initiative on women's health—a new documentary; a package of six programs; 12 "info-minutes" featuring Geraldine Ferraro, Wilma Mankiller, and Joycelyn Elders, a "yellow pages" from the National Women's Health Resource Center containing names and addresses of activist groups; a brochure called "Six Health Issues of Concern to Every Woman"; six free articles for distribution by PBS stations; $10,000 cash payments to stations; and combining feminism with promoting health-care policy. The series argues that domestic violence is a major health-care problem. Cigarettes are targeted—but not the health risks of high-fat Ben and Jerry's Ice Cream or caffeine-laden Starbucks coffee.

Another series aired this year, *Medicine at the Cross-*

roads argued against expensive "miracle drugs" and high-tech surgery in favor of community centered care and preventative medicine—a cost-reduction strategy favored in the Clinton plan.

Support for the Clinton Industrial Plan

2. ECONOMIC PLANNING: PBS has just aired a multi-part series called *Challenge to America* hosted by Hedrick Smith, which argues for long-range industrial planning similar to that used by Germany and Japan, views long held by the Clinton administration in contrast to free-market viewpoints of the Reagan administration. Japan and Germany are currently in worse economic shape than the United States or Great Britain.

Support for Clinton administration
Feminist Affirmative Action

3. "GENDER EQUITY": A good example is *Frontline's* recent *In the Game* about women's sports on campus and the demand for equal funding with men's sports—a subject of constant litigation and legislative interest and part of the feminist agenda. Complements women's health issues described above.

Support for Clinton Crime Bill

4. CRIMINAL JUSTICE: CPB has just funded a "youth violence initiative" to the tune of $200,000 as part of a package including a program hosted by Bill Moyers and outreach activities. No doubt this is keyed into the "prevention" aspect of the crime bill before Congress and its multibillion dollar programs for social spending. NPR, as is now well known, hired death-row inmate and Black Panther Abu-Jamal as a commentator. After an outcry, his commentary moved to CPB-funded Pacifica radio and NPR announced it will get a different death row convict as a featured commentator on *Fresh Air*.

Support for Clinton Immigration Policy

5. IMMIGRATION: On June 7, *Frontline* aired *Go Back to Mexico! Frontline* has previously aired attacks on GM for exporting jobs to Mexico prior to the NAFTA vote and an attack on Honda during a trade dispute with Japan in the Bush administration—both viewpoints of the labor unions in the Democratic party.

Support for Clinton Welfare Policy

6. WELFARE: On Friday, May 6, PBS broadcast *Mak-*

ing Welfare Work, with Walter Cronkite, looking at the "human side of this complex issue." On April 26, PBS aired a Ford Foundation-funded special called Building Hope: Community Development in America—in blatant violation of PBS conflict-of-interest and underwriting guidelines since Ford was the sponsor of the CDC programs promoted in the film—promoting Community Development Corporations as a solution to urban blight, blaming Reagan budget cuts for the failure of these notoriously corrupt and ill-considered boondoggles. No *Frontline* this year has centered on the outright criminality of many overseers of the "poverty plantations."

—*Laurence Jarvik*

Fiscal Questions About Public Broadcasting

The Corporation for Public Broadcasting uses taxpayer money to fund programs that make millions of dollars for well-connected private companies and individuals. A single celebrated PBS children's program generates more annual revenues than the National Hockey League, but none of these millions are shared with taxpayers who fund the shows.

CPB's budget is at an all-time high and has doubled since 1980. Because CPB is not subject to the Freedom of Information Act—it is "a private corporation funded by the American people" rather than a federal agency—the public cannot find out how much money is being made from the taxpayer-funded system. So far, it has been spared any congressional scrutiny of its funding practices.

Private, for-profit businesses doing business with public broadcasters are making considerable profits selling merchandise connected with PBS shows. Among the merchandise are games, toys, clothing, books, videocassettes, records, and computer games. There are also two catalogs dedicated to PBS merchandise, *Wireless* and *Signals*, with an estimated gross of $77 million a year.

☛ BARNEYGATE: THE EXPLOITATION OF CHILDREN'S PROGRAMMING
As the largest specialized PBS audience, children are by far the most profitable PBS market. PBS children's programming

provides free advertising and marketing for these companies selling associated toys and merchandise. One series, *Sesame Street*, alone generates almost $1 billion in sales annually. Yet none of these sales find their way back into the public treasury.

This is perhaps the most profitable area of PBS merchandising. The following are some revenue estimates based information from a trade publication, *The Licensing Letter:*

Sesame Street generates $800 million annually in gross licensing revenues. It has been on the air for 25 years. Parent "nonprofit" Children's Television Workshop has five for-profit subsidiaries, a $58 million stock and bond portfolio, and pays top executives who handle licensing $600,000 a year. According to Raugust, Major League Baseball only pays from $200,000 to $500,000 annually for executives handling a business that is more than twice as large.

Barney is making $500 million a year after two years. Although they have a new agreement with PBS, not one penny will be returned to the U.S. Treasury.

Shining Time Station earns over $200 million per annum after three years.

According to the Broderbund Software annual report, *Where in the World Is Carmen San Diego?* returns $20 million in income per annum, which reflects gross sales one can estimate at more than $100 million (the computer game is also promoted via a Fox animated program featuring the same characters).

PBS shows generally do better merchandising products in the marketplace than their commercial counterparts. By way of comparison with the for-profit world, $100-200 million a year is considered "a very strong property" by those in the business. Only the top grossing merchandise even comes near PBS levels.

For example:

Teenage Mutant Ninja Turtles averaged some $850 million a year over seven years, compared to *Sesame Street's* $800-million annual average—the same figure gross as the entire National Hockey League. At an estimated $1 billion last year, *Sesame Street* licensing compares with the same grosses for mega-hits *Jurassic Park* and *Aladdin.*

Barney compares to the *California Raisins,* at $500 million last year, and *Star Wars,* which has averaged $433 million annually over the product lifetime, but is not quite as big as Perry Ellis, at $750 million.

Shining Time Station and its star product, Thomas the Tank Engine, compare to Beatrix Potter merchandise, which yields $250 million annually. Beatrix Potter has been merchandising since 1903. It does better than *Star Trek*, which has made $1 billion over the lifetime of the series.

Of course, the *Turtles*, the *Raisins*, *Star Wars*, Beatrix Potter, *Star Trek*, the National Hockey League, *Jurassic Park*, and *Aladdin* don't get annual congressional appropriations to pay for their advertising and promotion budgets. It is clear that licensing revenues from PBS-associated merchandise are in the same ballpark as commercial products. Yet there has been no accounting to the American taxpayer for total revenues garnered by PBS promotion or the value of the PBS franchise in this lucrative market.

New children's series announced for PBS include *Bill Nye the Science Guy* (a co-production with for-profit Disney), *The Magic Schoolbus* starring Lily Tomlin (co-produced with for-profit Scholastic, Inc.), and *The Puzzleworks* (co-produced with for-profit Lancit Media). Each of these has the upside potential of *Barney* or *Sesame Street*, according to those familiar with the business.

Yet not one penny of public broadcasting's children's television revenues are returned to the American taxpayer who makes this multi-billion-dollar bonanza possible. Instead, the profits go to television producers, toy manufacturers, and giant corporations. Incredibly, public television comes begging to Congress pleading poverty even while it sits atop a billion dollar a year gold mine—a gold mine exploited by small group of politically well-connected insiders.

These same insiders donate to politicians who can help their business ventures receive continued government subsidies. For example, David Britt, president of *Sesame Street*'s parent company, Children's Television Workshop (CTW) gave $500 to Sen. Daniel Inouye. Inouye is chairman of the Senate committee responsible for the Corporation for Public Broadcasting and the rules affecting children's television on commercial networks. CTW founder Joan Ganz Cooney gave $1,000 to Sen. Tim Wirth, who sat on the same committee. Cooney donated $250 to Rep. Nita Lowey, who sits on the House committee that appropriates funds to public broadcasting. Cooney contributed $500 to President Clinton's campaign. Cooney also appointed Hillary Rodham Clinton to the board of CTW. A photograph of Cooney with President Clinton is prominently displayed in her office.

At the very least, the mixture of big business, government regulation, and campaign contributions raises the shadow of impropriety—the possibility of special treatment, favoritism, and cronyism—affecting federally funded broadcasting that can generate billions of dollars in revenue.

☛ MOYERS' MILLIONS

Before Bill Moyers left CBS News to come to public broadcasting, he was making $20,000 a week—more than $1 million a year. Yet he makes far more than that from public broadcasting. Moyers has admitted to raising more than $15 million for his private, for-profit, production company. In addition, Moyers has earned untold millions from speaking fees, book royalties, and videocassette sales. A legal action filed over *Joseph Campbell and The Power of Myth* estimated that series grosses, including various ancillary revenues, totalled over $20 million. Moyers also employs his wife and has employed his son. Add in his other popular series—*A World of Ideas I & II, A Gathering of Men,* and *Healing and the Mind,* for example—and you can imagine the total Moyers empire totaling approximately $100 million.

However, taxpayers cannot find out precisely how much Moyers has benefited at their expense because he has consistently refused to make his earnings public. Indeed, his privately held company will not even release his salary, let alone his company's earnings.

Public broadcasting has resisted all attempts to open its financial arrangements to public scrutiny, unlike the National Endowment for the Humanities, which has publicly reported that Ken Burn's series, *The Civil War,* has returned $1.5 million to them. CPB does not even require a return of the investment, much less a share of the profits from the series it funds.

☛ LOUIS RUKEYSER'S "SWEETHEART DEAL"

Another publicly subsidized multimillionaire, *Wall Street Week* host Louis Rukeyser started a newsletter last year estimated to be a $10 million-a-year operation. After Sen. Dole blasted the deal in a floor speech, Rukeyser agreed to share some of his revenues with Maryland Public Television. However, not one penny goes back to the U.S. taxpayer, whose treasury subsidized his stardom.

☛ PBS PROVIDES FREE ADVERTISING FOR SELECTED BOOKS AND VIDEOS

Book publishers and video distributors are among the major beneficiaries of PBS cross promotion. Among the most dramatic cases is that of *The Civil War*. Alfred A. Knopf is estimated to have sold some 750,000 books at $50 each, a total of $37.5 million. An estimated 250,000 cassettes were sold by Time-Life Video to the home market, and PBS Video sold thousands more to schools and institutions, adding up to over $12.5 million. Yet, while the National Endowment for the Humanities has managed to recoup some $1.5 million, the Corporation for Public Broadcasting has only recovered a few hundred thousand dollars for American taxpayers. It is obvious that without the added value of public broadcasting—and its blockbuster scheduling and promotion—*The Civil War* would never have had the success it achieved.

One cannot gauge the value of the hours of airtime provided the show. Certainly publishers would have to spend millions to purchase comparable "infomercials" on cable or network television. But in this case, the taxpayers take the risks and absorb the costs, while private companies reap all the profits. Instead of sharing in the windfalls from hit shows, PBS is reduced to lobbying Congress for government handouts and holding degrading on-air begathons to meet station payrolls.

In addition to *The Civil War*, other PBS subsidized bestsellers—exposure to PBS's book-buying demographic almost guarantees a spot on the *New York Times* bestseller list—have included Richard Attenborough's *Life On Earth*; Bartlett and Steele's best-selling *America: What Went Wrong?*; William Greider's *Who Will Tell the People?*; Michael Wood's *Legacy*; self-help works from the likes of hugely successful Leo Buscaglia and Les Brown; and titles such as *Fat or Fit, The Frugal Gourmet, This Old House, Crockett's Victory Garden, The New Yankee Workshop,* and *Yan Can Cook.*

☛ STARS SELL THEIR ALBUMS AND CDS ON PBS

During pledge week, major stars are featured in specials,

with the publicity sending album and CD sales soaring. Most famous is Yanni, the New Age Greek sensation. Other musicians who have appeared on the taxpayer-subsidized network include: Carly Simon, Paul Simon, James Taylor, Frank Sinatra, Liza Minelli, and Peter, Paul, and Mary. This year, *Great Performances* plans to promote Julie Andrews's return to Broadway, airing a documentary featuring her new album. While viewers may pledge to their local station, none of the major record companies involved return the value of the promotion to the taxpayer.

☞ HOLLYWOOD STUDIOS BENEFIT FROM PBS SUBSIDIES AND PROMOTION

Several *American Playhouse* productions have involved deals with major studios. *Stand and Deliver* was a Warner Brothers co-production, *The Thin Blue Line* was done with Miramax films, *Tales of the City* with Britain's advertiser-supported Channel Four. Now, the series has signed an exclusive multimillion dollar deal with Hollywood's Samuel Goldwyn Company, giving a private company access to the promotional value of public broadcasting.

Meanwhile, Ted Turner has paid $20 million for the right to distribute PBS videos through his for-profit company. Yet while Turner might do better than the previous PBS distributor in the $30-million-a-year market, again there is no return to the American taxpayer who makes it all possible.

☞ QUESTIONS

Do the American people have any idea of the size and scope of the private fortunes being made from public broadcasting?

Do the American people know how the chosen few who benefit from free advertising and promotion—not to mention subsidized production and distribution—are selected?

Even *Washington Week in Review* host Paul Duke has admitted that federal funding is not needed. He told *The Washingtonian* in June:

> The federal contribution is already down to about 13 percent. I'd like public broadcasting to be able to air its educational and cultural

programs without any federal funding whatsoever, but that takes more corporate underwriting. In all the documentaries and news
specials I've done over the years, I've found
corporations much easier to deal with than
the public broadcasting bureaucracy.

One thing is clear. Before Congress reauthorizes CPB,
it should conduct a serious investigation, including a General Accounting Office audit of all grant recipients and public hearings into the management of the system, to determine
the value of the services rendered and possible revenue
streams which are now diverted to private gain. The Corporation for Public Broadcasting and all its grant recipients
must be brought under the provisions of the Freedom of Information Act. Provisions must be made for the return to the
taxpayers of a reasonable share of the fortunes made from
public broadcasting-related merchandising.

Until the persistent questions of "Barneygate" are
answered, there can be no confidence that any money appropriated to public broadcasting is money well spent.

—*Laurence Jarvik*

BARNEYGATE

O f all the leaders and celebrities that came to Capitol Hill
in 1993, few did so with the fanfare of Barney, the
smiling purple dinosaur known to millions of America's children from the PBS series *Barney & Friends*. And thanks to an
article in *The Washington Post*, we now know why Barney
smiles so much.

You see, Barney isn't just a dinosaur—he's a cash
cow. According to the *Post*, sales of Barney merchandise
could reach $500 million per year, and the licensing fees mer-
chandisers pay for the privilege of making the more than 200
Barney products could be as high as $50 million per year. I
don't have any problem with that. From what I understand,
Barney & Friends is an excellent program, Barney is a lovable

character, and more power to his creators for producing jobs and capitalizing on his blockbuster popularity.

What I do have a problem with is the fact that despite putting up $2.25 million between them—much of it tax dollars—to launch *Barney & Friends* last year, the taxpayer- supported Corporation for Public Broadcasting and the Public Broadcasting Service haven't seen one dime from Barney merchandise. That's right, the American taxpayer helped make Barney into a multimillion dollar enterprise, but the Public Broadcasting System supported so handsomely by the taxpayers doesn't get a cut of the sales of Barney backpacks, Barney slippers, Barney socks, Barney lunch boxes, Barney videos, Barney bedside lamps, Talking Barney, or the scores of other Barney items available at a toy store near you.

CPB officials say they are concerned, and they should be. Eugene Katt, CPB's senior vice president for programming, told the *Post:* "Barney has been a lot more successful than we anticipated. We'll take a much harder look at licensing and profit sharing. Some income should be used to the benefit of public broadcasting." Children's television activist Peggy Charen concedes, "It seems idiotic to have all that product and no return to public broadcasting."

But "Barney-Gate" is just the tip of the iceberg. The *Post* article has exposed a problem that some of my colleagues and I took a lot of heat for discussing last year—the enormous taxpayer-subsidized profits of the children's television workshop, the well-heeled but so-called nonprofit corporation behind the fine program *Sesame Street*, not to mention the enormous revenue from merchandising associated with programs such as Bill Moyers' *The Power of Myth, The Civil War, Wall Street Week,* and *The Frugal Gourmet.* But if you want to get to the bottom of all this profiteering, you can't— public broadcasting isn't subject to the Freedom of Information Act.

If there was ever an area where Vice President Gore's "reinventing government" program was needed, this may be it. Maybe it's time for taxpayer-supported public broadcasting to drive a hard bargain with some of the profiteers making millions of dollars in licensing fees off of taxpayer-supported programs. According to the *Post,* a successful toy licenser argues that "PBS could negotiate deals that would bring it $10 million to $15 million per show each year." It seems only reasonable that before the taxpayers are asked to give public broadcasting a raise, a sincere effort ought to be made to share in the merchandising profits generated by taxpayer-subsidized programs or to phase out taxpayer subsidies for programs that clearly don't need them.

Again, make no mistake, this senator and Barney are friends, and there's absolutely nothing wrong with making a buck. However, it is time that this happy dinosaur's financial arrangement with the taxpayer-supported public broadcasting went the way of the Ice Age.

—*Sen. Bob Dole*

PART IX
TWO SOLUTIONS

THE FUTURE OF PUBLIC BROADCASTING

The problem at the heart of the present conflict over the perceived bias in public broadcasting is the misconception of mission by public broadcasters themselves. At the recent conference of the Central Educational Network, Michael Tracey, director of the Center for Mass Media Research at the University of Colorado, made the following observation:

> For me the most telling and disturbing discovery, as I have tried to understand the institution of public television, has been the deep ambivalence towards the public-as-audience. One gets a very real sense that the people in public television view American culture and society as something to be kept at arm's length, a dark and dangerous continent smothered by corrupted values and ethics, peopled by the fallen of mass culture, beyond redemption. Public television is to be a protected zone, safe and serious and pure, a kind of televisual green-lung amidst the devastation.

What Tracey characterizes as ambivalence on the part of public television towards its public is more accurately characterized as an *adversarial stance* towards its public—or, at least, that large element of its public that is not in a state of permanent war with American society and culture. It is this adversarial stance that produces the cultural isolation of public broadcasters and their present political problems.

This is even more obvious in Tracey's account of public broadcasters' reactions to current critics:

> Those who broadly define themselves as the friends of public broadcasting appear to regard these...attacks as badges of merit. They define the significance of the institution by the significance of those who assault it. If one is being attacked by the Republican leadership or by right-wing intellectuals... one must be doing something right.

Now whatever else may be said about this reaction, it is inappropriate and self-defeating for a public medium, publicly funded, and thus dependent on the support, or at least the forbearance, of that same Republican leadership and those same "right-wing intellectuals." It is not that public broadcasters cannot or should not have political and cultural attitudes that are liberal and/or elitist. It is that the *institution* itself cannot conceive its mission to mean advocacy of a partisan vision (however "enlightened" or politically "progressive"). If it understands its mission in a partisan fashion, it will inevitably find itself locked into an adversarial stance towards the very audience and community its looks to for support. It cannot back itself into such a corner and hope to survive.

Unfortunately, such partisanship is now an integral part of the self-understanding of many public broadcasters. It was on full display at the recent public-television conference in San Francisco, where the implicit and often explicit assumption of the thousand broadcasters present was that the mission of public television was to function as an agency of (progressive) social change.

Thus, in a crystallizing moment at the conference, moderator Charlie Rose asked PBS president Bruce Christensen the following question:

> Let me raise this question David Horowitz and others have raised. He says public broadcasting carries a strong liberal bias that violates a provision for strict balance in the

Public Broadcasting Act of 1967. I would like to turn to Bruce to respond to that, because that is part of the body of criticism that was aired on the floor of the Senate.

Christensen replied:

If you say our documentary programming has a liberal bias, and you define liberal as an argument for change or against the status quo, the answer is obviously, "Yes, our [documentary] programs argue for change."

The most important fact about this statement is that it was the first time any public-television official had admitted that documentary programming on the PBS schedule is in fact biased. For more than a decade, in celebrated controversies over *The Africans*, *Days of Rage*, and a series of documentaries celebrating Marxist revolutionaries in Central America, PBS officials generally (and Bruce Christensen in particular) denied that there was any bias in PBS documentaries—even a bias in favor of change. But that was before Congress spoke. We welcome Bruce Christensen's belated admission—that the objectivity and balance mandate has hitherto not been observed—as a first step in correcting the problem.

The second important aspect of Christensen's statement is its conflation of the specific and partisan description "liberal" with the general and neutral category "change." This goes to the core of the problem of mission that lies at the heart of the present conflict.

The documentary programs criticized by COMINT and others argued in behalf of Marxist revolutions in Central America, PLO guerrillas in the Middle East, and socialist solutions to Africa's problems. If public broadcast officials continue to define "liberal" to mean "change," and "change" to mean Marxist revolution or radical "solutions" to social problems, then there will be no end to the bias in public-television programming and no respite from its cultural isolation and political troubles.

The problem inherent in the prevailing conception of public broadcasting's mission surfaced in other ways at the

PBS conference. Bob Larson, general manager of Detroit public television, talked for example about the importance of "serving the needs of gays and lesbians." This was a powerful theme of several other speakers as well and was strongly affirmed by applause from those attending. These attitudes reflected a strong and articulated commitment of those assembled to the principles of diversity and tolerance and inclusion for all Americans. Well and good. This is an appropriate and important mission for public broadcasting. But would Bob Larson also have spoken of "serving the needs of Christian fundamentalists," a constituency practically invisible to public television audiences, except as an object of ridicule and scorn, yet representing a major component of the viewing public? And would the public broadcasters present have cheered him on? Certainly not. The same would apply to a proposal to serve the needs of any of America's religious communities, or any of its constituencies to the political and/or cultural right.

The problem, in a nutshell, is a conception of mission that puts public television on one side of the political and cultural barricades that now divide America's publics. As long as this conception prevails, public broadcasting will wind up somewhere in the firing line, squarely on those barricades itself.

Is there a way out of this impasse? Is there an alternative conception of mission that will allow public broadcasters to (1) honor the congressional mandate for balance and (2) feel comfortable with themselves? Can they meet the congressional requirements for balance and, at the same time, be satisfied that in their professional work they are acting to elevate the public consciousness and the culture in general? We think there is.

The mission of public broadcasting, as it relates to controversial public issues, should be to affirm and extend the foundations of America's pluralistic community.

In the last three decades, America has become increasingly divided. Public broadcasting is uniquely positioned to help heal these wounds in the body politic and reunite America's warring communities in a forum characterized by democratic dialogue, tolerance, and mutual respect. Relatively free of commercial constraints, public broadcasting is able to devote itself to the "long form" and to seek the higher intellectual ground. It is a medium specially suited to provide the kind of forum that can strengthen the fabric of a national community, that can emphasize (in Arthur Schlesinger's formulation) the *unum* in the *pluribus* of *e pluribus unum*.

This mission cuts right across the current debate. On this agenda (and perhaps this agenda alone), conservatives and liberals can agree. Liberals emphasize the *pluribus*, the importance of inclusion; conservatives emphasize the *unum*, the importance of the structure. Over differences in emphasis there can and will be disagreement; but disagreement is very different from ideological war.

Let us take, as an example, one of the most volatile and difficult issues of conflict, that between the religious orthodox and the gay community. The mission of public broadcasters should not be to resolve this conflict but to civilize it, by encouraging dialogue and respect and by emphasizing the tolerance that underpins America's pluralistic contract, the civic value that makes it possible for Americans to coexist with one another. Coexistence will not be furthered by excluding one party from the dialogue, as is presently the case. Nor will it be encouraged by programs that assault a particular community (as was the case with *Stop the Church*).

Other problems of the current schedule—those specifically affecting Republicans and Democrats—will be even easier to resolve within this revised concept of a public-broadcasting mission. It is exclusion that has created the present ground of bitterness that underlies the current conflict.

The problems that now beset public broadcasting will remain insoluble, however, if present conceptions persist. Thus, if conservatives are dismissed as selfish, complacent defenders of an unjust status quo, and if public broadcasters continue to understand their mission in terms of promoting "progressive" change, then public programming will maintain its present bias, and the conflict over its future will continue on its current destructive course.

We hope this will not be the case. We hope public broadcasters will consider these words and move towards a more appropriate conception of their role in shaping America's public space. We hope that they will begin to take serious steps to implement the congressional mandate to balance their program schedule. We turn now to the principles that would constitute steps in this direction.

PRINCIPLES OF BALANCE

We begin by noting what we have acknowledged in the past—that a significant portion of public broadcasting's schedule is already non-partisan, culturally enriching, and a striking achievement. In addition, certain current-affairs programs, widely influential, already observe the principle of balance. The *MacNeil/Lehrer NewsHour* is a liberal show with balance to the right; *The McLaughlin Group* is a conservative show with balance to the left. These two examples indicate that the principles of balance are neither obscure nor impractical. Nonetheless, in broad areas of the present public-broadcasting schedule, such as television's documentary series and radio's magazines of the air, the skew is far to the left and the principle of balance is all but ignored. With this preamble behind us, we are ready to begin:

1) Balance must take place within the public broadcasting schedule. The responsibility of public broadcasters is not to create balance in the society at large. This is a widespread view of those who currently see the mission of public broadcasting as that of an agency of social change. Thus, when COMINT criticized PBS for running two documentaries on Iran-Contra by Bill Moyers with no alternative view, Moyers responded that Oliver North had a whole week to present his case on network TV. Even if network commentators like Dan Rather, Peter Jennings, et al. were North supporters (which they obviously are not), that should not be an argument for excluding dialogue from public broadcasting itself. The congressional mandate is clear: Public broadcasting must balance its own schedule.

In any case, the effort to balance America's public space, by balancing the American media as a whole, is an impossible mission. It will only ensure the abandonment of any standard and the surrender of public channels to partisan purposes. The responsibility of public programmers is first and foremost to balance the programming for which they are responsible.

2) Balance is first of all a matter of creating parity between the views of Republicans and Democrats. Just as the effort to balance the views of the media in general is futile and serves only to undermine the very possibility of standards, so is the effort to balance all views in the political culture. There is certainly room for the presence of the whole political spectrum—radical views of the left and of the right (though only the left is now represented). But this is not the primary task of public broadcasting. Our two-party system has been successful for a reason. Compromise is the crucial political virtue in making pluralism work. The existence of two large parties creates a situation in which compromise must take place within the parties before they engage each other. The structure of the American political process drives the debate towards the center of the spectrum, the place where we all can co-exist. If public broadcasting is to strengthen our civic culture it should reinforce its central virtues not undermine them. Radical voices have a place on public channels, but the more important responsibility of public broadcasting must be to balance the mainstream voices in the public debate.

Finally, it was not radicals but Democrats and Republicans who created the public-broadcasting system by drafting and passing the 1967 Act. It was Democratic and Republican legislators who put the provision for objectivity and balance into the act precisely because it was their intention that the system they were creating should work to strengthen—and not undermine the political culture that had created it.

3) Balance must be established between comparable time slots. Not all television hours are equal. This is an obvious proposition presently recognized in all programming decisions—except those pertaining to balance. A half hour of William F. Buckley and a half hour of *TechnoPolitics* on Saturday afternoons does not balance an hour of Bill Moyers' prime-time shows.

4) Balance must be established between comparable formats. Different television formats have different impacts. Talking heads shows like *Firing Line, Tony Brown's Journal*, and *The McLaughlin Group* are different in nature from documentary shows like Bill Moyers' *The Secret Government* or *Frontline*'s *High Crimes and Misdemeanors*. In the former, the audience presumption is that opinions are being stated; in the latter, the audience presumption is that a historical reality is being documented. Moreover, documentary shows like *The Secret Government* have a post-air life in video cassette and educational formats. Any effort to create programming balance must recognize these differences and take them into account.

5) **Balance must be established between programming formats.** Series must be balanced with series. Series afford producers the opportunity to provide commentary on current affairs in a timely fashion and over an extended period of time. The impact of a series is immeasurably greater than that of isolated, one-time-only shows. Therefore, it is inadequate to balance segments of series only with isolated "rebuttals" or alternative views.

There are presently more than half a dozen regular PBS series that cover current affairs, including *Frontline, POV,* Bill Moyers' *Listening to America, Conversations with David Frost, The American Experience,* and Alvin Perlmutter's election special. All of these are produced from the Democratic and liberal side of the political spectrum. A priority requirement of any serious policy to balance the current PBS schedule must be the funding of conservative series comparable to this lineup.

6) **News shows must be internally balanced.** There are three prime-time national news-magazine shows on public broadcasting channels—*MacNeil/Lehrer, All Things Considered,* and *Morning Edition.* Only one of these, *MacNeil/Lehrer,* is reasonably balanced.

NPR's news magazines are heard by more than 12 million people. Because of the quality of that listening audience, the news magazine's influence is far greater than even this number suggests. Yet NPR has a relentlessly left-wing bias, a fact established by media studies and content analysis and by the kind of impression registered on regular listeners—listeners like Sen. Robert Dole, who, in turning on NPR, says he feels he is "listening to the Democratic National Committee." Such impressions lie behind the Senate debate over bias in the medium.

When the problem of balance becomes this obvious, it cannot be solved without a change in management. The problem of NPR's news magazines begins with NPR's top executive personnel. NPR's president, Douglas Bennet, was a functionary in the Carter administration. NPR's managing editor of news and information, John Dinges, and senior news analyst, Daniel Schorr, are well known members of Washington's liberal establishment. One can go down the roster without changing the view. There is no Republican or conservative presence in the upper management of NPR news, or in middle management for that matter. Where is the Bruce Fein or Terry Eastland or Gordon Crovitz or Suzanne Garment to balance a Nina Totenberg or Neal Conan or Linda Wertheimer? Without conservative personnel in senior management positions, it is unlikely that the liberal cast of NPR news will change.

7) **Funding must be reasonably balanced throughout the system.** In 1988, Congress allocated $24 million to the Independent Television and Video Service, a lobby of left-wing film documentarians. Notwithstanding that ITVS has squandered a significant portion of its grant on bureaucracy and administration and produced nothing to date, its existence creates a serious imbalance in the public-television system. The problem of ITVS needs to be confronted directly. It should either be defunded, or reorganized to bring it into conformity with the basic principles of the 1967 Public Broadcasting Act.

These are the principles of balance which should inform any serious effort to restore integrity to the public broadcasting system. In addition to these principles, however, there must be a program of *action* to put them into effect.

A PROGRAM OF ACTION
The first priority of reform must be:

1) **The establishment of an institutional mechanism at the Corporation for Public Broadcasting and throughout the public broadcasting system, down to the station level, for implementing the principles of objectivity and balance.**

The model for this mechanism should be the standards and practices departments that have been established on commercial networks. The following description of these departments is from Les Brown's *Encyclopedia of Television*:

> Standards and Practices Department—unit at each of the networks responsible for clearing all material to be aired, in accordance

with industry codes and the company's own standards of acceptability and good taste; in effect the network censors. On the station level, such a department might go by the name of Continuity Acceptance. The department's staff reads all scripts, monitors programs in productions and screens the completed shows, as well as all commercials, for violations of broadcast policy. Neither programs nor commercials may be aired without the department's approval, which often requires that producers delete scenes or words or even, in the script stage, whole episodes.

Since balance need not take place within the limits of a particular show, the standards and practices departments of public stations should make programming recommendations to the station, to PBS and to CPB, which would promote the balance principle. These departments would also act as clearing houses for audience feedback, now lacking in the system.

2) Balancing imperatives must have teeth. (A) The Corporation for Public Broadcasting must enforce negative financial sanctions as well as provide positive funding to promote balance. (B) It must exert its influence throughout the system.

(A) The contracts between the Corporation for Public Broadcasting and the stations that receive Community Service Grants are presently closed to public scrutiny. It is a fair assumption, however, that they include clauses that require the stations to conform to the provisions of the Public Broadcasting Act. Stations in violation of these provisions should be denied CPB grants.

The Pacifica stations for example, are notoriously political entities with a partisan agenda. The Corporation for Public Broadcasting should immediately put these stations on notice that they must take steps to conform to the balance doctrine of the congressional mandate. If they fail to take such steps in a timely fashion, they should be denied further CPB support.

(B) The complex structure of public broadcasting allows for endless evasions of responsibilities, as everyone familiar with it knows. In the recent authorization battle, entities like NPR and Children's Television Workshop issued misleading but technically accurate claims that they did not receive any government funds "directly." This kind of game-playing may be understandable and fair practice in political conflicts, but it will destroy any effort to bring integrity to the system. To insure such integrity, the Corporation for Public Broadcasting must recognize and exert its influence at the end points of the cash flow and not merely at its entrances to the funding system.

If NPR, for example, should fail to create greater balance in its administrative personnel and programming structures or in its national news magazines, the Corporation for Public Broadcasting should withhold a portion of the grants it makes to participating NPR stations, comparable to the acquisition fees the stations pay to NPR for those programs.

If the Corporation for Public Broadcasting were to follow the principles and procedures outlined above, it would function as the watchdog of the entire system and the guarantor of its integrity. If it were to accomplish this task with suitable diligence and rigor, it would obviate the necessity of congressional intervention, thus providing the "heat shield" protection of programming independence that was its original mandate.

—*David Horowitz*

PUBLIC TELEVISION
AT THE CROSSROADS

The direct role played by partisan politics in public broadcasting highlights the basic problem of having a government-supported television network dependent on congressional allocations for its lifeblood. So long as Congress pays the bills for public television, members of powerful committees will be tempted to interfere with what is produced and broadcast. And so long as the Corporation for Public Broadcasting is accountable for the expenditure of tax monies, it will be involved in programming.

Long before he arrived at the Supreme Court, Justice Antonin Scalia spoke about the problem of public broadcasting in a 1973 panel discussion recorded in Harry Ashmore's book about the television industry, *Fear in the Air*. Contrary to the conventional wisdom in 1973, which held that a centralized PBS was a necessity, Scalia pointed out that there were alternative structures possible and said PBS "could set up a system or systems without having the whole thing in control of one centralized network."

Scalia noted the irreconcilable conflict between fiscal responsibility and the First Amendment in any government funded media effort. He said:

> I find here people who profess to be deeply concerned over the problems of government control of the media but who also ardently support a scheme to establish a national television network, with a centralized system of news and public affairs programming that is dependent on the government for its operating income.
>
> The fact that we can talk about more independence for the press on the one hand, and on the other hand say, but what we really need is a government funded national news operation, strikes me as wild. It is just wild...If you are going to have CPB in charge, then CPB is going to take the responsibility. I think that is inevitable.

The conflicts within the system have never been resolved. Indeed, as the public-television monopoly has withered over time, the infighting between warring factions has grown more intense. The reason for this conflict is directly related to the birth of public broadcasting in the age of the monopoly of television networks.

PUBLIC MONOPOLY

The present system of public broadcasting was designed in the '60s, when the three major networks had a monopoly on national programming in this country. With the cooperation of ABC, NBC, and CBS, who did not want competition for advertising dollars, the Public Broadcasting Service became a noncompetitive "niche" programming service, filling the cracks in the network schedules without threatening network market shares.

In 1967, the Carnegie Commission on Educational Television defined the mission of what would become the Corporation for Public Broadcasting. *Public Television: A Program For Action* provided the specific rationale for the Public Broadcasting Act of 1967. It stated: "Public Television... includes all that is of human interest and importance which is not at the moment appropriate or available for support by advertising and which is not arranged for formal instruction." The original definition excluded both instructional television and sponsored programming because these were viewed as inappropriate for public television.

Thus, from the outset public television was seen as a creature of the network system, filling a broadcast schedule left unfilled by mass media in 1967. The noncompetitive nature of public television built into the very definition of the service and public broadcasting was, in many ways, intended to protect the network monopoly from the threat of a cabled future of hundreds of specialized channels.

Given the tremendous expense of operating a television-broadcasting system in the '60s, it was thought that only regulated monopolies could provide the economies of scale necessary for national television service. Newton Minow's condemnation of commercial television as a "vast wasteland" was seen as justification for the government to support what former FCC commissioner (now PBS president) Ervin Duggan recently called a "high-minded" alternative to the pedestrian fare designed for the lowest common denominator of the American mass audience. In the words of the Carnegie Commission report, public television would provide "a civilized voice in a civilized community" as an alternative to mindless network programs.

Posed in such altruistic and educational terms, offering the promise of uplift and enlightenment, the Public Broadcasting Act sailed through Congress and became law on November 7, 1967. The Corporation for Public Broadcasting began business with a mission of promoting the greatest achievements of Western civilization to the American public.

Today the situation in the broadcasting industry has changed dramatically. With the breakup of the network monopoly and the advent of cable to such an extent that approximately 90 percent of American homes today are passed by cable lines, fewer and fewer types of programming meet the original definition of public television since advertising and commercial services are providing more and more types of programs. Ironically, much of this advertising and sponsorship has actually gone to public television. Yet, in order to preserve the privileges of a '60s-style monopoly status, public television has been trying to finesse the issue of advertising and sponsorship, complete rejection of which is the only rationale for government support given in the original Carnegie Commission report.

Reliance on a monopolistic model of network television has led to a corrosion of the original ideals of the public broadcasting enterprise, which in turn has contaminated the entire structure of public broadcasting. Four years ago, producer Frederick Wiseman—whose award winning films include *Titicut Follies*, *High School*, and a recent portrait of Aspen, Colorado—testified before the Senate communications subcommittee regarding the Public Telecommunications Act of 1988. He told the committee there was a cancer at the heart of the public-television system because of the process utilized by the Corporation for Public Broadcasting to award grants. He warned:

> Public television is a mess. The fact that it is a mess is not a secret. Everybody knows. What is strange is that nothing is done about it. People working in public television seem to be incapable of taking corrective action. They are stuck protecting their own baronies, and battles over turf occupy time and energy that should go into programming....
>
> The result is that quality, which should be the only criterion, is the least relevant consideration in programming. Personal politics, the buddy system, jealousy, and pop ideology dominate the panel's deliberations....

Make no mistake. These are not just my parochial views reflecting my narrow self-interest. They are widely shared by station presidents, managers, and programmers, as well as by independent filmmakers. There are differing views about what might or should be done. But there is a wide consensus on the failure of the present system.

Wiseman suggested that public television be reformed along the lines of the English Channel Four—which, although Wiseman did not emphasize the fact in his testimony, is a private commercial channel supported by advertising sales. Wiseman noted that "most competent professionals would not consider working in public television in its present form" and called for a drastic reorganization to establish personal responsibility and accountability on the part of PBS and CPB employees.

Partly as a result of Wiseman's testimony and the lobbying efforts of numerous groups, a reorganization of public broadcasting began in 1989. As part of this effort, CPB was to concentrate on long-range planning. Programming decisions were centralized at PBS under a chief programming executive, Jennifer Lawson, and the Independent Television Service was established, intended to generate work by independent producers.

However, the Public Broadcasting Service—despite (or perhaps because of) its new "programming czar"—has failed to secure a number of important programs for its national program service. It failed to generate any programs at all from the now scandal-marred Independent Television Service. A grant from the Markle Foundation to cover the 1992 elections collapsed and instead went to Ted Turner's private cable channel, CNN. When Texaco announced a new performing-arts showcase at a Los Angeles press conference hosted by then NEA chief John Frohnmayer, it was for the Bravo cable channel. The BBC proclaimed that it would showcase its programming on cable channels such as Bravo and A&E. Ted Turner scored another coup by presenting Richard Attenborough's spectacular new animal series *The Trials of Life*. And, in an item that should greatly interest Washingtonians, Fox Television announced it had hired P.J.

O'Rourke to handle its 1992 election coverage.

It is clear that deprived of its monopoly status for providing cultural programs, and deprived by ideology and statute of potentially vast revenues from advertising sales, public television simply can not compete in the long run for the quality talent necessary to produce and present quality television.

ECONOMIC DECEPTION

In addition, the business and programming practices of public-television executives are distracted by an overly bureaucratic system and conflicting mandates from Congress. Without a clear sense of mission and without the incentive of an honest profit motive, the temptation to squeeze advantages out of inflated overheads and "insider trading" is a constant problem. Despite some improvements in management since 1988, public television is still, in Wiseman's words, "a mess."

The Corporation for Public Broadcasting has been unable to fully supervise the local recipients of Community Service Grants in much the same way it has been unable to prevent or remedy the ITVS scandal. A 1978 CPB audit found that local Washington station WETA had violated the rules and commingled funds, but no penalties followed.

Public television's franchise of upscale and educated viewers has allowed stations to use the revenues from pledge weeks and "non-commercials" for all sorts of curious things without direct accountability to the public or to the CPB. A 1987 *TV Guide* article quoted producer David Stone: "Look around WNET. See the offices and modular furniture, the decor, and you'll see how much has been put into the outward trappings and how few facilities there are for the actual production of television programs." Like the profligate monopoly-era networks that gave them birth, the noncommercial public-television stations have a lot of overhead. Stone estimated that the overhead charges could reach as high as 40 percent at some stations, a fact not well-known to most donors.

But using donations for fancy offices and other perks is just the tip of the iceberg. There is the appearance of impropriety in programming practices, as well. One modest deception is presenting imported programming as American made. This is a somewhat peculiar public television practice stations call "re-versioning."

Here's a hypothetical example of how it works. A foreign documentary is purchased in what is called a "co-production" from the BBC. Such a purchase is most often actually a direct sale, since BBC contracts rarely allow more than ten minutes of a program to be changed from the British version. In order to make the program seem domestically produced, this English show is then stripped of its British commentary at an American station, such as WGBH in Boston. Then, an American narrator adds an American-accented commentary instead of the British one. Frequently there are some minor edits in the picture. Finally, the local station logo for WGBH and the national PBS logo are added to the program.

When the show is broadcast on PBS, perhaps on a series such as *Frontline* or *Nova*, the viewing public is unaware of the foreign origin of the program except for a discreet credit at the end of the broadcast. In this case, the casual "tune-in" viewer has no idea the show was originally made by the BBC. In a sense, the presenting stations are trying to claim credit for production work they have not done simply by changing the soundtrack and adding credits. Overhead costs of this type of simple translation from British English to American English sometimes run as high as $100,000 an episode—certainly not the best use of scarce production funds, especially when paid for out of tax dollars.

Most notable of all the routine deceptive practices on the part of public broadcasting, however, is the sale of commercial air time on what is supposedly a noncommercial service. This is not a new phenomenon.

In 1983, Michael Kinsley called attention to the ridiculousness of public television's claim to be noncommercial. In a *Harper's* article entitled "None Dare Call It Commercial" he wrote, perceptively:

> It's really a miracle, when you stop to think about it. Like the virgin birth. Like turning water into champagne, drinking it, and having it too.
>
> The spectacle of this old hooker [public broadcasting] announcing that she has discovered a method of going all the way

without losing her virginity is pretty comical, because there's nothing especially non-commercial about public television...in many ways public broadcasting is more ensnared in commerce than the so-called commercial networks.

In his drollest manner, Kinsley went on to cite a fundraising letter from New York's Channel 13, which offered him, for the sum of $50, "the Thirteen Tote Bag. Carry it proudly. It's the tote with the most cachet in town." In addition to mocking the hype and commercialized snob appeal of public broadcasting, Kinsley chided Channel 13 for its annual fundraising auction, which in 1983 spent $1.3 million to raise $1 million in pledges. He also savaged the dishonesty of the usual pledge-week fundraising pitches:

> The place where the veneer of non-commerce is so thick that you can see right through it is in the production and financing of the major PBS network shows. Though they like to scare you during pledge week by saying that your favorite shows, such as *Masterpiece Theatre*, will go off the air unless you send in money, these shows in fact generally cost PBS nothing...Because underwriters supply them for free.

Herb Schmertz, who headed Mobil's public-relations efforts, was just as blunt. He said that the use of *Masterpiece Theatre* during pledge weeks was clearly deceptive and misleading. "It's not truth-in-advertising," Schmertz stated. This sort of institutionalized deception in fundraising for public broadcasting sets a pervasive moral tone that cannot help but trickle down, Watergate style, throughout the system. And, unfortunately, there are all too many abuses that have made their way into newspapers (and undoubtedly others which have not).

The head of Jacksonville station WJCT was reportedly forced to resign in 1990 over a scandal involving the misuse of auction funds, for example. Apparently he was accused of personally profiting from the annual fundraiser and pocketing proceeds that donors thought went to the station.

On a larger scale, Pittsburgh station WQED—one of the largest in the public-television system—was the recent focus of a multi-part newspaper investigation of station finances that revealed, among other questionable practices, that station president and CPB board member Lloyd Kaiser (whose company car was reportedly a Mercedes) had been receiving salaries from both the non-profit corporation and for-profit entities contracting with WQED. Unable to get certain financial information from WQED, a reporter requested documents from the Corporation for Public Broadcasting, including records of a rumored fraud investigation. Her request was denied. In the published story, CPB chairman Marshall Turner was quoted as telling the reporter: "There are some things the public doesn't need to know." The *Post-Gazette* headline read "Station is Wary With Financial Data."

The revelations published in the *Pittsburgh Post-Gazette* produced strong reactions against public television among the general population. A published letter to the editor from Rich Kienzle of Greensburg, Pennsylvania—entitled "Publicly Disgusted"—showed public anger not only at allegations of financial misconduct but also at the arrogance and condescension of the public-broadcasting establishment's attitude towards the very public it was supposedly serving:

> Congratulations to the *Post-Gazette* for exposing WQED President Lloyd Kaiser's ego-powered, troubled empire...Kaiser believes Pittsburgh viewers don't pledge because this is a blue collar, aging, underpaid and undereducated region. What a shrewd way to encourage donations. Tell people that despite the region's high-tech industries, sophisticated health care facilities, and universities, they're too old, poor, and dumb to understand QED. Can you say "elitism" boys and girls?
>
> Did Kaiser ever consider that people don't donate because of WQED's lousy programming? Aside from children's shows, it

often seems like *Pee Wee's Playhouse* for would-be intellectuals. Viewers respond to quality PBS shows like *The Civil War* but WQED and WQEX, while downplaying local shows, offer Lawrence Welk reruns, bad British soap operas, bizarre discussion programs and a glut of dull how-to shows.

Former Corporation for Public Broadcasting board member Richard Brookhiser is right. No one scrutinizes public television because it is presented as virtuous. During pledge breaks pompous QED staffers patronizingly remind us of public TV's superiority as they beg money and hawk trinkets like TV evangelists. I don't feel government belongs in broadcasting. The private sector can provide quality programming. They do it on C-SPAN, the Discovery Channel and the A&E Network, without all the self-righteousness.

The mess at WQED, reported by the *Pittsburgh Post-Gazette* was not the only problem in the stations of the public broadcasting system. Even more serious trouble than the newspaper expose was brewing for public broadcasters. In early 1991, the FCC dramatically punished misconduct by San Francisco's public station KQED, one of the most highly regarded public-television stations in the nation. KQED was stripped of its license for sister station KQEC because, in the words of the FCC decision,

...KQED committed serious misconduct by lacking candor about and misrepresenting the reasons for deactivating KQEC beginning in January 1980. The Commission found that KQED's board of directors adopted a resolution authorizing the deactivation of channel 32 [shutting down KQEC] as a means of this approach [saving money] knowing that the Commission had previously expressed disapproval of prior action by KQED deactivating channel 32 for budgetary reasons. Because the Commission found that KQED committed serious misconduct, it denied renewal of KQEC.

In other words, the FCC found that KQED had taken KQEC off the air for long periods of time in order to save money, despite having been warned not to do this by the FCC itself. KQED then misrepresented the situation to the FCC, saying it had done so for technical reasons.

The charge of "misrepresentation" is among the most serious that the FCC can bring, and license removal is one of the most serious penalties the FCC can deliver. Such a charge is regarded so seriously because misrepresentation reflects on the character qualifications of the license holder to serve the public "interest, convenience, and necessity" as mandated by the communications act of 1934. If a station ownership and management is found to be lacking in good character, under law the station has no right to any broadcast license.

Although the FCC decided it had been bad, KQED was not found to be quite *that* bad, and so was not stripped of all its licenses. Nonetheless, the FCC held that this was a case where good programming did not mitigate the effect of lack of candor with the FCC and warned KQED "although the denial of KQED's other licenses is unwarranted on this record, we expect KQED to take whatever steps are necessary to ensure that no further misconduct occurs. In this regard, we will carefully scrutinize any indication that further misconduct has occurred in the operation of those stations."

On February 13, 1992, I wrote to CPB general counsel Paul Symczak to inquire as to whether the CPB—in its role of supervising the community service of local public-broadcasting stations—ever exercised oversight relating to the "misrepresentation" found by the FCC as part of its supervision of the $2 million Community Service Grants provided annually to KQED. I asked for copies of documents relating to the KQEC matter. As of this date, I have received none.

CONFLICTS OF INTEREST

How is it that no one at CPB saw the problems at KQED coming before the FCC stripped the KQEC license? And how could a public broadcaster even think to risk its good reputation for high-mindedness by a low-minded lack of candor with the FCC?

Perhaps one cause of such problems in public television is the incestuous nature of a system described by former PBS president Larry Grossman as "a system no one in the outside world understands or can penetrate. It is a system that ensures that public television will remain mired in second-class status with a top-heavy, expensive and stifling bureaucracy, a handicap in attracting or retaining truly creative and talented people and an incapacity to make timely program decisions." Another public broadcasting insider, himself a former CPB board member, described the public broadcasting community as "like Biosphere II. They sealed the hatch in 1967 and no one has been permitted in or out since."

Overly insulated from contact with the outside world, protected by powerful politicians from intense scrutiny, the hothouse environment of public television encourages cronyism, favoritism, and deception—perhaps even self-deception.

Despite the organizational changes made since 1989, Grossman's statement, like Wiseman's earlier one, remains true. In the public-television system, the insiders wear many hats despite numerous rules and guidelines designed to prevent conflict of interest. They sit on a system of interlocking boards of directors that govern organizations with extremely complicated financial arrangements practically impervious to outside scrutiny. In addition, many of these organizations give money to each other without congressional oversight.

Henry Cauthen, for example, the head of South Carolina Educational Televison (funded by the Corporation for Public Broadcasting), sits on the board of CPB and on the board of the Public Broadcasting Service (which CPB also funds) and on the board of the Public Television lobbying group America's Public Television Stations (which local stations fund) and on the board of Public Television Playhouse (the production company for *American Playhouse* that CPB funds) *and* on the board of the American Documentary, Inc. (producer of the controversial documentary series *POV* and also funded by CPB). Yet Cauthen seemingly perceives no conflict of interest.

Sharon Rockefeller is the wife of a sitting U.S. senator active in Democratic Party affairs; and she sits on the board of both CPB and PBS and is president of WETA. In a breath-taking political move that transcends even traditional cronyism, according to *The Washingtonian*, Rockefeller had chaired the WETA search committee for a new station president—and she then used the post to select herself for the job.

Henry Becton, whose station WGBH presents *Masterpiece Theatre* and *Mystery!*, also sits on the board of the supposedly independent *American Playhouse*. His station presents the documentary series *Frontline*, and he sits on the board of directors for *POV*, supposedly an independent and alternative documentary series.

Clearly such interlocking directorates do, in fact, present the appearance of conflict of interest and must surely play a role in the apparent lack of competition for drama, documentary, and other programs in the public broadcasting "biosphere."

Even the so-called "independents" championed by Congressmen Markey and Waxman are pretending to be outside the system while they actually participate in the magic circle of PBS bureaucracy in the traditional manner. Lawrence Sapadin was managing director for *POV* in New York while simultaneously serving as chairman of the board for the Independent Television Service headquartered in St. Paul, Minnesota.

The late Marlon Riggs, who made controversial documentaries such as *Tongues Untied* and was supposedly an "alternative" voice, was funded by both *POV* and ITVS. He also sat on an official program advisory board reporting to chief programming executive Jennifer Lawson at PBS before his death in 1994.

The Corporation for Public Broadcasting pays thousands of dollars a year to *Current*—the trade journal of the public-broadcasting industry owned by a cartel of public-broadcasting stations.

PUBLIC FOR PROFIT

The desire for public television to increase its income while maintaining its halo has led to many stations developing a split personality. The non-profits create for-profit subsidiaries to raise money and subsidize their overhead. This sometimes results in big business for for-profit subsidiaries by the non-profit PBS and NPR stations. And the appetite for profit in the non-profit sector can be as voracious as that on Wall Street. In fundraising for public television, it often seems "greed is good."

Minnesota Public Radio, for example, reports grossing $77 million from the operation of its for-profit trading company that manages two mail-order catalog businesses: *Wireless* and *Signals*. *Signals* is managed under contract to Boston station WGBH. The Minnesota broadcaster recently bought a Minneapolis radio station from the commercial sector for $12 million with some of its profits, a move opposed by Jim Wychor of the Minnesota Association of Broadcasters, who accuses Minnesota Public Radio of unfair competition for advertisers.

Many other stations and public-broadcasting institutions run for-profit businesses. In Washington, D.C., WETA owns WETACOM, a commercial provider of telecommunications services. On a national level PBS has PBS Enterprises, whose PBS Home Video line grossed $30 million last year. PBS Enterprises provides tele-conferencing and satellite-data services for clients such as Bell and Howell and *Post-Newsweek*. PBS has also announced joint ventures with cable operators such as the Discovery Channel.

New York's Channel 13 presents the *Charlie Rose Show* in partnership with The Learning Channel. Such public-private deals are not uncommon and continue to spread throughout the system. *American Playhouse* had a deal with Warner Brothers for *Stand and Deliver*. *The Civil War* was distributed in a deal with Time-Life, now a division of Time-Warner.

Most famous among those who know how to work the PBS system for profit is Bill Moyers. He heads his own for-profit company called Public Affairs Television Inc. It occupies office space at New York's Channel 13 for an undisclosed rent. When Andrew Ferguson wrote his *New Republic* expose "Bill Moyers: The Power of Myth," he was unable to determine the extent of Moyers income from public television, writing "the flow of funds within the hermetic world of public TV is one of its tightest secrets."

When I wrote to Moyers myself requesting information on his use of tax money, I received a short reply stating "PAT [Public Affairs Television] is an independent, privately-owned production company—like so many others in the field—and our business affairs are none of your business." Moyers later told the *Los Angeles Times* that he had raised $15 million for Public Affairs Television from a variety of sources.

David Horowitz has termed the system used by Moyers and others in public broadcasting "reverse money-laundering." In one case he found Moyers had provided his private company with $4 million from the MacArthur Foundation through a process where funds were cleansed of their non-profit character through a complicated *and perfectly legal* series of pass throughs. In the MacArthur case, he described Moyers operation like so:

> How do you do this? By having your private company, Public Affairs Television, not take the money directly from MacArthur. Instead, you get them to earmark the money for you, but to pay it to public stations WNET and WTTW, which are non-profit, tax-exempt institutions. Unlike your company, they have no shareholders who might profit personally from the investment of philanthropic capital. WNET and WTTW then hire you as a private entity, on a for-profit contract basis. Thus, the same capital, which was not supposed to be available for profit making companies (like yours) or to enrich private shareholders (like you) is made available for just that purpose. It is all perfectly legal. And perfectly immoral.

Moyers is forced to conduct the type of enterprise described above because of the structural flaw of public television's ban on advertising and commercialism. Moyers and other public television producers such as Ken Burns do in fact sell books and video-cassettes through public television—directly through so called "book tags" and indirectly as a result of the publicity given by the shows themselves. Yet because of the officially non-commercial status of public broadcasting, such a reality must be denied, and public television cannot allow market forces to generate greater revenues for the system. An almost Soviet-style black market is the result, complete with the Orwellian Newspeak. Sponsors are called "underwriters," spot advertising is called "enhanced underwriting," and the profiteers in this closed system pretend to do charity work. Worst of all is the pattern of institutionalized deception and stonewalling that results on the part of public broadcasting executives, stations managers, producers, and funders in order to protect from public scrutiny a system that, as Justice Scalia has pointed out, is a living contradiction.

SOLVING THE PROBLEM

The sad history of apparent monopolistic practices (even as the real monopoly of public television vanishes with cable, satellite, video cassette), manifest corruption of the noncommercial ideals, and rampant greed in exploiting the system found in public television will only be broken when public broadcasting is privatized.

Hodding Carter, certainly no conservative critic, once said to *New York Magazine's* Edwin Diamond of PBS: "It's the perfect American screwed-up system, combining the worst of both worlds—bureaucratic Washington and opportunistic capitalism." But there is a simple solution Carter did not give. Separate the two. That will end the screw-up.

As Stanton Evans said: "What is needed on both sides of this debate is a further step to the outright abolition of tax-funded television....there is really no reason to have such a system in the first place."

The best solution to the problem of public television is to privatize it, to sell the Corporation for Public Broadcasting to the American Public. In that way, public television can continue to operate on the local level much as before. The average viewer would probably not even notice a change in the schedule the day his membership contribution became an investment in a public company. Privatization of public broadcasting will help solve the deficit while encouraging efficiency, excellence, and truly free speech in the marketplace of ideas.

The philosophical case for a true marketplace of ideas has perhaps been made best by the British writer Sir Kingsley Amis:

My case is not that arts subsidies from public money are unjust because they make the poor pay for the rich, true as that is, nor that they encourage waste in productions of opera and dramas (though, they do) nor even that they inevitably attract "the idle, the dotty, the minimally talented, the self promoters," as a distinguished poet put it when resigning from the Arts Council some years ago. I say that such subsidy damages art.

Such subsidy damages art, because, as the British author John Pick adds in his gloss on Amis, "the artist is judged worthy of state aid by a committee, and is paid in advance. Thus the public at large has no voice in the arts and the artist has no incentive to interest, engage, or please the public. The artist's main incentive is to demonstrate that his or her work is avant-garde."

Against the view that pits artist against audience, Pick notes that: "those whose utterances were of interest only to themselves and who could not be understood by anyone else, were once not called 'real artists' by most people, but were more probably thought to be mad...Nor were painters once thought to be worthy of state support simply because nobody liked what they painted." The state subsidy system, argues Pick, "bestows the title of composer, painter, or poet upon those whom it subsidizes, and plainly some state arts bureaucrats do not think that the absence of listeners, watchers, or readers seriously tarnishes their judgment."

Pick's view is that state subsidies *harm* art because what is paid for in advance is decided...

at best by a committee of well-meaning but secretive bureaucrats, or at worst by a *clique*, sensitive only to some prejudged notion of what is, according to their secret codes, innovative, avant garde, and new. The artist is thus not just relieved of any obligation to interest and please at least some of the general public, but is also encouraged to please the subsidizers by demonstrating that his work is difficult, advanced, displeasing to the majority and therefore in need of public subsidy. The bureaucrats will generally help things along by announcing that there is nevertheless a need and an articulated demand for this kind of baffling art and that it will, once subsidized and developed, attract business, improve inner cities, bring communities together, bring the tourists in, demonstrate a can-do philosophy, and simultaneously soothe, stimulate and educate one and all.

The absurdity of conventional arguments for federal funding of the American public-television establishment mirrors the ludicrous nature of the British Arts Council as criticized by Amis and Pick. The solution to the problem of public television is, as mentioned earlier, simple. In America, as in England, allow Adam Smith's invisible hand to pick and choose the best our culture has to offer.

—*Laurence Jarvik*